ONASSIS AND CHRISTINA

The Amazing Story of a Fabulous Dynasty

Also by L. J. Davis

NONFICTION

Bad Money

FICTION

Whence All But He Had Fled
Cowboys Don't Cry
A Meaningful Life
Walking Small

ONASSIS AND CHRISTINA

The Amazing Story of a Fabulous Dynasty

L. J. DAVIS

LONDON
VICTOR GOLLANCZ LTD
1987

First published in the U.S.A. 1986
under the title *Onassis: Aristotle and Christina*
by St. Martin's Press, New York

First published in Great Britain 1987
by Victor Gollancz Ltd,
14 Henrietta Street, London WC2E 8QJ

The following publishers have generously given permission to use
extended quotations from copyrighted works: From *Jackie Oh!* by
Kitty Kelley © 1978 by Kitty Kelley. Reprinted by permission of
Lyle Stuart Inc. From *Cows, Pigs, Wars and Witches* by Marvin
Harris © 1974 by Marvin Harris. Reprinted by permission of
Random House, Inc. From *Point of Departure* by James Cameron
© 1961 by James Cameron. Reprinted by permission of David
Higham Associates Ltd. From Harriet Van Horne column, re-
printed by permission of the *New York Post*. From *Onassis* by
Joachim Joesten © 1983 by Joachim Joesten. Reprinted by permis-
sion of Harper & Row Publishers, Inc.

British Library Cataloguing in Publication Data
Davis, L. J.
  [Onassis, Aristotle and Christina.] Onassis and Christina.
  1. Onassis (*Family*) 2. Shipping—Greece—Biography
  I. Title
  387.0092'2   HE569.O5

ISBN 0-575-04034-3

Printed in Great Britain by
St Edmundsbury Press Ltd, Bury St Edmunds, Suffolk

For Earle and Frances

After a certain point, making money's just a
way of keeping score.
H. L. HUNT

CONTENTS

Photographic sections follow pages 80 and 208.

Acknowledgments

In writing a book with an uncooperative protagonist, an author needs a lot of help, and I am delighted to say that I got it. Dumb luck played its role, of course, as it always does; for example, it is unlikely that I would have been granted access to certain essential files in London without the timely intervention of Stephen Fay, the only journalist in England who knew who I was, and the book could literally not have been written without his providential assistance. Special thanks are also due to the London *Sunday Times,* and especially to Lewis Chester and Mark Ottaway of that paper, for their many kindnesses. I owe undying gratitude to Paul Anastasi, John Theodoracopoulos, Helen Vlachos, Constantine Haritakis, Helen Spironis, John Rigos, Stelios Pappadimitriou, and Professor Ioannides Georgakis in Athens. I believe I am correct in regarding Nicholas Gage's suggestion (that I gain access to the Onassis villas by feigning an automobile accident or a nervous breakdown) as a good ole boy prank, along the lines of releasing a cougar in a crowded hotel lobby "to see what will happen." Anyway, I didn't do it. Very generous help was also given by Dorothy and Judith Bobrow, Joseph Bolker, Kitty Kelley, Steven V. Roberts, Manuel Kulukundis, Jimmy Stewart, the late Constantine Gratsos, Roy Cohn, the Earl of Gowrey, David Willis, Dimitri Negroponte, Jim Hougan, John Broady, Lewis Bemans, Stanley Slotkin, Arianna Stassinopolous, Nancy Tuckerman, Ed Ross, Jamie Auchincloss, Rex Reed, and Alice, Lady Russell. Without their assistance, this book would not have been possible. While dialogue has in some instances been edited for both comprehensibility and continuity, I have never altered a person's tone of voice, nor have I improved on the information they gave me. What you see is what I got.

I suspect that my family is by now as weary of hearing about rich Greeks as it previously was of my discourses on the American plutocracy, but they have borne up splendidly, as have my long-suffering friends. Among the latter, I would especially like to single out Ernest Volkman, who offered much-needed support and invariably sound advice during a (in retrospect) preposterous crisis when it seemed that my work was all in vain, and Judith Rascoe, who acted as sounding board, straight man, proofreader, and rooting section; most important of all, she did not hesitate to be blunt when bluntness was needed. Among others, Michael Sissons, my British agent, weighed in with invaluable help on the London phase of the operation, while my American agent, Patricia Berens, knows precisely why she deserves my thanks. Jared Kieling at St. Martin's Press saved the project when all seemed lost; Clancy Sigal was a brick as usual; and I'm sure that John and Anthea Lahr will remember one special afternoon in their house in Hampstead, where they made an American visitor feel very much at home. As the book went into its final drafts, Lewis H. Lapham at *Harper's*, the late David Maxey at *Geo*, and Jane Amsterdam at *Manhattan, Inc.* were generous with the sort of assignments that keep the wolf from the door.

As for the others, the anonymous sources who are identified in the following pages only as "a friend of the family" or some similiar locution, I can only say that their contributions were essential, freely and in most cases generously given, and (although this will sometimes be hard to believe) largely well meant. You know who you are. So, I suspect, does Christina.

Foreword

In the end, when the last of the bodies had been carried into the wings, she stood alone on the stage, the unlikely protagonist in a drama that was originally supposed to have starred someone else. Before 1971, when Christina Onassis astonished the world (and her father) by marrying the "dinky millionaire," Joseph Bolker of Los Angeles, almost no one outside her family circle had ever heard of her. After 1975, with her brother, her mother, and her father all consigned to their graves, it was almost impossible for even the most casual follower of the gossip press to avoid the mention of her name and the description of her supposed exploits, some of which actually occurred and almost all of which were beside the point.

Largely ignored by journalists who concentrated with avidity on her growing obesity, her husbands, her neurotic tics, and her jet-set amusements, there existed an obvious but singular fact: She was the daughter of Aristotle Onassis, the legendary shipping tycoon whose fleet was larger than most of the world's navies and whose second wife was Jacqueline Kennedy, and the daughter of Aristotle Onassis had inherited Aristotle Onassis's brains. It was widely and somewhat lavishly commented upon that a conspicuous part of her legacy consisted of her stepmother, and when Jacqueline Onassis shortly departed from the family circle with a $26 million payoff, it was universally interpreted as a mighty victory for the presidential widow, even if the avarice implicit in the act did much to destroy what little remained of her reputation as a kind of American Madonna. In fact, though, the twenty-five-year-old Christina had just saved herself a considerable sum of money, while simultaneously opening the way for her own seizure of power within her late father's far-flung empire: The will was tainted, the possibility existed that Jackie could have demanded many millions more, and the stepmother's departure from the scene enabled Christina to carefully dismantle the serious restrictions her father had placed upon her participation in the shipping business. Aristotle Onassis should have known better; he had often remarked on the close resemblance between his daughter and himself.

They were alike yet not alike. Aristotle Onassis had been born into a comfortable merchant family in Smyrna, the principal city in the ancient band of Greek settlements that made up Turkish Anatolia. He fled the place in 1922, sixteen years old, penniless and disguised as an American sailor, when the troops of Kemal Ataturk recaptured the city from a Greek army that had been unwise enough to attempt the reestablishment of the old boundaries of Byzantium. He laid the foundations of his fortune as so many others had done, as an immigrant in a new country—in his case, Argentina —with the wit to exercise his brains and the nerve to test his luck, and he never forgot his origins. (If he had, there were others among the Greeks, perhaps less lucky but equipped with the priceless gift of an impeccable family line, who were more than willing to remind him that he was, after all, nothing but a Turk.)

Christina, by contrast, was born to great wealth and a measure of parental neglect that, though difficult to quantify, left deep and lasting scars. She and her brother were raised by servants, their parents being otherwise engaged. One hears little of Christina (and much of her father) until the point at which she bolted for California and married Joseph Bolker at the age of twenty, but after the departure of Jackie, one hears of little else. Though shy and indecisive by nature, she inherited the self-aggrandizing publicity apparatus assembled by her equally shy father, a man who was nevertheless uncommonly fond of seeing his name in the papers, and there were spacious sectors of the press that found few things more irresistible than a corking good Onassis story, even if the Onassis was the retiring Christina. At the same time, she did much to help matters along; in the years following her father's death in 1975, she seemed to be careening out of control. To appease the parental ghost and please his sister, she almost immediately married young Alexander Andriadis, a man she barely knew and one whose family, having disastrously backed the wrong horse in the hectic round of Greek politics, had developed a sudden and pressing need for $20 million. Andriadis's chief qualifications were that he was Greek and (for the moment, at least) rich, qualities by which her father had set much store when the subject of husbands was broached. The marriage, such as it was, lasted 14 months. In 1978, at the age of twenty-seven, she married a third time, to a Russian citizen and suspected KGB agent named Sergei Danielovitch Kauzov, and went to live with him in his mother's two-room flat in Moscow, an event that horrified her family, delighted the journalistic fraternity, and induced perturbation in the chanceries of the governments of the free world. Slightly more than two years later, she was divorced again. Next, she grew grotesquely fat.

This was the debit side of the ledger. On the credit side, and largely ignored by even her most devoted observers, she successfully preserved her inheritance in the midst of the worst world shipping crisis since the Great Depression, corrected her dying father's last mistakes in a manner he could hardly have bettered, and extracted three fine new vessels from the Russians and Bulgarians while she was married to Kauzov. By 1985, she was an established member of the Union of Greek Shipowners, the only woman ever admitted to its ranks.

There was, then, an almost schizophrenic quality to her life—the Christina who existed for public consumption, a pampered darling of wealth plagued by obesity, reported emotional instability, and foolish marriages, and the other private Christina who moved silently behind a wall of corporate secrecy erected by the best of her father's old advisers, either making all the right moves or listening only to the right advice. Her friends saw only the former Christina, an aging adolescent with more money than God (and even that was incorrect) concerning whom they would many tales unfold, some of them true—there were few deep thinkers among her friends. If almost no one saw the Christina who fought the Greek government to a standstill over taxes, pensioned off her stepmother, circumvented her father's will, and either supervised or consented to the purging of her company's most disruptive executives, it was at least partly by design. Her father had loved publicity, yes, but only publicity of his own choosing; he loved secrecy more, and Christina Onassis was a woman devoted to her father's methods.

"In Athens they know nothing and will tell you everything, but in London and New York they know everything and will tell you nothing," said one of my sources. He was a writer but, poor fellow, he was no investigator. The most successful conspiracies, including conspiracies of silence, consist of precisely one member, but Christina Onassis either knows or has dealt with many extremely talkative people. Moreover, portions of her life and the lives of those around her have been extensively documented, most notably in the London *Sunday Times* Insight Team's fine biography of her father (on which I have at times leaned heavily, though supplementing its findings with new research); Kitty Kelley's *Jackie Oh!;* and Arianna Stassinopolous's biography of Maria Callas. At times, because of Miss Onassis's reluctance to be interviewed, the project resembled an exercise in oral history as I shuttled between New York, Athens (where, as it happens, my friend was wrong: things are known in Athens), Monte Carlo, London, and Paris. At other times, because no understanding of the person Christina Onassis has become is complete without an understanding of her father, his fleet of ships, and his obsessions, the study lamp burned late. The result (to borrow a phrase from Max Beerbohm) is the only book I have ever written whose moral I know, and it is this: Money doesn't buy happiness.

Because of the money, and despite schooling in some of the finest (or at least, some of the most expensive) private schools on two continents, Christina never achieved anything that the more intelligent among her friends would have regarded as a liberal education. Because of the money (and, it should be added, because she was Greek), she spent the first twenty years of her life as a cherished commodity, a marriageable object destined to be put on the block and sold. Because of the money, she could never live a life of her own choosing with the first man of her choice—because, she found, she was unable to live without the money. Because of the money, her father was always absent, making it, defending it, and spending it. Because of the money, her mother, Tina, could indulge herself. Because of the money, Christina and her brother, Alexander, could be raised by servants. And because of the money, they could believe they would never die. This, perhaps, was the worst of all.

A researcher in the lives of the rich should always bear in mind Robertson Davies's dictum that the wealthy go to heaven, too. The knowledge does worlds of good when it comes to humanizing the subject matter, and also when it comes to understanding a small but fatal flaw in the beliefs of, specifically, Aristotle Socrates Onassis and by extension his daughter, Christina. On the subject of heaven, Aristotle Onassis had every reason to believe he was remarkably well informed. It was simply amazing, the things that money could buy. It was not until the last that he discovered that the things impervious to purchase were even more astonishing.

Their story begins with an ending, on a fabulous island during a day of rain, with the burial of a king.

PART ONE

The Father

CHAPTER ONE

A Homecoming

It could have been done with more dignity. Gratsos and Vlassopoulis and the professor had done what they could, but Jacqueline Kennedy Onassis had been smiling for days, wearing that fixed and dazzling habitual smile, almost a grimace now, that she assumed in the presence of the paparazzi and the public, and which, evidently, she now intended to wear to her husband's funeral. Aristotle Onassis had complained for years that she had no sense of proportion.

Smiling, she was first off the Olympic Airways 727 after it touched down at the military airfield at Aktion on the coast of Epiris on the Ionian Sea at two in the afternoon of a March day in 1975 that was filled with rain and shadow. The coffin bearing the pitifully wasted body of her husband was in the aircraft's hold; the press, as always, was waiting. She was followed down the ramp by her former brother-in-law, Senator Edward Kennedy, the man she had chosen, but not well, to protect her from the wrath and indignation of her husband's family. Senator Kennedy was sometimes not at his best in Greece. The rest of the immediate family, all that was left of it, a remnant of women, waited on the tarmac: Aristotle Onassis's three sisters, Merope, Callirhoe, and the cold, aloof Artemis, once Jackie's greatest—and only—champion within the inner circle, now her implacable enemy; and Christina, the daughter, the survivor and heir, stunned with sedatives, without makeup, and uncomely in her grief.

There had been many homecomings here, only one other—the day they brought back Alexander's body—as melancholy as this, but there would be no more: the entire NATO base, it seemed, appro-

3

priated for the personal use of the man his enemies called (but never to his face) the Old Turk; the private jet sweeping down from the sky; the waiting crowd of retainers and friends; the great yacht, a converted Canadian warship, riding at anchor off the coast. Over the horizon was the island of Skorpios. He had bought it because his rival, Stavros Niarchos, had one, because it had been cheap, and because he could see Ithaca from there. A homeless wanderer for most of his life, Aristotle Onassis had always felt a profound affinity for the island's king, Odysseus.

The atmosphere was tense; many things had come together as they prepared to see the old tycoon to his long home. Jackie and the others were met by the party from Athens: the watchful relatives her husband had subsidized for so long, forgiving much, and the associates he had gathered around himself in the course of the long adventure that began so many years ago in Buenos Aires, careful men who had forseen much, and who had laid their plans accordingly. The coffin was unloaded from the plane; some of the women placed small bouquets of purple flowers atop the waiting hearse; and then it was time to go. Cars and buses were lined up at the edge of the tarmac to take the mourners to the coast, where they would change to boats for the last stage of a journey that would end, as always, on Skorpios. Until the very last, its owner had believed himself immortal, but he had been proven wrong.

Smiling, surrounded by people who disliked her and were at pains to show it, Jackie guided her stepdaughter toward the limousine. She had never bothered to learn the appropriate meekness of a Grecian wife, but she knew all about funerals.

"Oh God," said Christina through a haze of sedatives. "Even now . . . how can you?"

"Hang on," said Jackie. "Take it easy now. It'll soon be over."

Senator Kennedy joined the two women in the back seat—the large assertive body, the famous face, a jarring American presence. Christina's father had had many American friends, but he regarded Americans in general as a pack of gangsters, and had often said so.

The car started. Costa Gratsos, the old tycoon's longtime friend and closest aide, later reported that Senator Kennedy leaned over and spoke. "Now," he said, or so Gratsos claimed, "it's time to take care of Jackie."

"Stop the car!" cried Christina. Bursting into tears, struggling with the door, she ran to take refuge with her aunts. Afterward, sources close to the family reported that she had been "cool" to her stepmother during the funeral because the senator had tried to discuss "financial matters."

"He looked upon the marriage as his greatest folly, I think," said Gratsos of Onassis the following year. "And he hated the Kennedys, not so much Rose as the rest, Teddy in particular. He felt cheated by life and blamed himself for being cheated. He had climbed to the top of the tree, and there was nothing there."

As the funeral party embarked at the fishing village of Nidri, the local women, dressed in the black of their own eternal mourning, crowded around to watch the celebrities. Even in death, Aristotle Onassis put on a good show. The coffin was placed aboard a launch, the family disposed themselves in a second launch, and the balance of the group followed in a ferry. The trip, as always, did not take long. Steven V. Roberts, who covered the event for *The New York Times*, remembers the willow tree that drooped over the water near the dock on Skorpios and how the day seemed all gray and green—the gray of the lowering skies and intermittent rain, the green of the island's lavish, almost sensual plantings brought from all over the world by the vessels of a merchant fleet larger than most navies: bougainvillea, cypress, and almonds. Near the chapel on the hill were the little farm and new pavilion some people likened to the Petit Trianon at Versailles. Aristotle Onassis had built them for his second wife, who was fond of horses. She had lost interest in them.

The procession was met at the dock by the Kennedy children, Caroline and John, Jr., and their grandmother, Mrs. Hugh D. Auchincloss; John, 14, had always gotten along well with his stepfather. Whiling away the time earlier in the day under the eyes of a press corps made vigilant by boredom and by what it considered a great waste of its time and talents, the children had driven around the island in a small cart. At 10:30 in the morning, as John Vinocur of the Associated Press telephoned a dispatch to his editors from the dining room of the Onassis yacht, they sat down to a late breakfast with Mrs. Auchincloss. As a rule, serious reporters viewed the Onassis beat with a mixture of resignation and cynicism for which their profession is renowned, but there was no telling what might please an editor. A few years before, *The New York Times* had solemnly reported that the world's most famous couple had celebrated the year's most important holiday with two Christmas trees, one on the bow of the yacht, and one on the stern. Shielding the receiver with his hand, Vinocur began to relay the latest scrap of news when he was interrupted by a voice of brass. "The Kennedy children's grandmother is not having breakfast at ten-thirty in the morning," announced Janet Auchincloss. "She ate hours ago."

It was always like that on the Onassis beat. Unless you watched yourself very carefully, sooner or later you might find yourself behaving like an idiot.

The free-lance photographers had stormed the beaches again, just as they had done at the wedding seven and a half years before. Meanwhile, on the nearby island of Levkos, a second echelon of mostly British journalists, excluded from the official media pool and banned from the proceedings, astonished their American colleagues by filing story after story describing an event that they could not see. Aristotle Onassis was buried as he had lived, and some would have said fittingly so, amid lies, tension, greed, farce, and the warfare of women.

To the slow tolling of the chapel bell and the snap of camera shutters, the coffin was unloaded from its launch. A procession formed behind it, Christina and her aunts first, the others strung out behind them, and they began to climb the hill. Snubbed and demoted to the second rank—a Greek wife would have taken pride of place, but a Greek wife would also have known how to compose her face in a proper expression of mourning—wearing oval dark glasses and leaning on the arm of her son, Jackie had come to resemble a death's head.

Led by Father Apostolous, the village priest from Nidri, the coffin and its escort reached the chapel courtyard, where it was greeted by seven floral wreaths on white tripods, one of them—white and pink carnations, pink hyacinths, and white lilies—bearing a ribbon that read, "To Ari from Jackie." The Americans and the British had called him that, and strangers of other nationalities had picked it up, even a few Greeks. Among themselves, his Greek friends always called him Aris or Aristo.

Four of the wreaths were from a Swiss bank.

"The courtyard was lined with hundreds of white lilies, their pots draped in red velvet," Roberts wrote for *The New York Times.* "On the terraced hillside behind the chapel, cherry trees blossomed pink. In the distance was anchored the *Christina,* Mr. Onassis's 325-foot yacht. Its Liberian flag was at half-mast."

The small chapel held sixty people. There was a scuffle at the door, no one can remember why or with whom; it was probably the photographers again. Professor Ioannides Georgakis, the scholar and diplomat Christina's father had appointed head of the executive committee at Olympic Airways—the only national airline in the world owned by a single individual—on the basis of little more than a single conversation, had brought a Byzantine lamp to place on the grave. It was shortly stolen.

"Father Apostolous read St. Paul's Epistle to the Thessalonians," wrote Roberts, "and a small choir sang several verses, including this one: 'I went to the grave and saw the naked bones, and I said to myself, who are you? King or soldier? Rich or poor? Sinner or just?' "

"Come and give him your last kiss," said the priest, and the mourners lined up to kiss the ikon on the lid of the coffin. One of Christina's aunts, overcome, was led away. Christina herself appeared dazed.

The coffin was carried back outside and placed in its sarcophagus as island servants and crew members from the yacht stood nearby with lighted candles. It was almost time now. Father Apostolous spoke a few more words. For the first time, Jackie seemed to lose her maddening composure. Christina stared at the open grave.

The coffin was lowered into the cement and plaster enclosure. On the opposite side of the building was the new wing, recently completed, that covered the tomb of Onassis's son, Alexander, who had been killed in a baffling air crash two years earlier, taking all his father's hopes with him. Under Greek ecclesiastical law, only a saint could be buried beneath the floor of a church; Christina's father, mad with grief, had buried her brother out-of-doors and extended the chapel. Now another new wing was planned.

The funeral party returned to the yacht. There were sixteen guest cottages on the island, but no one was disposed to linger. The men from Olympic Maritime and Springfield Shipping were eager to return to their offices in Monte Carlo and Piraeus, where they proposed to consult their own interests, and there were those among the relatives who were watchful behind their masks of sorrow, calculating their advantage. Christina would soon open the will. The girl was inexperienced, emotionally unstable, and widely believed to be unreliable. No doubt she would need the counsel of wiser heads, and strong arms to lean on.

As for Jackie, she had an appointment with her hairdresser in Paris.

Christina, too, had laid her plans, but they were not what her relatives and her father's men had come to expect, nor would they be much to their liking. She was alone in the world now. Her father was dead; so were her mother and her brother. Her late Aunt Eugenie, she was wrongly convinced, had been murdered. She hated her father's fortune, not so much the money itself but what it had done to them all, the way it had forced them to live, the intrigues and the deaths and the chaos, the nightmarish unreality and the misery. She was twenty-four years old; sometimes it seemed as though she had never known a moment's peace.

The ship's crew and the servants from the island were assembled on the spotless deck of the vessel her father had named for her. Here he had dwelt in state, looked down on by a genuine El Greco he had bought because his friends called him "the Greek," surrounded by the carved whale-ivory fittings that were a momento of a small adventure that had ended in a private war with Peru. When they were ready, Christina stepped before them and flung out her arms. "This boat and this island are mine," she said in her colloquial, adequate Greek. "You are all my people now."

She proposed to take charge. But she had yet to read her father's will.

CHAPTER TWO

The Ships

In the German port of Hamburg at precisely 3:26 in the afternoon of July 26, 1953 (it was noted in the press with a typically Teutonic passion for exactitude), Christina Onassis, aged two and a half, launched the largest oil tanker in the world. It was her earliest memory.

Chubby, wearing a white dirndl, surrounded by her family, and observed by between twenty to thirty thousand grateful citizens, shipwrights, and officials seated on grandstands erected for the occasion, she propelled the traditional bottle of champagne against the vessel's bow and pronounced her mother's name, Tina Onassis. Then her brother Alexander, aged five, pressed a button and the great ship slid down the ways as a cannon salute boomed across a harbor that still bore the visible scars of war. Theodore Schecker, the director-general of the shipyard, called for three cheers for the Onassis family, and the crowd roared its appreciation. As the two children of that family accepted the congratulations of the dignitaries and walked back to the big Mercedes that would return them to their hotel, they could be forgiven if they felt that nothing out of the ordinary was happening. Their uncle built ships, their grandfather built ships, and their father—who was, quite naturally, a hero; everyone said so—also built ships. It was an entirely typical Onassis launching. They had always been rich.

At 45,752 deadweight tons and with a carrying capacity of 15.7 million gallons, the *Tina Onassis* was not merely the largest tanker, she was the largest cargo ship ever built, a distinction she would hold until February of the following year, when the children's uncle, Stavros Niarchos, launched his *World Glory*. Aristotle Onassis built big, and he built lavishly. His first tanker, the 15,000-ton *Ariston*, constructed to his specifications in Sweden before the war (and equipped with the novel addition of a swimming pool), had likewise been the largest such vessel of her time, but she had long since been eclipsed in all respects as Onassis and his brother-in-law, together with the Americans Daniel Ludwig and J. Paul Getty, pursued ever grander economies of scale and the prestige of advanced design. On the *Tina Onassis*, the captain's cabin and the owner's suite were paneled in natural woods and furnished under the direction of Professor Cesar Pinnau, Hamburg's leading interior decorator. Other Greek shipowners had the reputation, in many cases justified, of stinting on the comforts of their crews, but by prevailing standards the crew's quarters aboard the *Tina* were almost luxurious. She was long and narrow—too long and too narrow, in the opinion of American naval architects—and she was equipped with the bright green decks and rakish funnel, designed by Onassis himself, that were her owner's signature. She could carry three times as much petroleum as the old T-2 tanker, hitherto the undisputed queen of the oil routes, and she could do so marginally faster and proportionally much cheaper, with a steaming speed of sixteen knots and a crew of sixty-four, not counting Captain Jack Poudiezo's wife, who traveled with him everywhere.

The *Tina Onassis* was not the first of her owner's German ventures, nor would she be the last. At $6.5 million, the vessel's cost was only a fraction of the sum, estimated at somewhere between $70 and $75 million, that he had invested in the shattered north German economy since his first postwar visit in 1949, earning him the personal thanks of Chancellor Konrad Adenauer. From Kiel to Hamburg, all across the non-Communist north, an Onassis launching was an occasion for municipal rejoicing, for salutes and bands and caps in the air as the great ships, each larger than the last, received the ritual baptism of wine and slid into the harbor. There were six 20,000-tonners on order or delivered at Weser-Hamburg, ten 21,000-tonners at Howaldt-Kiel, and two 45,000-tonners at Howaldtwerke-Hamburg, of which the *Tina* was the first. At each launching, as befitted his new status as local and national hero, Christina's father distributed gifts—lighters, brooches, scarves, handkerchiefs—emblazoned with his personal symbol. And as with all very wealthy men, stories had begun to stick to him, only some of them true.

He was only forty-seven, but he was said to dye his hair gray for business conferences and black for partygoing. He was said to have introduced the dry martini to Hamburg (years later, his daughter would receive credit for introducing backgammon to Hollywood). There seemed little doubt that he was a drinker of almost epic proportions. His habit of consuming alcohol in quantities at a somewhat staid Hamburg nightclub called Tarantella (in New York he favored El Morocco, often in the company of Greta Garbo, and in Paris he would later become a frequent guest at the Crazy Horse, where he was sadistically fond of watching the reactions of his guests, particularly if they were British, to the pornographic floor show), combined with the insomnia that had plagued him for years, produced late-night shouting matches with his crony, Captain George Koutsouvelis, over who was the greater shipping expert. (His children would be close to teetotalers; Christina, too, would find sleep elusive.)

His business methods became legendary: the endless haggling over prices and details, usually at night, usually in a restaurant, followed by the phone call the following morning to renege on everything, whereupon the performance would be repeated. "He would send in a private plane to pick somebody up to talk business," said Professor Ioannides Georgakis, the man he later tapped to be chairman of the executive committee at Olympic Airways, "give them three hotel suites instead of one, all at a cost of, say, fifteen thousand dollars, and then spend hours haggling over a few dollars. It was the battle that counted, not the deal. In business, he was a voyeur." (In business, his son Alexander would become a cypher. Christina would operate from behind a screen of aides.)

As with many very rich men who made their money themselves, the greatest part of his fortune was based on a single insight combined with a stroke of luck: the insight, in a world powered by coal, into the possibilities of oil, a business no Greek had ever seriously entered, and the luck of having been right. He had been poor once, selling neckties in the streets of Buenos Aires; he was determined never to be poor again. He had made his first real money there, in South America, but the fact was that almost no one but Onassis knew just how. The stories, some of which he told himself, were

various and conflicting; at least one tale had him running a string
of prostitutes that included the future Eva Perón. Despite his later
protestations to the contrary, his family had been prosperous in
Turkey, exporting the produce, opium, and tobacco of the
Anatolian interior. The family had been uprooted by the fighting
between the Turks and the Greeks and transported to Athens following the disaster at Smyrna, but although its circumstances were
reduced, they were not obliterated. Researchers peering back into
the Buenos Aires years of the young Onassis found him at work,
first, at the regional telephone company and later, using his father's
surviving connections, in the tobacco business, but none of this
explains how he rose in eminence and substance to a point where
he was appointed deputy Greek consul at the age of twenty-six, or
how a New York bank could declare his worth to be in the vicinity
of $4 million in September, 1940. And even this was a pittance
compared to the sums he would command by that miraculous summer of 1953, when his plans matured and he burst upon an unsus-
pecting world in a single astonishing outpouring of expenditure.

People who met him in later life found a man who was by turns
charming and irrational, extravagant and frugal, but they did not
encounter a deep intellect or one that was particularly well informed. Great entrepreneurs, like great artists, often defy explanation; it is rare to encounter the example of an H. L. Hunt, whose
petroleum fortune can be dated from the moment he made a
shrewd investment with $119 in his pocket and a letter of credit for
$30,000 from his haberdasher in his hand. In trying to unravel the
mystery of Aristotle Onassis and how he made his money, perhaps
the best explanation is the simplest. "When he was young, he believed he was stupid, you know," said a Greek-American woman as
she rearranged the hors d'oeuvres on her plate in a restaurant. "His
father, Socrates, was a stern taskmaster and an embittered man who
was profoundly disappointed in his son. It was my mother who first
convinced Aristotle that he had a head on his shoulders. Years later,
Ari told me that it all began at that moment, when my mother
finally persuaded him that he was smart."

Like one of Sherlock Holmes's deductions when it was explained
to Dr. Watson, the rest seems absurdly simple. In 1932, with the
$600,000 he had made in tobacco, he went to London, then the
center of Greek maritime activities, in search of two things he

lacked: information on the shipping business, and some ships. With the knowledge gained in London, he proceeded immediately to Canada where, in that worst of all Depression winters, he bought six splendid cargo vessels from the Canadian National Steamship Company for the fire-sale price of $20,000 apiece. Thus equipped, he was able to enter the sea lanes just as the world shipping business began its post-Depression recovery, and with the leverage and the profits of a successful fleet at his command (and with the not inconsiderable help provided by his new girlfriend, Ingse Dedichen, the daughter of an influential Swedish shipbuilding family), he was able to turn his attention to the next phase of his operation: oil.

Just how Aristotle Onassis came to be interested in the bulk transport of petroleum is another mystery. Not only was it a business ignored by most Greeks, but it was a Scandanavian specialty. There was little reason to think an outsider could prosper in the field. The greatest producing reserves were in the United States, a country that had little need for seaborne transport. Other known non-Communist reserves were concentrated in parts of the world that came equipped with brutal climates and long histories of political instability, like the Middle East, or equally brutal climates and long histories as closed markets, like the Netherlands East Indies. Coal, on the other hand, was everywhere. There was coal in England and there was coal in Germany. There was coal in India and coal in China. Even Japan, otherwise so deficient in raw materials, had coal. Indeed, if a rational man with his eye on the main chance were to have surveyed the world's energy sources in the late 1930s, there seemed to be enough coal in enough places to drive the wheels of commerce for hundreds of years. Oil, by contrast, was a vastly more finite resource; even the United States, with its comparatively abundant proven reserves, had only enough to last for a handful of years. The wise man would leave the business of hauling the stuff, what little there was of it, to the Norwegians, but Aristotle Onassis was not a wise man. He went to Sweden and began building tankers. Perhaps he had noticed something else about the petroleum situation in the late 1930s. No one really knew how much of the stuff there was, and it was almost literally as cheap as water. And if the industrial nations of Western Europe ever shifted from a coal-fired to an oil-fired economy, there weren't enough tankers in the world to supply their needs. A man with such vessels could name his price.

By 1953, the year his daughter christened the tanker named for her mother, his prophecy (if that was what it was) had come true and more than true. While he was not as rich as he would become, and while he was never as rich as he allowed some people to believe—comparing himself to his hero, J. Paul Getty, he once remarked: "Mr. Getty is in a rich man's business. He produces oil and carries it. I am in a poor man's business. All I do is carry it."— he had nonetheless reached a point where he could justifiably believe that the world was missing a wonderful treat in having failed to make his acquaintence. He proposed to announce that he had arrived.

When a very rich man decides to make his presence known, he usually does so in one of two closely related ways: He either erects a monument to himself, or he buys one. Aristotle Onassis proposed to do both. He would build the most spectacular yacht in the world, and he would buy the principality of Monaco.

In trying to explain Onassis's mind and peculiarities, especially his public extravagance and the frugality amounting at times to stinginess that he enforced in his private life, his detractors—and he had a few—offered a simple but beguiling explanation: He was a peasant, with a peasant's love of power and display and a peasant's lack of taste and a peasant's meanness. Perhaps there is some truth in that, and it is equally true that the wealthy of continental Europe have been measurably fonder of extravagance (and measurably less fond of public service) than their British and American counterparts. But perhaps, too, it is possible to go a little further and see a trifle more clearly. The course of behavior upon which Aristotle Onassis launched himself in 1953 resembles nothing so much as a familiar social aberration beloved of anthropologists, known as the Big Man Syndrome.

It is a phenomenon that has appeared as far away as the South Seas, but by far its most famous manifestation occurred among the Kwakiutl Indians of Vancouver Island, British Columbia, as originally popularized by Ruth Benedict in her seminal book, *Patterns of Culture*. This was the ceremony—actually, a gigantic party— known as potlatch.

Two ingredients were essential for a successful potlatch: wealth, and a local chieftan—the Big Man—in the grip of a nagging insecurity about his status. Anthropologist Marvin Harris's description of what happened next can hardly be bettered:

> Preparations for potlatch required the accumulation of fresh and dried fish, fish oil, berries, animal skins, blankets, and other valuables. On the appointed day, the guests paddled up to the host's village and went into the chief's house. There they gorged themselves on salmon and wild berries while dancers masked as beaver gods and thunderbirds entertained them.
>
> The host chief and his followers arranged in neat piles the wealth that was to be given away. The visitors stared at their host sullenly as he pranced up and down, boasting about how much he was about to give them. As he counted out the boxes of fish oil, baskets full of berries, and piles of blankets, he commented derisively on the poverty of his rivals. Laden with gifts, the guests finally were free to paddle back to their own village. Stung to the quick, the guest chief and his followers vowed to get even. This could only be achieved by inviting their rivals to a return potlatch and obliging them to accept even greater amounts of valuables than they had given away. . . .
>
> At the potlatch, the host chief would say things like, "I am the only great tree. Bring your counter of property that he may try in vain to count the property that is to be given away." Then the chief's followers demanded silence from the guests by warning: "Do not make any noise, tribes. Be quiet or we shall cause a landslide of wealth from our chief, the overhanging mountain."

With certain relatively trivial modifications imposed by time, circumstance, and cultural distance, much that was conspicuous about Aristotle Onassis's life after 1953 can be understood as a gigantic potlatch. Instead of candlefish oil, he burned money.

Until the very end of his life, his interest in charitable undertakings was small to the point of invisibility. He endowed no hospitals, subsidized no libraries, and patronized no art, although he had acquired an exhaustive knowledge of the ballet to impress a dancer in Argentina, learned to play Bach's inventions on the piano in order to shine at parties, and later (or so his banker, George Moore, claimed) became more expert on the subject of opera, which he hated, than Moore himself, and Moore was president of the New York Metropolitan Opera. Onassis once calculated that if he distributed nine million dollars among the people of Greece, he would have provided each citizen with the wherewithal to purchase a single cinema ticket. On the other hand, if he made a successful nine million dollar investment, he would create nine million dollars' worth of wealth and jobs, and he would also reinvest his profit— performing, as it were, the important wealth-distributing function of the potlatch. George Moore believed that there was something to be said for this view. "In all my years in banking," he once said, "I've only met a handful of people who had that kind of entre- preneurial zest—Getty, Ludwig, Livanos, Onassis—their aim was the accumulation of wealth. In a sense you could argue that these people are necessary and that society should make sufficient conces- sions to enable them to function. Maybe they should be spared the burden of taxes because of what they do. It may seem unfair, but life is unfair."

A proper potlatch requires a proper setting, and the setting itself should reflect the Big Man's disdain for cheeseparing and financial prudence. Accordingly, Professor Pinnau was a busy man during that summer of 1953. The *Tina Onassis* was launched, but she was not yet ready for delivery; there was a myriad of details to oversee in the final fitting out of the cabins entrusted to his care. At the same time, there was the equally pressing matter of Mr. Onassis's new yacht, and on the subject of his yacht Mr. Onassis was a very particu- lar man indeed. Still, he was a client who could evidently afford to be; before the vessel was finished, it would cost more than $4 mil- lion.

The vessel had begun life as the *Stormont,* a 2200-ton Canadian frigate of warlike mien and no pretensions to grandeur whatever. All really rich men, Onassis knew, had yachts, and the richer the man, the more splendid his seagoing hostelry. If he ever read a book, nobody remembered what it was, but he kept well abreast of the usual periodicals, the business press, and the glossy society sheets that he scanned for the clues that governed his developing social life, and on the subject of yachts these latter publications were in singular and disturbing accord. When it came to personal vessels, it was widely agreed, his brother-in-law and fellow ship- owner, Stavros Niarchos, was very well equipped.

Niarchos—he had married Tina's older sister, Eugenie—was, in fact, the owner of the largest privately owned sailing ship in the world and also one of the most beautiful, the *Creole*. Like the *Stormont,* she had begun life in another incarnation, as the *Viva,* built by the distinguished British firm of Nicholson & Cooper, and had fallen on hard times during the war, when the Royal Navy used her as an anchorage for barrage balloons. Niarchos refurbished her in the revived German yards at the unprecedented cost of two million dollars, an expenditure that Onassis was now, thank heavens, well on his way to bettering. Stavros Niarchos was a dedicated anglophile who affected a Mayfair accent of such paralyzing intensity that many people, meeting him for the first time, believed he had a speech impediment. Embarked aboard the *Creole,* he flew the colors of the Thames Yacht Club, to which his wife belonged but he did not. Some observers thought it was the flag of British Honduras.

Onassis already owned the *Olympic Winner,* a converted whaling craft equipped with a raised platform for his Piaggio seaplane, but he was clearly outclassed. It was a novel experience. Until now, his brother-in-law had been the distinctly junior partner in their relationship—the younger (by three years), the latecomer to fortune, the less rich—and their soon-to-be-celebrated rivalry had been more tacit than explicit. Yet that such a rivalry existed, and uneasily at that, their friends did not doubt for a moment, although opinion was divided on its precise cause. Some said it was because they had married sisters. Others, going further—and noting, for example, that Niarchos had been conspicuously absent from Onassis's wedding reception in 1946, suggested that the heart of the matter resided in Niarchos's belief that he had married the *wrong* sister. Still others also blamed Niarchos, but for a different reason: He could not abide the fact, they said, that his brother-in-law was richer and more successful, whereas Onassis found it difficult to dislike anyone, even (and this was most unusual in a Greek) the Turks.

Whatever the truth of the matter, it seemed clear that the brothers-in-law had attempted to defuse or at least control the situation by competing directly only at the card table, where their talents were closely balanced, and choosing areas of specialization. Niarchos excelled in the social graces and in sports—the most difficult ski slope at St. Moritz was renamed "the Niarchos Run"—while Onassis led the way in business, or so he believed. "Niarchos was far closer to the sea in a romantic sense than Ari, for all Ari's rubbish about having salt blood in his veins and so forth," said Sir John

Russell, a British diplomat who knew both men well. "Stavros loved
the sea for itself, but for Ari it was just something on which his
tankers sailed. He used to say he had no time for games, which was
how he saw Niarchos's sailing." But Niarchos's *Creole* was more
than a mere plaything; it was a symbol, and Onassis believed himself to be an expert in the matter of symbols. "Keep a tan even if
you have to use a lamp," he wrote years later in W. Clement Stone's
Chicago magazine, *Success Unlimited.* "To most people a tan in
winter means only that you have been where the sun is, and in that
respect, sun is money. Live in an elegant building—even if you have
to take a room in the attic—where you will rub shoulders with
wealthy, successful people in the corridors and on the elevators.
Frequent luxury cafes even if you have to sip your drinks. Soon you
will learn that many people with money are very lonely. If you are
short of money, borrow it."

Another consideration shaped his thinking. In 1953, he was laying
plans that, if successful, would make him the wealthiest and most
powerful man in the world—at least, that was his hope—but the
money would lose much of its luster if he lacked a proper forum for
its display. Fortunately, as often happened—he was always lucky,
and he knew how to use his luck, even his enemies granted him that
—an opportunity had arisen that would provide him with a bully
pulpit while enabling him to upstage his relative by marriage. An
American racetrack owner made the *Stormont* available for a mere
$50,000 (where it would not be noticed, he always liked to save what
money he could). Onassis called in Professor Pinnau, opened his
checkbook, and set about converting the vessel into what one
writer subsequently called "a three-hundred-and-twenty-five-foot
hull of dazzling indifference to the outside world." She would be
named the *Christina,* after his daughter. (And in 1979, following
instructions left in his will, his daughter would give it to the president of Greece. Some said she did so because the vessel needed an
extensive refit. Others spoke more briefly on the subject. "Christina," said one of her friends, "doesn't like boats.")

The specialists at Howaldtswerke-Hamburg labored under only
one constraint: Mr. Onassis demanded perfection in all things concerning his new yacht. When he detected ripples where the rakish
new bow joined the old hull, he ordered it torn off and the work
redone. When he discovered knots in the wooden screening that

covered the metal bulkheads—screening that, in turn, would disappear behind oak paneling—he ordered it replaced immediately. Without imparing the ship's seaworthiness, a way had to be found to accommodate his Piaggio, a sailboat, a hydrofoil, and the speedboats that his son Alexander would shortly begin to smash one after the other. He insisted on a sunken bath of Siena marble, on a massive air-conditioning plant, on forty-two radio-telephones, on a mosaic dance floor that lowered hydraulically and became a swimming pool. Other men's yachts had staterooms; the *Christina* had suites, nine of them, each named for a Greek island. (The Ithaca suite was usually reserved for the most favored guest. Sir Winston Churchill occupied it, and so did Maria Callas.) The floors were covered with thick Smyrna rugs; the electric doors opened and closed silently.

In the bar, the stools were upholstered with the scrotums of whales, the handrail was whale ivory, and the footrests were the teeth of sperm whales—the fruits of a whaling fleet that he had recently dispatched to the southern Pacific. In the bar, too, one of the walls consisted of an enormous map, executed by a Berlin cartographer, on which small models of Onassis ships could be moved about by means of electromagnets, demonstrating the world-spanning extent of the host's holdings while enabling the guests to play at being the host himself.

The fireplace in the smoking room was inlaid with lapis lazuli at a cost of four dollars a square inch. The sliding doors were antique Japanese lacquer; the railing that led to the deck was marble. (With all the added weight and despite the best efforts of the German craftsmen, it was small wonder that the *Christina* was top-heavy.) There was a surgery and a movie theater. For the dining room, Marcel Vertes executed paintings depicting the family as the Four Seasons, with Alexander and Christina representing Spring. In the original scheme, the artist had chosen a derelict huddling in a snowbank in New York's Central Park as his motif for Winter, but Onassis believed he detected his own features on the beggar's face and a skating scene was swiftly substituted. The hero of the potlatch was by definition insecure about his status.

The *Christina* was to be more than a pleasure craft; it was to be the family home. To a Greek, his native island, his village, or his province were localities of profound and almost mystical significance, defining an important part of his identity, influencing his friendships and business relationships and choice of a marriage partner, and frequently occupying a prominent place in his will when he died. But Aristotle Onassis had been born in Smyrna, now Turkish Izmir, a foreign city in a foreign country. In the sense that most Greeks understood the term, his all-important birthplace no longer existed, and he was adrift. It was a condition that he did much to abet. He owned a villa in Montevideo and maintained a permanent suite in the Plaza Hotel in Buenos Aires. In New York, there was the exquisite little bandbox of a house at 16 Sutton Square, a wedding gift from his father-in-law, the fabulously wealthy Stavros Livanos. In Paris he had recently acquired the top-floor flat at 88 avenue Foch, conveniently near the Livanos residence in Paris. (Stavros Livanos was a dedicated family man. He would want to see his grandchildren frequently.) With the well-known Onassis obsession with symbols and the outward forms of wealth, these were all addresses that he would have called "prestigious," but they were not real homes. They were places where he could sleep beneath a roof when he was in town, places where he could park his wife and children when he was away on his frequent travels, and although they were comfortable enough, all of his acquaintances agreed that he did not generally live in state when he was ashore, and they commented on the fact. An exception to the rule was the beautifully decorated house in New York. But the house on Sutton Square was around the corner from 25 Sutton Place, which Stavros Niarchos had furnished with great care.

On the subject of his nationality, Onassis was precise. "As a Greek, I belong to the West," he told *Fortune* magazine. "As a shipowner, I belong to capitalism. Business objectives dictate the details of my operations. My favorite country is the one that grants the maximum immunity from taxes, trade restrictions, and unreasonable regulation. It is under that country's flag that I prefer to concentrate my profitable activities. I call this business sense."

In 1953, his most ostentatious residence—albeit a rented one— was the Chateau de la Cröe on the tip of Cap d'Antibes in the south of France. (Stavros Niarchos maintained a residence nearby, in the Chateau de la Garoupe.) Built in 1930 by a British nobleman, and resembling a cross between the Petit Trianon and the American White House, it nestled in the midst of twenty-five acres of pine-clad grounds, gardens, swimming pools, tennis courts, and beaches, with Yakimour, the home of the late Aga Khan, and the estate of the film star Martine Carol as its closest neighbors. At one time or another, it had housed the Duke of Windsor, King Farouk of Egypt, King Umberto of Italy, King Leopold of Belgium, and Queen Helena of Greece. Its corps of servants included a butler, a housekeeper, a valet, a ladies' maid, three other maids, two chauffeurs, two cooks, and a scullion. Here, as in New York, he affected some pomp. It was even possible that he considered turning it into his principal abode—it was up for sale that year—but his wife thought otherwise. As far as Tina was concerned, a great deal of the bloom had departed from the place when she discovered her husband in what she believed to be compromising circumstances with one of her old school friends at a nearby chateau. De la Cröe was no longer divine, her favorite term of approval. It would have to go.

The yacht would be the perfect replacement.

Perhaps it was for the best, after all. The vessel, with its mobility, was unlikely to tie him down in a country whose taxes, trade restrictions, and regulations might turn to his disfavor at any moment. Governments, he suspected (and was about to discover for certain), were unreliable. Instead of returning to his home, his home would meet him whenever he put his airplane down near a suitable harbor; top-heavy though the *Christina* was, it could even cross the Atlantic. Celebrities being fond of yachts, it would also act as a powerful lure for the people whose company, he discovered, he had begun to crave. He was no stranger to the company of the famous, of course. Garbo was his friend, although when it came to the exact nature of the friendship, his friends either did not know or would not say. He had looked in on Hollywood during the war, and he was careful to live in all the proper places and cultivate the proper people. The company of the powerful and the notorious had always been a comforting assurance that his life was on the right track, but with the stupendous efforts of his German period almost behind him and his fleet of tankers becoming a reality, he proposed to launch a bold new initiative. He proposed to take the rich and famous and dazzle them with his splendor and his wealth, something he had never done before. For this, the yacht would be indispensable. Many men had chateaus.

Moreover, the yacht would be a gallery in which he could display the perfection of his family life and the depth of his devotion as a father. A portrait of his daughter adorned the mantel in the vessel's library, and photographs of both children were scattered here and there, smiling testimony to the habitual joy experienced by his fortunate offspring. Christina's dolls were dressed by Dior, a typical Onassis touch that was much admired by the sector of the press that interested itself in such things, although it was never very clear how (or whether) she was expected to play with them. Similarly, the walls of the nursery were decorated with fifteen panels especially painted by her father's favorite artist, Ludwig Bemelmans. It was not a playroom. It was her father's idea of a playroom, one that was totally outside his personal experience but also one that was calculated to put his bank account on prominent display. The children's reaction to it was never recorded.

No doubt their father meant well. No doubt the extravagance of the children's quarters was also meant to express the extravagance of his affection for them. It was indisputable that his love for his offspring was as much a part of him as his nose and his teeth, and that was the whole trouble with it: He regarded them as parts of himself. They would do what he wanted. They would mirror his achievements, but they would not have achievements of their own. They would figure in his plans, but they would not make plans. His life was changing. His children, like everything else he touched in the long, amazing summer of 1953, were symbols of that change.

Their music box was disguised as a Monte Carlo slot machine. And thereby hung another tale.

A father who did few things by half measures, especially if there was publicity involved, Aristotle Onassis was about to become known as the Man Who Bought the Bank at Monte Carlo. (His shipping business, conducted with obsessive secrecy, experienced his generosity but not his extravagance. He once demanded to know why one of his ships used twice as many light bulbs as another.) In fact, what he had done was rather simple. Monaco was then a tax haven. It was also centrally located between the oil fields in the Middle East and his major markets in northern Europe. It therefore seemed eminently logical for him to establish a headquarters there, or at least as much of a headquarters as he would ever have. (By preference, he conducted his operations from wherever in the world he happened to be, but even an Aristotle Onassis required an office staff.) When he confided his plans to his French banker, he learned an interesting thing. A controlling interest in the famous casino (and therefore, in effect, in the entire principality, since it could be argued with persuasive force that Monaco was in fact the casino) could be purchased for about $3 million, or roughly the price of a used T-2 tanker. The deal was not unprecedented—Basil Zaharoff, the munitions king, had done the same thing some years previously—but it was irresistible. That the place already had a titular monarch in the form of His Serene Highness Rainier III presented no obstacle. Quite the contrary. In 1297 the Grimaldi family and its retainers had disguised themselves as monks and seized the domain by force, but the dynasty's warlike impulses had been long since dispelled. The current prince was never so happy as when driving at madcap speed along the dramatic roads of the seacoast with his friend of the moment, an actress, named Gisele Pascal (an effort spearheaded by the American publishing tycoon Gardiner Cowles to marry Rainier off to Marilyn Monroe had failed), and the famous casino, which provided him with an important part of the funds that enabled him to pursue his simple pleasures, was badly in need of new funds and fresh energy. The prince—whom Onassis shortly took to calling "that boy"—would be no trouble, while the citizens of his realm, all 2000 of them, would doubtless welcome the return of good times. Quietly, so as not to drive up the price, Onassis agents began to purchase shares in the relevant entity, the Société des Bains de Mer et Cercle des Étrangers—SBM for short—on the Paris Bourse.

Later, when the reporters flocked around, Onassis waxed rhapsodic about his first glimpse of the principality's incomparable skyline from the ship that was taking him, a young and penniless refugee, to the land of opportunity in South America. His resolve to make himself the master of Monaco, he implied, was forged on the spot. At the same time, he was careful not to mention that there was an intriguing but eminently practical consideration that may have motivated his investment. From the point of view of Aristotle Onassis, the benign Monégasque tax climate would be vastly improved by the acquisition of a nearly moribund gambling operation that would require a vast infusion of new funds and which, with careful management, might never turn a profit.

Yet when he spoke glowingly of the place Monte Carlo occupied in his heart, he spoke the entire truth. Not even his closest friends pretended that he was entirely rational, but he rarely made a major move without mixed and often intricate motives. Cut off forever from vanished Smyrna, a stranger in Greece, a foreign-born citizen in Buenos Aires, and a visitor everywhere, he had finally purchased a usable past that was, he believed, exactly cut to his measure. Far more than his beloved celebrities, Monte Carlo invested him with the power of its history and its myth. Control of the SBM meant control of the casino and proprietorship of its legends, all those tattered ghosts of which he was now the eager custodian: White Russian princelings squandering the plunder of one-sixth of the world beneath the murals of innocent milkmaids; adventuresses with tiny silver pistols in their muffs; British peers in boiled shirts; suicides on the beach; and the bar bills of ruined gamblers on his cuff, all the beau monde at his tables and the world at his feet. With the casino came the Hotel de Paris with its violet mansard roofs, its lobby ceiling adorned with mermaids, seahorses, vaguely anthropomorphic amphibians, and the shells of giant sea turtles, and the cream of gilt of its Salle Empire where he could dine every night in one of his rumpled suits as he conducted his business over a telephone with his battered old notebook spread out before him on the spotless cloth. "He was in heaven every time he came into the Salle Empire," recalled one of his bankers. "It was like a diamond that belonged to him." He had long ago learned not to hiss at waiters when he wanted to attract their attention.

It took his representatives only forty-eight hours to complete the takeover of the SBM at the annual summer meeting. While Onassis paid his respects to the young man whose country he had just bought, orders were given to convert the first three stories of the beaux arts Winter Sporting Club at 17 avenue d'Ostende into offices for the executives and staff of Olympic Maritime, with living quarters for the family on the floor above. The old nightclub was conveniently located around the corner from the center of his new holdings; a quarter of a century later, reporters cooling their heels in the hotel as they waited vainly for an interview with Christina could look down and see her bathing suit drying on the terrace railing. Her father's rooms, where he would be photographed as he labored at his desk, were to be furnished in the antique French style and decorated with glass cases, but the children's nursery (which no one outside the family circle would see) was adorned with what one subsequent visitor disdainfully called "tacky duck-type wallpaper." ("Appalling bad taste," she added.) It was wise not to go overboard with these things, especially when they were not in public view.

From the windows of the Sporting Club, anytime he chose, he could look out over the perfect oval of the harbor, la condomaine, blue as an idol's eye and awaiting the ornament he would shortly provide—the great pleasure craft he had named for his daughter. (Sometimes it seemed as though he had named his daughter for his yacht.) As he flew north to Hamburg, where he proposed to preside over the *Christina*'s launching, he could congratulate himself on many things. It had been a summer of momentous events and many fine coups. Not the least among them was the fact that in his take-over of Monte Carlo he had just betrayed his brother-in-law. In clear defiance of a highly specific written agreement between them, he had Monte Carlo in the palm of his hand, and he was not inclined to share.

It was the first of the two great blunders of his life.

CHAPTER THREE

Rivals and Children

Even before (in the words of Onassis's early biographer, Joachim Joestin) "the public took to associating Niarchos and Onassis as it might associate Abbott and Costello, Simon and Schuster, or A&P," the two Greeks made an odd, almost perfectly mismatched pair, almost as though they were the separate halves of a single divided personality. Aristotle Onassis was shaped like an oil drum (his old friend, the shipowner Basil Mavroleon, preferred to describe him as a monkey), perspired constantly, wore clothing that never seemed to fit, drove himself relentlessly, and suffered from an acute insomnia that was relieved only by brief intervals of deathlike sleep. ("I think it was more than mere insomnia," Professor Georgakis once remarked. "I think there was something else involved, something, well, Jungian. It is possible that he was afraid of what he would encounter there, in sleep.")

Stavros Niarchos was as handsome as a film star and lithe as a cat, and he knew how to wear his clothes. Like his brother-in-law, he had once been poor, although never so poor as Onassis had been in Argentina. Because he was an Athenian, he had never lost his roots, but because he was an Athenian (and here he resembled his relative by marriage) he was something of a curiosity in the shipping business; the men of Athens, like the men of Smyrna, rarely followed the sea. He was forty-four years old in 1953, and he was rich. But he was not as rich as he wanted to be, nor was he as rich as he believed he deserved to be. Most important, he was not as rich as Aristotle Onassis.

"Niarchos was a snob," said Helen Vlachos, an Athenian newspaper publisher and his one-time friend, "the best kind of snob. He was attracted toward quality, he wanted to enjoy the highest standard of living and meet people who knew all about it. Stavros Niarchos was untypical because his dreams of power and riches progressed much farther than just plush living and the obsequious smile of headwaiters in the exclusive nightclubs of the world. He was clever enough to realize that he had a lot to learn about manners, food, art, sport, and clothes."

Onassis refused to grasp any more than the rudiments of any of these. "He wanted history to start with him," said Professor Georgakis. "You have a definite impression of B.C. and A.D. in Ari's life. When he spoke about his youth, he never mentioned friends by name. His adventures were never joint ones, whereas most people's recollections of their youth involve stories in the first person plural. A.D. begins about the time he made his first million. After the advent of Jesus Christ there are vivid recollections of joint ventures."

Yet despite his lack of cultivation, Onassis was celebrated for his wit, and his personal charm was legendary. "Stavros Niarchos was the most boring intelligent man I ever met," says Helen Vlachos. "If he had something on his mind, he never stopped. I remember once when he got into a quarrel with Lady Russell, Alice Russell. He'd rented Alice Russell a flat in New York, and there was a dispute about rent. He came to Athens for the weekend, and somehow it happened that I had lunch with him, I dined with him, and *he never spoke of anything else for forty-eight hours!* My husband and I nearly went mad."

Niarchos was a royalist. Onassis knew little of practical politics but considered himself a liberal. Niarchos was often unintelligible, turned few memorable phrases (he was, in fact, among the least-quoted of plutocrats), and he grew increasingly reclusive with the passage of time. Onassis, though he never lost the accents of his native Anatolia, was fluent in Spanish, English, and French. "Onassis's sense of the natural balance of a spoken sentence," wrote Randolph Churchill, "is uncannily acute." He was the most agreeable person at any social gathering he happened to attend, and he commanded the intense loyalty of men vastly more cultivated and far better educated than himself. (A full year after Onassis's death, George Moore, the distinguished banker, burst into tears as he reviewed their friendship.) Niarchos, on the other hand, impressed many people, even those who considered themselves his friends, as a cold man, aloof, suspicious, and hostile. He demanded the obedience of his subordinates, ruled his shipping empire by fear, and frequently inspired contempt. And when he met Aristotle Onassis in London before the war, he owned little more than the clothes on his back.

The details of their first meeting do not appear to have survived; it was not, apparently, a memorable one. Niachos wore impeccably tailored suits and drove a red Bugatti, but fortune had not smiled on his first twenty-seven years. His father had lost the family money in the stock market, compelling young Stavros to begin his working life as a clerk in his uncles' prosperous flour-milling business in Piraeus, a job with little future at a time when most other prospects were dim. His tastes were expensive—helped along, no doubt, by the membership he enjoyed in the Athens Yacht Club, courtesy of his uncles—and his ambition was keen, but his purse was short. Like Onassis, he saw great possibilities in ships. It was not only in Canada that splendid vessels were selling for the price of a Rolls Royce in the late 1930s, and Niarchos, too, sensed the impending revival of world trade. But it was an opportunity he could only grasp at second-hand. He persuaded his uncles to purchase six small cargo vessels and found himself installed as the manager of a modest fleet, a clerk no longer but hardly the shipowner of his dreams. In his new capacity he had inevitably gravitated to London, still the center of a great civilization and a great empire, still the maritime capital of the world, still a place where a clever young man could make his own luck. And Stavros Niarchos was clever, everyone granted him that.

The war was good to both Onassis and Niarchos, but in significantly different ways. When Onassis arrived in New York aboard the S.S. *Samaria* in June, 1940, nervously clutching the deeds of his ships during lifeboat drills, two of his new oil tankers were interned in Sweden and a third had been requisitioned by the Norwegian government, yet he came through the hostilities without losing a single vessel. He would be nicely positioned to take advantage of the postwar boom that he, virtually alone of the maritime Greeks, foresaw.

As for Stavros Niarchos, the war was the making of him. He saw service on a destroyer in the North Atlantic and was later posted to Washington as an assistant to the Greek naval attaché, but with his genius for following in the footsteps of his future brother-in-law he, too, was soon in New York, where he rented an apartment from Harry Hopkins, the presidential adviser, and discreetly tucked away his drug-hazed second wife, Melpomene, in a bungalow on Long Island not far from the country retreat that Onassis and his Swedish mistress, Ingse Dedichen, had taken in the village of Centre Island. (In 1930, Niarchos had eloped with the daughter of Admiral Constantine Sporides. The marriage had lasted less than a month.) Somehow he was able to scrape together enough money to buy a small Great Lakes ore carrier and an old freighter converted into a primitive tanker. Both were placed on the Atlantic run, both were torpedoed and sunk, and Stavros Niarchos was suddenly a wealthy man; the insurance settlement on these and other losses came to an estimated $2 million. He was still an upstart and, for the duration of the war at least, an exile from his German-occupied native land, but he was no longer a poor one. And in New York, no less than in London, he knew how to make his own luck.

It was inevitable that he and Onassis would be thrown into each other's company. They knew each other from London, of course, and they had their Long Island houses. Ingse Dedichen, who was fond of pottering, even did a spot of gardening work at the Niarchos place, and there is a 1944 snapshot of Onassis, Niarchos, and Melpomene relaxing with a Turkish waterpipe on a suburban lawn; the picture of camaraderie (although in truth the expression on Niarchos's face is more than a trifle maniacal). Superficially, their tastes were actually similiar, even if Niarchos's were more refined, and their business interests were identical, although Onassis's apparently unsinkable fleet was larger. And each of them, for identical reasons, had found himself drawn to the salon of sorts that was maintained in a suite at the Plaza Hotel by Stavros Livanos, the acknowledged dean of the numerous Greek shipowners then resident in the wartime safety of New York.

Because Stavros Livanos was very rich, he was naturally of interest to ambitious younger men who had chosen the same line of work as himself. Yet, although he did not possess an intricate personality, he simultaneously represented a social dilemma that both Onassis and Niarchos found themselves confronting, and a possible solution to it.

Fifty-three years old in the war year of 1943, Stavros Livanos was a man who seemed devoid of any striking qualities but his money, of which he had a great deal, and his ships, of which he had a great many. Short, nondescript, and colorless, he resembled (wrote Onassis biographer Joachim Joesten) "any Greek grocer." He was a native of Chios, an island that was formerly the personal property of the Ottoman sultana and the birthplace of most of the European-trained physicians in the Turkish empire. Livanos in his time had been the youngest chief engineer and the youngest ship's master in the Greek merchant marine, and although he no longer personally followed the sea, he retained his papers to the end of his life. It was the rule of thumb in the tightly-structured world of the Greek maritime aristocracy that a man was not properly a member until his family had three generations in ships, and the family of Stavros Livanos had precisely that. His grandfather had owned a caïque, a light skiff common to the Aegean. His father, George, had been one of the first Chiots to own a steamship, a 2800-ton formerly British vessel that he staffed with his sons. Following the outbreak of the First World War, George Livanos dispatched Stavros, who had served against the Turks in the Balkan Wars of 1912–13, to London with instructions to open a branch office. Diligent and persistent—some would have said driven—the young man developed the habit, never broken, of working twelve hours a day with an intensity and singularity of purpose few of his peers could equal—or would want to. In 1926, when his father died, the family enterprise was renamed S. Livanos & Co., although Stavros Livanos was by no means the oldest son or the only one with maritime experience.

His father had made it his policy to buy his vessels strictly for cash; with Stavros Livanos, buying vessels for cash became a religion. Making the fullest use of his practical experience as engineer and captain, he personally supervised the construction of each of his ships; at the end of his life, in the early 1960s, he still traveled from shipyard to shipyard, haggling over details, examining the minutest portions of the work, and cloaking his movements in a secrecy that was remarkable even by the taciturn (not to say slightly paranoid) standards of his nation and profession. He had few outside interests. In middle age he developed an enthusiasm for golf and bridge—one reason for the almost daily gatherings at his rooms in the Plaza was, apparently, the need to ensure that he would always have a foursome for his game of cards—but his life was otherwise bound up with his fleet, his fortune, and his family.

Livanos was not immune to the habits of backbiting and intrigue that came as naturally to most Greek shipowners as their daily meals. During the war, Basil Mavroleon sued him in England for defamation of character, won two thousand pounds, and forced Livanos to donate it to charity. It was an altogether satisfactory settlement, not least because it parted Livanos from a sum of money. When his contemporaries thought of Stavros Livanos, especially if they were not thinking of him kindly, the thing that came first into their minds was his legendary stinginess.

André Embiricos and his prominent Andros Island–based clan of shipowners had lost three of their six vessels by 1942, but they nevertheless donated their previous year's profits to Greek war relief, devised a new convoy system, and surrendered their yacht. No such gestures were forthcoming from the far wealthier Stavros Livanos. He would walk miles to save a taxi fare; when he traveled to a distant seaport, he would sleep aboard one of his ships rather than pay for a hotel room. Of personal extravagances he had none, except the chauffeured limousine he had maintained in London for the convenience of his children, Eugenie, 16 in 1943, Tina, 14, and George, 8. And it was precisely here, with his children, that his detractors believed that he was about to encounter a distasteful problem. The girls were rapidly approaching the age when the daughters of Greek shipowners were expected to marry. Their husbands, of course, would expect dowries.

Livanos himself had married when he was in his thirties; his bride, Arietta Zafirakis, the daughter of a prosperous merchant, was fifteen. In a society that held that a bride should be half her husband's age plus seven years, she was young for a man so old, but not by much; among the seafaring families, girls commonly married in their teens.

Both then and later, the Greek shipowner was rare who encouraged either independence or a broad view of the world among the female members of his family. "They are very much under the chador, I think," said Helen Vlachos years later, seated behind her polished desk in the offices of her Athens newspaper, an outspoken woman who had been exiled by the military junta that had run the country in the mid-1960s and early 1970s, only to return in triumph when it fell. "I believe that we have three special tribes of humans in Greece," she continued. "One is the royals, one is the gypsies, and one is the shipowners. They have a different set of values; they really believe they are different from us, that they have another blood. The shipowners live as they did a hundred years ago, in Smyrna or someplace, where the weight of the women's jewelry represented the size of the husband's fleet. And it still does." Among the shipowners, it was the son who would inherit and who was therefore to be educated in the arts of commerce and the realities of the world, skills whose very possession might destroy the prospects of a daughter. A girl was to take something with her into her marriage, adorn her husband's table, make herself agreeable to his friends, bear his children, maintain an orderly home, and serve as the hostage in the somewhat uneasy alliance between the two families.

Stavros Livanos was not inclined to innovate. His children were born in England and were therefore British subjects, but that was the usual thing in those days. When the girls became old enough to go to school, they were driven to daily classes in London's Holland Park and later sent to board at Heathfield in Oxfordshire. They learned their sums and letters and acquired the crisp accents of their classmates; there were French and Greek lessons and piano instruction for Eugenie, but their world went no further than the immaculate thresholds and manicured lawns of their immediate surroundings. When they were home, the weekly round was punctuated by Sunday services at the Greek Orthodox Cathedral, and the yearly cycle brought them an annual vacation on Chios, to which their father remained powerfully and typically attached. Tina learned that some things, usually very expensive ones, were "divine," and that other things, usually cheaper and less pleasant, were not, and there her education ended. (When her own daughter's turn came to be educated, Christina would fare little better.) "I doubt if she even knew that poor people existed," said a friend of the family. "Poor, that is, in the sense that they had less money than she did."

With the beginning of the London Blitz in 1940, Tina's father moved the family to Montreal and enrolled the girls in the Villa Maria, a suburban convent. But Montreal, it seems, did not serve Stavros Livanos's needs. In 1942, joining many of his fellow shipowners, he moved his family and his operations to New York, took the rooms at the Plaza, enrolled Eugenie in Miss Hewitt's Classes, and sent Tina, thirteen and mad for horses, off to board at school in Fairfield, Connecticut. Then he settled in to tend his interests and wait out the war.

The others began to gather at his suite in the afternoon, the Greek shipowners resident in New York, of whom he was the richest and the most senior—friends who might one day be enemies, former enemies who were presently friends, all of them refugees now, well-heeled victims of a century of displaced persons. For them at least, the experience of being uprooted was not unique. It was true that they had never been farther from the homeland than this, but their history was one of constant movement. Their ships were frequently small and often old, and numbers of them were now at the bottom of the sea, but there was nothing unusual about that, either; confronted with an epidemic of sinkings in the Greek merchant navy in the 1920s, Lloyd's of London had imposed a penalty premium on the insurance it sold them.

Their memories were long, vivid, and unpleasant. When their families had begun to build their fleets in the 1830s, the year the motherland gained its independence from the Turks, Athens was a village dominated by a thirteenth century Frankish watchtower and the modest stucco palace of the new German king, and the port city of Piraeus was a field of rubble surrounding the monastery of St. Spiridon. The nautical families, islanders most of them, had their headquarters on Hydra then; later they moved to Spetsai and finally to Syra in the Cyclades, where the largely Catholic population enjoyed the protection of the French and therefore had been spared the ravages of the wars of independence. From Syra, they dispatched trusted family members to London, just as Livanos's father had done, where they opened offices on St. Mary Axe near the Baltic Exchange and prepared to dine on the crumbs beneath the Empire's table.

They were not trusted and they were not liked, although there were exceptions. In all but name, their ships were part of the British merchant navy, but their reputation for seamanship, reliability, and honesty was poor, and their crews were regarded as maltreated, insolent, light-fingered, and downright subversive. Traditional British xenophobia completed their isolation. Cut off from Greece by distance and from British society by their nationality, their customs, and their somewhat too supple business practices, they made a virtue of necessity and developed a peculiar outlook of their own.

It was an oddly schizophrenic existence. They kept up the old ways and spoke Greek in the home, but like Stavros Livanos they sent their children to British schools. They bought their clothes on Savile Row and their yachts (if they could afford them) from Camper and Nicholson, and they lived as close as possible to Eaton Square. Their first loyalties were to their families, their ships, their native islands, and themselves, and their lives were governed by a handful of simple and tested principles. Like mercenaries, they would serve a power that was greater and more urgently in need of their services than their homeland. They would take their advantage where they found it, and they would not hesitate to seize it; inconvenient laws existed to be circumvented. No condition was permanent. Prosperity was invariably succeeded by slump, nations fell, great fortunes decayed, dynasties crumbled. Only the sea was eternal; as the old proverb reminded them, it sometimes grew sick, but it never died. As long as the Socialists and Bolsheviks were held at bay, as long as a shrewd man held on to his ships and his wits, there was always a way to make some money. And no man was truly one of them if he lacked three generations in the trade.

They had already lost their fleets twice, the first time in the Turkish wars and again, confiscated by the British and sunk by the Germans, in World War I. Now, in New York in 1943, they were losing their fleets again. There were many things to discuss in those afternoons in the rooms of Stavros Livanos—the possibility of finding a decent tailor in America, the progress of the war, the latest sinkings—but there was really only one thing *worth* discussing. The Royal and American navies were finally gaining the upper hand in the Atlantic, not without a fearful cost in merchant tonnage, and it was important to read the future with some accuracy. The shipowners thought they knew what it would bring. They had been fooled after the last war by the boom of 1919–20 and had rebuilt their fleets only to be staggered when the bottom fell out of the market in 1921. No doubt the same thing would happen again when the present war had run its course. Perhaps there would be a boom; certainly there would be a slump. Caution was the watchword of the day, caution and restraint. Aristotle Onassis disagreed.

He and young Niarchos were curious fellows, especially Onassis. Privately, the two were called "the parachutists," a pair of men as different from each other as could be, who had dropped from nowhere, as though they had fallen from the sky. It was true that they owned ships and were Greek, or at least Niarchos was—Onassis, it seemed, had most recently been an Argentinian—but they were Greeks of the wrong sort. They came neither from the islands nor from any of the mainland seafaring communities, their families were not known (for all practical purposes, Onassis's family seemed all but nonexistent), and their fathers—a bankrupt? a tobacco merchant?—had neglected to form any of the essential alliances. Well, it was wartime, and in wartime one made allowances. Things would be different with the return of peace. There were always vacancies in the shipowners' lodge, but only for men with the right sort of credentials.

It could not be said that young Mr. Onassis—he would soon be forty—was a disagreeable fellow, for all his strange talk about tankers. With one exception, he did not press his views upon men who, they would be the first to admit, possessed wiser, more experienced, and far more socially secure heads than he. In truth, he listened more than he spoke, seemed to be aware of his place, treated his betters with due deference, respectfully plied them with questions about their experiences in the business and their methods of operation, and seemed to understand much of what he was told. When he chose—and he chose often, despite the occasional seizures of shyness that seemed to take him, when he would fall silent and look at his hands—he was delightful company, an attentive companion with a rich fund of anecdote. There was no denying that his life had been an interesting one, and he knew how to tell a story. Most recently, for example, he and his friend Costa Gratsos—who *was* a member of the shipowner's fraternity by dint of his family background—had briefly gone into the whaling business in California, where they had persuaded the bored antisubmarine sailors who cruised offshore in big Coast Guard blimps to spot their prey for them. In San Francisco, Onassis had apparently developed quite a serious attachment for Geraldine Spreckels, the sugar heiress, although nothing came of it, and it was known that he had looked in on Hollywood, where he had been seen in the company of Paulette Goddard, for one, and Veronica Lake, who later claimed that he had proposed. She turned him down, she said, because of his piercing black eyes.

In short, there were worse companions, inexperienced newcomer and parvenue though he was. Indeed, there was only the one small matter on which he seemed to forget himself. In the teeth of the wisdom prevailing among the merchant aristocrats who gathered in the rooms of Stavros Livanos, he was convinced that business would boom after the cessation of hostilities, and he said so. In time, he would say so with greater and greater vigor. It would become the one thing, in addition to the accident of his birth, that would bar him forever from full membership in the charmed circle of the shipowning elect. In time, his prediction, and the vast fortune he believed could be reaped when it came true, became almost a mania with him.

It was never clear just how, exactly, he came to be romantically involved with the younger Livanos girl, although Onassis himself claimed to remember the exact moment when his infatuation (if that was what it was) formed. It was at 7:00 P.M. on Saturday, April 17, 1943, or so he said. Later it was given out that he had first set his cap for the older girl, Eugenie, and only eventually settled on Tina, but it was a match about which many things would be said. The New York Greeks had not lost their fondness for gossip, and speculating about the affairs of Stavros Livanos was an agreeable way to pass the time, especially after he became so comically entangled with the parachutists. For, yes, Stavros Niarchos was also in the picture, and it was asserted with authority that he had originally had his eye on Tina, not Eugenie. (What happened to Melpomene, his second wife, is equally mysterious.) It was further stated that Stavros Livanos, although delighted that his daughters had attracted the attentions of a pair of young comers who would require nothing very great in the way of dowries, was superstitiously anxious to have Eugenie married first, lest the marriage of her younger sister doom her to the permanent blight of spinsterhood. Another version of the tale would have Onassis taking Tina for his own but airily throwing Eugenie to Niarchos as a consolation prize. In any event it was here, almost everyone agreed, that the celebrated rivalry had begun.

Tina's version of events, although woefully incomplete, at least had the advantage of being clear. Her first meeting with her future husband was brief, she said, and hardly a meeting at all. She was a month past her fourteenth birthday, and she was on crutches; her leg, injured in a riding accident, was in a cast. Her mother and sister were with her, and the rooms at the Plaza, as usual, were full of men. "To me, he was just one of my father's friends," she said, "younger and better looking than most of them, nothing more. My leg bothered me and I did not pay much attention to my father's visitors. But later Ari and I compared notes and it turned out that he was one of the two younger men—the other was called Stavros Niarchos—and he vividly recalled seeing me. It was, he said, the moment he fell in love with me." Later, to commemorate the occasion, he sent her a gold coin of Alexander the Great inscribed with the date and the initials T.I.L.Y. Tina, I love you.

Among the shipowning Greeks, once they got their teeth into the story, there was a certain amount of speculation about Onassis's motives. There was, for example, the question of whether or not he was actually in love. "Ari?" said his friend Basil Mavroleon in 1976. "What can I say? No. Perhaps Tina was in love. She was a young girl, you know. She had been brought up like all Greek girls, to love and respect her husband." (If this were so, it was a lesson that she conspicuously failed to convey to Christina.) It would soon become clear that Onassis was rarely a man to do things for the simplest, most obvious reasons or even for a single one. In any event, marriages among shipowners were only incidentally affairs of the heart. Onassis was in the process of making a discovery that may, in fact, have astonished him: The possession of money was not enough. Of money he possessed a good deal, and he proposed shortly to place himself in the way of a good deal more (although it is doubtful that even he could have imagined the sums that would one day be his), but he was aware that it had not brought him acceptance by men he regarded as his peers and even, when it came to business, as his inferiors. It was not a dilemma unique to Aristotle Onassis, for many self-made men have made a similiar discovery, and it was never very clear how conscious he was of his feelings, for he was a man who did not develop the useful habit of examining his thoughts and emotions until very late in his life. Nonetheless, his courtship of Tina marked an important watershed. As one observant witness remarked, he was a much nicer person before the war, and the war had brought him Tina. The parachutist Onassis had listened to the established Greeks for quite long enough, absorbing their secrets and their methods of operations as he deferentially smoothed their egos. As the son-in-law of Stavros Livanos, he would be one of them, or so the logic went. And he did not merely propose to join their ranks. He proposed to lead them.

He was good when he was in the company of other men, but he was at his considerable best with women, especially if the woman in question was inexperienced, distressed, or confused. He had attached himself to Ingse Dedichen, the daughter of a Scandanavian shipbuilder, when Dedichen was experiencing the traumas of divorce. Now—or, more precisely, when the war was over and it was safe to travel—Dedichen would be pensioned off with a subsidy of $500 a month, an outright gift of $35,000, and an apartment in Paris. (She was still there, still subsidized, in a flat in Neuilly only a few blocks from the hospital where he lay dying twenty-nine years later.) He laid siege to Tina by treating her to his colorful autobiography, although he doubtless left out some things and changed others. (He was especially fond of portraying his father as poor and humble, whereas his father had been nothing of the sort, and he could hardly have told her about Dedichen and Veronica Lake, among others.) By a happy chance, the Livanos family vacationed near his house on Long Island, which gave him a heaven-sent chance to exhibit both his manly form and new-found skills on waterskis. It was important to win the girl to his side, of course, but these were also the sort of motions that one went through as part of the ritual of courtship. The actual match would be arranged by the father of the bride and the prospective groom. Stavros Livanos could hardly protest at the inappropriateness of a union between a middle-aged man and a child, grotesque as it might seem to outsiders, since Stavros Livanos had accomplished just such a feat himself only a few years before. And there was no denying that the prospective groom was very well fixed.

On December 29, 1946 in the Greek Orthodox Cathedral in New York City, Aristotle S. Onassis, forty, bachelor and shipowner, was married to Tina Livanos, sixteen, heiress, with Archbishop Athenagoros presiding. The newly wedded couple immediately departed for an extended honeymoon in South America, where Mr. Onassis's business interests urgently required his personal attention. A year later, in November, 1947, the twice-divorced Stavros Niarchos married Eugenie.

"It did not go down well," Basil Mavroleon recalled later. "Not because we saw a new dynasty, but the girls were so much younger than their husbands. Old Livanos was much criticized for throwing his girls at these chaps." Nor was it felt that Onassis and Niarchos had married for money. "On the contrary, it was the other way around. It was Livanos who married for money to avoid paying a dowry. What did he give? A ship apiece? Whatever it was, it was nothing. Nothing." Actually, this was not quite fair. Each of the girls came equipped with a large personal fortune. But it was easy to believe the worst about Stavros Livanos and, as usual, Livanos kept his own counsel.

He also chipped in with the house on Sutton Square, arguably the most exquisite, if small, personal residence in New York City. Its ownership was shrewdly vested in the specially created Tina Real Estate Company; perhaps out of habit, Stavros Livanos preferred to leave only the faintest of trails. His daughter, he could be sure, was in good hands. In all the years she was married to Aristotle Onassis, she touched her personal fortune only once, to make a minor purchase in Paris. Like most Greeks, her husband had no respect for a man who could not support his wife.

If Onassis had hoped, however—and there are indications that he did—that his dazzling match would improve his position in the expatriot Greek community, he was sadly mistaken. To date he had made remarkably few false moves in his life, at least that anyone knew about, but if he believed that marriage to Stavros Livanos's daughter would be his ticket to power among his fellow men, he had misread the situation badly. That Stavros Livanos himself had power was evident from his ships, his hangers-on, and even the gossip that attended his offsprings' marriages. But it was a crude sort of power, the power of a man who knows a secret—how to make money—that other men devoutly wished to learn. Real power, the kind that moves men, resided elsewhere among the London and now the New York Greeks, most conspicuously in the person of

Manuel Kulukundis, "the Eagle" as they called him. It was Kulukundis who had been a moving force behind the establishment of
the Union of Greek Shipowners, the trade association that made at
least a show of cleaning up its members' business practices and the
main reason why the "Greek penalty" was lifted by Lloyd's. It was
Livanos who cut the largest deals during the 1920s and 1930s, but
it was said that Kulukundis cut the shrewdest. And although Onassis
claimed credit for inventing the flag of convenience (the wonderful
maneuver whereby one evaded many taxes and regulations by sailing one's ships under the colors of some cash-starved country like
Panama or Liberia), there were those who believed that when the
shipowners finally erected a statue to their true benefactor, it would
bear the likeness of Manuel Kulukundis. A tall, soft-spoken, pipe-
smoking man who sometimes executed talented nautical watercolors while speaking with his aides, he was generally regarded as
representing the very best the seagoing Greeks had to offer and
often served as their ambassador to the world. If Onassis was to gain
a position with the New York Greeks, it was Manuel Kulukundis
whose favor he must seek. And if the truth were told, although
Manuel Kulukundis was the first to acknowledge the newcomer's
obvious abilities, there was something about Aristotle Onassis that
disturbed him. The others had always said that he saw further than
the rest of them.

Actually, it was central to the growing debate between Onassis
and the Eagle that the far-seeing Kulukundis had missed something
that lay at his very feet, while Onassis had not. Indeed, Onassis was
driven into a virtual frenzy by the man's blindness. As he had
uncannily anticipated, an opportunity had developed in the early
postwar years, the kind of opportunity that happens rather less than
once in a man's lifetime, a chance that, if seized and properly
exploited, could make a man into another Vanderbilt, another
Rockefeller. With the benefit of hindsight, it seems like an obvious
thing, but as is often the case with such moments, it was not so very
obvious at the time—except to Aristotle Onassis and a handful of
others, among whom was his brother-in-law, Stavros Niarchos. Everyone knew that the major oil companies had begun to develop
their major finds around the Persian Gulf in the 1930s. Everyone
also "knew" that the Swedes and the Norwegians could handle the
business, as they always had. Aristotle Onassis was not everyone.

(He and Niarchos were briefly in business together during those early postwar years. It is likely that they discussed the situation then.)

Onassis saw his opportunity in the fact that the war had decimated and in some places obliterated the industrial base of Western Europe. As the countries there rebuilt themselves with the generous and soon-to-be forgotten assistance of the United States, they naturally did so with the very latest in available technology, most conspicuously but by no means exclusively in Germany, which the victorious Allies had briefly thought to turn into a factoryless landscape of peasant crofts and shepherd's huts. And this technology not only ran on oil, it used oil as an ingredient in the manufacturing process, vast amounts of oil, the oil that was waiting beneath the sands of Arabia. Simultaneously—and this was the part, Onassis knew, where everyone would get rich if only they would pay attention—the major oil companies were impaled upon the horns of a dilemma. They, too, were in a position to grow rich, but they were undercapitalized. They could either expand their production, or they could build the fleets of tankers that were necessary to haul the product to market, but they could not do both.

Onassis stood by to help with his tankers, by now restored to his ownership, and so did Daniel Ludwig, an elusive American entrepreneur whose foresight had been as good as his own. But as things stood, Ludwig and Onassis could not possibly meet the demand for tonnage that would soon develop. The flow of petroleum from the Gulf to Europe would be unimaginable; it seems likely that Onassis, positioned as he was to take advantage of a somewhat slower technological change, had not imagined it. But he believed he knew where he could find some of the ships he now so desperately needed if he was to become wealthy beyond his wildest dreams.

The Americans were virtually giving them away. During the war, they had equipped themselves with a large fleet of Liberty cargo ships and T-2 tankers, which they were now, with the good-hearted obtuseness for which they were famous, distributing to private owners in allied countries, at a discounted price and on highly favorable terms. One of these allies was Greece, whose merchant fleet had seen its usual hard wartime service. The trick, then—it was as plain as the rather substantial nose on the Onassis face—was to persuade his fellow shipowners to take their full allotment, especially the vital tankers. It was time for Aristotle Onassis to assume the leadership of the maritime Greeks.

Casting aside the deference he had carefully maintained during the war, he spoke to everyone who would listen and to some who would not. Obviously, if the Greeks took the ships and then distributed them, it would be the only chance he stood of laying his hands on some of them, but he was more than willing to share. When Europe recovered its momentum, there would be plenty of work to go around. And yet the established shipowners remained dubious. They were still anticipating a slump, and they were used to buying their ships in Britain. The T-2s had been developed from a design pioneered by Daniel Ludwig, and the hastily assembled Liberties had been welded together rather than riveted in the fashion to which the Greeks were accustomed. The man who hastened into such unknown waters was often the man who drowned.

Watching the opportunity of a lifetime slip away, or so it seemed, Onassis completely forgot himself. His tongue and his business sense got the better of him. He informed his elders that their caution was foolish, the bargain was irresistible, and the ships were finer than any they had ever owned. As it happened, he was perfectly correct, but the circumstance was unlikely to contribute to his popularity. It was time, in fact it was past time, to put young Mr. Onassis back in his place.

It was never very clear just what was said. Years later, seated in his office in a beaux arts New York townhouse where the walls were adorned with his latest watercolors, Manuel Kulukundis would talk around the subject. Onassis believed he had been called an upstart and, worse, an Anatolian and a South American, terms well designed to awaken the paranoia that was never far from the surface of his mind, as it often is in the minds of men who have achieved wealth without power. He was reminded that his ships sailed under the Panamanian flag; he was further reminded that, unlike the others, he had suffered no losses. Worse yet, it appeared that he had done his missionary work too well. The Greeks, led as always in those days by Manuel Kulukundis, took the Liberties and the T-2s as well, but there were none for Onassis. Seeking to share the wealth, he had created competitors.

Onassis retaliated as best he could. He dispatched a cable to the Greek government accusing the overseas Greeks of making no contribution to their country's welfare, which was patently absurd. With the help of Costa Gratsos (although Manuel Kulukundis would insist forever afterwards that Onassis had written it himself), he also composed and circulated a manuscript laying sharp business practices and shady dealings at the feet of the shipowners in general and the Kulukundis family in particular, and he published an excerpt from it, entitled "An Open Letter to Manuel Kulukundis," in New York and Athens. Kulukundis would never forgive him.

Meanwhile, it remained essential for Onassis to lay his hands on some tankers. His emotions, as he sat without a proper ladle on the shores of what was surely a bottomless lake of money, can only be imagined. As it happened, Daniel Ludwig had again shown the way, although he had shown it to Onassis's bankers and not to Onassis himself. The bankers were perfectly willing to lend Onassis the money to purchase the thirteen Liberty ships he eventually obtained on the open market, but they were unable to oblige him in the matter of tankers. Instead, they directed him to the Metropolitan Life Insurance Company of New York.

In the immediate postwar years, insurance companies like Metropolitan Life were flush with funds and eager to send some of them on adventures, and the persuasive Mr. Onassis had just such an adventure in mind. The scheme he concocted, perfecting Ludwig's invention, was often complex in its details but, like most successful plans, basically simple in outline. He would begin by obtaining a charter from an oil company that granted him the right to haul a quantity of its product for a specified number of years. With the charter as collateral, he would then obtain a loan from the insurance company. With the loan, he would build a tanker. The tanker, carrying the chartered oil, would pay off the loan, and the profits it generated over the balance of its working life would belong to Onassis alone. He had, in effect, devised a method of obtaining a fleet for free, and he generously passed along the secret to his brother-in-law, who later professed his scorn for it, although he used it himself. "Niarchos would say to me, 'Don't believe Onassis when he says he has money,'" says Helen Vlachos. "'Onassis doesn't have money, he has debts. Don't believe him!'" It was an opinion that Niarchos shared with his father-in-law, although Stavros Livanos put his own peculiar spin on the ball.

"I had lunch once with Livanos in Paris," says Jimmy Stewart,

Onassis's longtime insurance broker. "We transacted some business, and then he said, 'What do you think of my sons-in-law, Ari and
Stavros?' I said that I liked them both; they were very different
people, obviously. 'Ahh!' he said. 'They're not shipowners, they're
bankers.' " Stavros Livanos, as always, bought for cash.

But whatever one thought of it, Onassis's plan had one single,
great advantage: It worked.

Soon, Onassis was able to diversify. Perhaps remembering his
wartime whaling venture with Costa Gratsos and the fun they had,
he now converted some surplus Canadian corvettes into a whaling
fleet, equipped it with German crews and renegade Norwegian
gunners—the Norwegians held the secrets of their trade very
closely, but not closely enough—and despatched it to the Pacific
with instructions, which were obeyed, to ignore the international
hunting season and kill everything in sight—cows, calves, endangered animals, everything. He also began to dabble in real estate.
Here, however, he encountered Stavros Niarchos—specifically, he
encountered him at the luxurious Hotel Plaza Athenée in Paris, a
property that had attracted their mutual but separate attention.
They knew each other well by now, and perhaps, too, they had
learned something of themselves. Their brief postwar partnership
was behind them, and they would not repeat the experiment. At
the same time, in a way that Onassis was never quite able to put into
words, they had become essential to each other. In later years,
when their greatest battle was a thing of the past and the press had
made their celebrated rivalry more famous than it probably deserved to be, they would still sit down at the table together and, as
Onassis said, "behave ourselves for the sake of the ladies." Alexander would become close to his Niarchos cousins, and rumor
would place Christina on the brink of marriage with young Philip
Niarchos. (She would also come to believe, mistakenly, that her
Uncle Stavros had murdered her aunt, or so she said.) And Onassis
himself freely admitted that, alone, he would have gone far, but not
as far as he went when goaded by the competition of Stavros Niarchos.

But for the time being it seemed wisest to put off the clash that
was probably inevitable. In 1952 they signed a formal pact of neutrality that defined the rules of play if their real estate ventures
again converged. Since they shared a clear community of interest,

it seemed better and more economical to consult with each other and share the spoils rather than compete. Curiously, it was Stavros Niarchos, the man with a plausible claim (despite his obvious anglophilia) of being the more thoroughly Greek of the two, who evidently forgot that there were other ways the game might be played. "In Greece, it is common practice for Tom and Harry to form a league to bugger Dick," says Constantine Haritakis, an Athens antiquarian and friend of Onassis. "A month later, Harry will have joined Dick to bugger Tom. I am qualified to say this objectively because I myself am basically British." Stavros Niarchos may have believed that their struggle would come about despite the pact of neutrality. The evidence indicates that he never suspected that it would occur, in part, because of it.

To Tina, it all seemed like a great game, at least at first. "It was funny," says one of her friends. "Tina would tell me, 'Today, my father is richer than Niarchos and Onassis!' Then, a few days later, one of the others would be richer." Tina was small, soft-featured, and blond (her sister was small, soft-featured, and dark), and for all her short life—until the very end, when drugs and grief had eroded her face and her eyes had become the eyes of a woman who has seen a ghost—she remained much as she had been on that night when she came hobbling into her father's suite at the Plaza: a pretty little girl, spoiled and shallow, with no true center of her own.

"The two sisters were quite different," says Helen Vlachos. "Tina was a flirt, Tina was living around, Tina wanted success, Tina was dressing up in jewels and probably drinking. Eugenie was the ideal Victorian wife." Tina was a child bride, the daughter of a child bride, and she never grew up. "Onassis always treated Tina like a child," says a friend of the family. "He always behaved as if he had three children. He never thought of Tina as a wife; he used to bounce her on his knee and play with her as though she were a little girl."

"She was not well educated, you know, and she was not a conversationalist," says another friend. "I remember her entering a crowded theater once, radiant and blond—she dyed her hair, of course, all the Livanos women are naturally dark, but she stood there like a vision. Then she opened her mouth and began to speak, and the room emptied."

She soon had children, of course, for no Greek shipowner was complete without the descendants who would inherit his fortune, carry on his work, and thus confer upon him a species of immortality, but their arrival was more a footnote to their parents' lives than a punctuation. Alexander was born at the Harkness Pavilion in New York City on April 30, 1948, and Christina followed at the same hospital on December 11, 1950. Their father was not overly fond of Americans and grew less enthusiastic about them as time went on —in later years, he preferred to surround himself with self-confident Britons and, as always, Greeks—but his children were American citizens nonetheless and quite properly so, American citizenship having replaced subjection to the British crown as the shipowners' nationality of choice in the postwar world. (Tina herself had become a naturalized American by a special if distinctly minor act of Congress during the war. Onassis, as always, traveled on his Argentine passport.) The children's credentials having been thus arranged, their parents carried on much as they had before, as if, in fact, they had no children whatsoever, or their children had no needs.

Their father traveled, staying away from home as much as he was there, pursuing his profitable activities and invariably calling their mother promptly at nine from wherever in the world he happened to be. Their mother was still seen in the places where it was important to be seen—and occasionally photographed for the magazines and newspapers—in Paris and St. Moritz, where she maintained a chalet, and New York. Indeed, the marriage changed in only one respect, but it was a crucial one. Now that Tina had produced a male heir and a marriageable daughter, her husband slept with her less and less, and he finally abandoned the practice altogether. In his bitter last years, he would regret that he produced no second son. Alexander would be dead by then, leaving him half-mad with grief. Christina would have irrevocably lost his trust. Why, he would wonder aloud, was she alive and Alexander gone, when it should have been the other way around. And he wouldn't seem to mind who heard him say it.

For the moment, however, things were much as they had been, although by no stretch of the imagination could they be described as normal. From the beginning of the marriage, he had made it his practice—as he had made it his practice with Ingse Dedichen—to discuss his extramarital adventures with his young wife, but he does not seem to have invited her, as he invited Ingse, to critique the performances he described. "I want to be unfaithful to her before she's unfaithful to me," he explained to a friend who reproached him, not so much for his infidelity as for the brazen way he went about it. If that was his motive—and he gave no other—he not only got his wish but witnessed the fulfillment of the prophecy it contained, and he himself had established the essential conditions. "He always left her," says one of her friends. "He was always away, traveling, and she was left alone. She was very young. And naturally, being alone, she started leading her life too." For the time being, although this would change, she preferred the company of handsome young Swiss ski instructors.

Like many of the maritime wives, she was curiously accident-prone. ("All those Greek women!" exclaims an American who knows many of them well. "Always hurting themselves! Why, do you suppose?") She broke her leg a second time in 1954, while skiing at St. Moritz, and by her own account she did so without leaving her feet: "I'm probably the only person in the world who managed to break a leg standing up," she said at the time. In March, 1956, driving in the Engadine Mountains with her friends Countess Marina Cigogna and Sandy Whitelaw, the British skiing champion, she crashed into a Swiss military vehicle and broke her nose and both cheekbones. The injuries of her companions were minor but Tina was hospitalized. It was clear that her face would have to be reconstructed, and Stavros Niarchos was soon at her side. Niarchos insisted on the finest care, the best men, and over the protests of the attending physician he carried her off by helicopter to Geneva. The experience nearly killed her; she had developed a thrombosis in her leg. It was the last time she ever flew.

With the benefit of hindsight, there were those who professed to read the future in this episode, but in fact both she and Niarchos would shortly develop quite different romantic interests. In the early 1950s, however, she seemed quite content with her ski instructors and a life that involved the making of purchases and small talk in roughly equal measure. Her disillusionment with her husband lay in the future, where many things were hidden. The life she led was not unusual for a woman of her station, times, and class, except for her extreme youth—she was twenty-four in 1953, the year her husband acquired his yacht and his casino, and thereby shaped their destiny—and her comparative solitude. True, it was not an existence that was designed to stimulate the life of the mind, but there is no evidence that Tina's mind had much in the way of a life, although she was plainly not stupid. There was a social calendar to pursue, balls and shows to attend, and the houses of friends to visit, houses that were not so very different from the houses of one's own. As for her admirers, in a woman of her position and English upbringing, a little cheating was acceptable provided it never got out of hand. It made for mildly interesting talk in a circle of people whose principal topic of conversation was themselves. She found it intriguing that she was named for the goddess Athena. And there was one thing that she most definitely was not. She was no mother.

Of the two children, she clearly preferred Alexander, but her attentions were a mixed blessing; as he grew older, her feeling for him evolved into a jealous posessiveness that resembled neurosis more than it did affection. She was slowly becoming addicted to the barbituates she took to dull the pain of her injuries, and to bring the sleep she seemed to find elusive (her sister, too, would sail that private sea), and perhaps it was better that she chose to raise her offspring in the English fashion, through the medium of hired servants, although of them all Christina was fond only of Marie Therese, her brother's governess. And yet, in retrospect, it seemed that the attention of the servants was only marginally preferable to no attention at all. When asked what was the one thing Alexander and Christina most remembered about their childhoods, their friends answered with one voice. "The neglect," they said.

The children's paternal grandparents were long since in their graves; the Livanos grandparents had established a residence near the fifteen-room Onassis flat at 88 Avenue Foch in Paris, where Onassis occupancy was only a sometime thing. In any event, their grandmother Arietta—"very funny, a little gaga, you expected to find her wearing a babushka," in the description of one of Christina's friends—was increasingly absorbed in the dynastic ambitions that, she hoped, would one day make the Livanos family supreme among the maritime aristocracy. Christina, in particular, would be hearing more about that subject in due time. At the Chateau de la Cröe, before Tina tired of it, there were two spirited thoroughbred horses, a gift from the king of Saudi Arabia, that occasionally in-

duced raptures of gush in the people who wrote about such things
—such lucky children, they said—but there was no evidence that
the horses were ever ridden and, in any event, they were hardly
able to supply the missing element in the children's lives. This, such
as it was, could only be found in Athens, where their father had
recently purchased two villas in the suburb of Glyfada and made
one of them available to his sister Artemis and her husband, Professor Theodore Garofalidis. Artemis managed the Onassis household,
took the children when their parents entertained, and tried to
create something resembling a normal home life for her niece.
"Artemis was childless, a proper, old-fashioned woman," says a
friend of the family. "She lavished on Christina all the affection she
was capable of giving, but actually she treated her rather like a pet
animal." But at least she tried.

"Onassis was a terrible father," said Basil Mavroleon. "Alexander
was brought up by a henchman, Koutsouvelis, and Christina was
brought up by her Aunt Artemis. He had no family life as the
Greeks understand it."

As the children's features developed, it became clear that they
had inherited none of their mother's physical beauty. Each had
their father's great prow of a nose, and Christina had inherited the
deep, chiseled lines beneath the eyes that made her father's gaze
so penetrating but which only made her own face seem wizened
and prematurely elderly. She might one day, with luck, be striking,
but she would never be pretty; her hair was oily and hard to manage, and she had a tendency to gain weight. She had a good mind
—by the age of seven, or so she later claimed, she was fluent in
English, French, and Greek, although in truth her Greek was only
passable at best—but she was a moody child, withdrawn and subject
to tantrums, and she was not easy to like. She treated the servants
badly (it would become a lifelong habit, and one that caused her
much remorse) and was disliked by them in turn, and she avoided
the company of her brother. And presently, the servants began to
put it about that she was hopelessly neurotic.

At the age of three, Christina abruptly stopped speaking; not a
word could be gotten out of her. Alarmed and completely out of her
depth, Tina took her to Zurich and consulted specialists who announced that the child was suffering from mercurial mutism, a
malady remarkably few pediatricians have ever heard of, although

the Zurich analysis of its cause was accurate enough as far as it went. It commonly occurred, Tina was told, in overprotected children, and it would clear up in time. If Tina was also told that it was usually associated with very angry children, and with children desperately trying to attract the attention of their parents, she did nothing about it.

Her father was no help. From an early age, he taught both children to regard themselves as unique, inhabiting a treacherous and rapacious world where other people would find them interesting chiefly because of their money, which those other people would want. "His inner conflicts were expressed in the way he treated the children," observed Professor Georgakis. "He was not a master of pedagogy. You must consider the contrast between his own education and the one he expected his children to have. Onassis was brought up in Asia Minor by his grandmother Gethsemane, a deeply religious woman from the interior who couldn't even read Greek. He was sent to church every Sunday, and even his clothes were blessed with incense. He went to a good school, but he was a little devil, not good at his lessons. His father, Socrates, was a stern and authoritarian man, and his grandmother protected him. . . . He'd grown up in a medieval environment, and as a founding member of the jet set he had to educate his children in New York, Paris, and the Côte d'Azur. With Ari, education was aggression."

His method, especially with Alexander, alternated between moments of extreme, frightening, mostly verbal violence when he demanded blind obedience and unquestioning acceptance of his views, and other moments when he overwhelmed his offspring, especially Christina, with great addictive waves of love, admiration, and gifts. He called his daughter "chryso mou," my golden one, but when he was asked what he wanted for his children, he said, "I wish happiness for my son." His son. Like Tina, Christina would serve her purpose when the time came—of course he would supervise the nuptuals, having chosen the groom—but it was in his son that his hope resided. In that, at least, he was typically Greek. In the maritime families, it was not uncommon for the birth of a male heir to lend new focus and fresh purpose to the activities of the head of the household, who now concentrated his energies on building a praiseworthy inheritance for the son whose mind, tastes, and outlook he would now shape until there emerged a reasonable facsimilie of himself. But Aristotle Onassis apparently believed that this minor miracle, the development of his son, would occur without his continuous and active intervention, as he pursued the personal life that continually absorbed him, dropping into his children's world on occasion to see how things were getting on. In short, he seemed to expect not a minor miracle, but a major one. He expected his children, especially Alexander, to grow up exactly as he wished, without his assistance, and he was infuriated when he discovered that the desired result was not being achieved. After all, he had paid for it, hadn't he?

Under the circumstances, it was not surprising that Alexander and Christina began to develop qualities more common to the children of the very poor than the offspring of the rich. They, too, were often alone and left to their own meager devices. (The servants, they soon discovered, were just that: hired help to whom very little in the way of obedience was owed.) They knew very little of the outside world and were given few opportunities to learn. (Christina would attempt to repair the oversight.) In the absence of their parents they enjoyed great freedom (Alexander would soon run wild), but it was also a freedom that was largely false, defined and controlled as it was by their father's fortune, their father's purposes, and their father's ambitions. As much as any ghetto children, they were at the mercy of an outside force, and they were never equipped to lead any other kind of life, as Christina would one day discover to her dismay. They experienced feelings of omnipotence combined with feelings of total helplessness, exhibited an inability to postpone gratification or to distinguish between impulse and reason, confused possessions with merit, revealed a broad ignorance of life as it is commonly lived elsewhere on the planet, and seemed dominated by a kind of solipsism that made it difficult for them to see where the family money left off and the rest of humanity began. "I was always surprised by the things Christina knew—and the things she was ignorant about," said one of her former classmates. "She had no idea what things cost. Her dolls were dressed by Dior in the latest fashions from Paris. But I don't believe she'd ever been inside a taxi, let alone traveled on the subway. Think about that for a moment! To be *that* remote from ordinary life—it's spooky, don't you think?" Alexander once remarked that the two men he most admired in the world were his father and Howard Hughes.

In the embittered last years of Aristotle Onassis, one of his greatest regrets was that he had never spent enough time with his family; if he had, he seemed to believe, perhaps he could have defeated the future and outwitted the fate he had prepared for himself. But in 1953, launching his great tankers and his yacht, buying up Monte Carlo and preparing to harvest money as though it were a crop, he was deep in his heroic period, the Horatio Alger years that he would always remember as the happiest and most satisfactory period of his life. At the age of forty-seven, all his predictions fulfilled, he was about to cross the border into the country of the super rich, a sparsely (and quite selectively, he believed) inhabited terra incognita whose dim outlines he discerned with all the romantic avidity of the Buenos Aires necktie peddler he had once been. (Yes, and he had also trundled a wheelbarrow through the streets of the city, bearing a load of sand concealing trinkets that children, if they paid him for the privilege, could search for.) First National City, his New York bank, would shortly estimate his probable cash flow for the coming decade of the 1960s as somewhere in the vicinity of a billion dollars. In the Pacific, his killer ships ravaged the surviving whale herds. In Saudi Arabia, in murky partnership with Dr. Hjalmar Horace Greeley Schacht, the only top Nazi to have been raised in Brooklyn, he was laying plans that he confidently expected would make him the richest and most powerful man in the world. Later, there would be time for his family. Later, there would be time for everything. Then Stavros Niarchos struck.

It was his own fault. Onassis put on a bold face and tried to claim otherwise, but it was he who had broken their 1952 pact of neutrality with his majority interest in the facilities at Monte Carlo, and peace could not be restored, nor did he try. Niarchos, too, had laid covetous eyes on the diminutive but glamorous principality. He knew of his brother-in-law's plan to buy up the necessary stock; Onassis had told Niarchos himself, and in accordance with their agreement, Niarchos had advanced Onassis the money to purchase his share of the deal. Onassis claimed that Niarchos's money was a loan and repeated as much to the arbitrator Niarchos called in to settle the matter. Onassis lost the case, paid his brother-in-law 130 million old francs, and dismissed the matter with a nonchalant "one hundred thousand or one hundred million francs, it's all the same to me." But Stavros Niarchos was not a forgiving man.

For the first three years of Christina's life, her father had neglected his children while he built his fortune. For the next three years, he neglected them as he tried to save it. Before then, there had been no one to blame for the barren, servant-dominated life they led. Now, as their father swept down on the family, railed against the schemes and plots of his brother-in-law, and raced away again to meet some fresh threat to his diminishing resources, the author of the mischief was identified at last. The children's hidden antagonist, flushed from cover by their father's cleverness, was their Uncle Stavros.

CHAPTER FOUR

War

In May, 1954, Ray Taggart, the man who managed the Washington, D.C. office of Robert Maheu, the celebrated and enigmatic private investigator, received a telephone call from Stavros Niarchos's British solicitor, L. E. P. Taylor. The message was brief: Taggart was to stand by for instructions. A few minutes later, a Niarchos messenger was at the door bearing a stack of dossiers, a photograph, and the details of an assignment. Taggart was to arrange a tap on the business telephones of the man in the photograph. The man in the photograph was Aristotle S. Onassis.

The man whose agency had been chosen for this delicate task was in many ways the perfect foil for the plan of destruction that Niarchos would shortly evolve. Maheu, an accomplished investigator whose career had begun in the FBI and who would later serve as general factotum to the eccentric (some would say quite mad) Howard Hughes, possessed two qualities that were perfect for the job at hand: His contacts with the Central Intelligence Agency were excellent, and he was very good at making himself invisible. It would be many months and one lawsuit later before Aristotle Onassis even learned of the existence of Maheu, his brother-in-law's chief tactician and deadliest instrument.

The immediate task was not a difficult one, but it proved to possess certain features suggesting that there were powerful forces at work, forces that desired nothing in this world so much as the undoing of Aristotle Onassis. New York in 1954 was a city wide open to wiretaps, as Onassis was probably aware. John Broady, a well-known private investigator, employed wiremen who could hook into the conversations of an astonishing 125,000 telephone subscribers on the Upper East Side, including the United Nations, and he would shortly go to trial for it. (Broady, a minor figure in the hall of mirrors that was Aristotle Onassis's life, later claimed he was instructed to forget everything he knew about Onassis operations in Argentina.) Maheu's team, however, had every reason to believe they enjoyed special protection, if not total immunity. The tap itself was installed in that spring of 1954 by three employees of the New York Telephone Company. While it operated, Maheu's men lived at the National Republican Club on East 40 Street. Their field headquarters for the operation were the offices of Schenk & Schenk, an insurance firm whose premises had been engaged with the assistance of Robert Judge, a prominent contributor to the Republican Party. Presumably these were the fruits of maintaining an operation that enjoyed the personal patronage of the incumbent vice-president of the United States, as this one did. Almost two decades later, after having ascended to the presidency following an unanticipated eight-year delay, Richard M. Nixon would again reveal a keen interest in clandestine and illegal activities.

The Maheu wiretap, as it happened, found nothing.

If, from this point on, Onassis found himself at grips with an unseen adversary in the form of Robert Maheu, it was not because he had failed to put himself on guard, nor did he lack for warnings. Indeed, only three months earlier, in February, he had been arrested and briefly jailed for violating the Ship Sales Act of 1946, and his case was even now pending in the courts—something that might have alerted him to the possibility of governmental high-handedness. It was just that, like many people before and after, he expected the government of the United States to honor its ideals, obey its own laws, and play fair. Forever afterward, he would regard most Americans as little better than gangsters, and if anyone made so bold as to question the conspiracy theories with which he embroidered his leisure hours, he would point to the events of the 1950s and rest his case.

Onassis was not a student of politics, but he was certainly aware that the nation in which he had enrolled his children was embarked upon a great postwar Communist hunt that had already unmasked, or so it was believed, the Rosenberg spy ring while simultaneously

ruining many totally blameless lives. And while he was no student
of psychology, he was equally aware that at such times of national
hysteria, the public mind seeks scapegoats. Nor was he in any doubt
as to who some of those scapegoats might be: the maritime Greeks,
himself among them, with their flexible loyalties, equally flexible
business ethics, and rather too conspicuous prosperity—a prosperity based in provable but relatively small degree on hauling goods
to Communist harbors in American-built Liberty ships that had
been given to them by the Americans themselves, at a loss and on
favorable terms. (By 1954, the vessels of his father-in-law, Stavros
Livanos, had visited Communist ports some twenty-eight times on
one occasion or another.) There was great danger here, Onassis
knew, and he was right. The so-called "Red trade" had inevitably
attracted the attention of the ubiquitous Senator Joseph McCarthy,
compelling Manuel Kulukundis and Stavros Livanos to hasten to
Washington and discuss matters with a young McCarthy aide
named Robert Kennedy. Although it was not illegal for a Greek (or
an Argentinian) to trade with Communists, Onassis was not engaged in the traffic, and he was at pains to say so. Back in 1950, the
first year of the Korean War and, coincidentally, the year investigators from the Department of Commerce began to pore over his
books, he had gone so far as to offer his whaling and tanker fleets
to the American government with himself enrolled as a "humble
sailor." The offer was refused; in fact, the offer was regarded with
some suspicion. After all, he was the son-in-law of Stavros Livanos,
and Stavros Livanos *was* engaged in the Red trade, even if his
son-in-law was not. And the United States government, or so Onassis soon came to believe as a result of the Ship Sales Act case, had
decided to discover just how fond of his son-in-law Stavros Livanos
was.

   He had gotten into trouble by taking a certain step openly and
with the consent of his lawyer, Herbert Brownell, who had left
private practice in 1953 to become, by supreme irony, the attorney
general of the United States. This now put Brownell in the position
of prosecuting Aristotle Onassis for the crime of having taken his
advice. And in the late 1940s that advice had been both simple and
to the point. Once the surplus vessels from the wartime merchant
fleet had been distributed to such deserving allies as the Greeks
(Onassis owned nineteen of them by 1949), the Ship Sales Act of 1946

forbade the sale of tankers and other strategic vessels to foreign individuals. However, Brownell's law firm had pointed out, it was perfectly legal for a foreigner to take an interest in an American company that owned such vessels, provided the interest did not constitute a majority holding. As it happened, in 1953 Onassis made the acquaintance of Edward Stettinius, Franklin Roosevelt's last and Harry Truman's first secretary of state, whose place in history had been assured when he continued the practice, which had been encouraged by Roosevelt, of approaching the president for daily instructions. (Truman replied that if the secretary of state didn't know what he was supposed to do all day, then Truman would find himself a secretary of state who did.) At the time he met Aristotle Onassis, Stettinius had two great goals in life. He was eager to assist certain of his friends whose patriotism, he said, had caused them to neglect their personal interests, and he was equally eager to do something for Liberia, a country in whose fate he had interested himself.

Onassis was happy to oblige on both counts, although not quite in the way the ex-diplomat had anticipated. In short order, he made Liberia into the owner of the most popular flag of convenience in the world, and he put forward a plan that would enable Stettinius and his friends, who included Admiral of the Fleet William F. Halsey, to become rich precisely as Onassis himself had done—on an investment of nothing. The Stettinius group, Onassis suggested, would purchase forty T-2 tankers. Onassis would put up a quarter of the money, $20 million, and cheap federal mortgages would pay for the balance. The ships would be placed in service in the booming oil trade, the mortgages would be paid off in five years, and the owners could then decide whether to continue in the business or sell the fleet—at, needless to say, an enormous profit to themselves. It was foolproof.

It was also a trifle too bold. Neither Stettinius nor his associates could bring themselves to believe that it was workable, legal, or both, but more than one train of thought had begun during those fateful discussions at Stettinius's Virginia estate and the Onassis townhouse on Sutton Square. Onassis went on to establish U.S. Petroleum Carriers and its subsidiary, Victory Carriers, with other, more visionary (and less visible) American partners and a less ambitious program. Meanwhile, Stettinius and his group purchased five tankers on terms that were more to their liking and with the assistance of Stavros Niarchos—launching a chain of events that would result in temporary exile for Niarchos and ten minutes of jail for Aristotle Onassis, and which eventually involved a cast of characters that included Vice President Richard Nixon, the National Security Council, the State Department, the major oil companies, two kings of Saudi Arabia, the British foreign office, Lloyd's of London, and the Republic of Peru.

The first blow fell in October, 1953, when a federal grand jury handed down a sealed indictment against Onassis. It was not entirely unexpected. Stavros Niarchos, presently cooling his heels in London, had been the subject of a similiarly sealed indictment since April, and it took no great exercise of genius to conjure up the probable contents of both documents. They would charge violations of the Ship Sales Act, of course. Now, as each of Onassis's American-flag vessels made port in the United States, it would be visited by a customs officer who would hand its captain a letter placing it under arrest. A federal marshal operating under the supervision of a deputy United States attorney general named Warren Burger— who eventually controlled so many Niarchos and Onassis ships that his colleagues began to call him "Admiral" Burger—would then post an official letter of attachment. The ship's master would be deputized and instructed to carry out his duties, the crew would be paid by the United States Treasury, and the vessel's profits would be deposited with an on-shore custodian, who would retain them until the case was resolved.

Onassis would soon convince himself that he was the victim of a Republican plot, and there were indications that he was not far wrong. The previous administration had investigated him and found nothing; it had, in fact, bestowed its blessing on his methods through the Maritime Administration. But the Republicans had come to power in 1952 after a long drought and in a vengeful mood, and the right wing of the party was eager not only to apprehend the Communists it saw lurking everywhere but to make its anger and frustration felt by the Democrats, of whom Stettinius was a prominent example. The road to Stettinius led, or so it seemed, through Stavros Niarchos, and it was hardly possible to bring Niarchos to book without attacking Aristotle Onassis, whose involvement with American-flag vessels was, if anything, even greater, and who appeared to be the author of the entire scheme. That both Niarchos and Onassis were married to the daughters of the powerful Stavros Livanos was an irresistible added inducement to litigate. With the example of the brothers-in-law before them, Livanos and the other Greek shipowners were likely then to subscribe to an important goal of American foreign policy, the old Republican fantasy that the Soviets and their satellites could be starved into capitalism and democracy by cutting off their trade.

Onassis, ever the man of action, was inclined to fight. If he read the situation correctly, there was no case against him. He owned no more than 49 percent of any of the ships that were at the source of the contention. United States citizens demonstrably owned the other 51 percent, the attorney general of the United States had given the transactions his approval when he was in private practice, and it was clear therefore that he, Aristotle Onassis, was the aggrieved party, and not the federal government. He had pressing and highly confidential business in Saudi Arabia and it would not wait, but as soon as he had completed his transactions there he flew to Paris for legal consultations, sent Tina and the children to St. Moritz, and flew to New York in February, 1954 against the advice of his attorneys and without any clear idea of the reception that awaited him beyond the assurance, hardly comforting, that he would not be arrested at the airport. Perhaps it was not without a feeling of grim satisfaction that he wired Attorney General Brownell and placed himself at his disposal.

There arose a mildly colorful story that he was arrested while he was eating lunch at the Colony Club. Actually, he was at the club when federal marshals arrived at his offices with the warrant. The following Monday he traveled to Washington with a corps of lawyers headed by Ed Ross, surrendered himself to the federal attorney, and was fingerprinted and photographed. (At one point, Ross found himself watching the proceedings from a holding pen that he shared with the big news items of the day, the surviving members of the Puerto Rican terrorist unit that had just shot up the House of Representatives.) Finally Onassis stood before Judge Bothila J. Laws. The charges were read; they were what he expected. He pleaded not guilty, posted $10,000 bail, received the judge's instruction—later modified—to remain in the United States, and departed, angry but confident. This, he was certain, was nothing he couldn't handle. It was time for the dickering to begin. And when it came to dickering, there were few better men than Aristotle Onassis.

A few days later, he walked into another office in the capital city, his mood much improved. "Mr. Burger," he demanded, "what is the ransom?" He was prepared to bargain with the government, man to man.

In Europe, well beyond the reach of federal writ, Stavros Niarchos was also preparing to contact the American government, although his approach would be significantly different. Niarchos, by what means it was never clear, had recently obtained a copy of something called the Jiddah Agreement. Reading it, he realized that he was now in a position to give the United States something it wanted very badly, although it gave no sign that it was aware of the fact. Stavros Niarchos could give the Americans his brother-in-law.

Although the aftermath of the battle that was about to begin would form one of the four great facts of Christina Onassis's existence—the others were the ghetto of her father's fortune, his intricate personality, and the death of her brother—Stavros Niarchos's current dilemma, like that of his hated rival, had begun with an innocent and apparently legal business transaction. Niarchos, too, had desired to lay his hands on some surplus tankers, and to this end he had founded the North American Shipping and Trading Corporation, retained 40 percent of its stock, and distributed the balance to four American partners, one of whom, his American-born sister, Mrs. Andrew Dracopoulos, gave him effective control of the company. Meanwhile, certain of Stettinius's American investors—later called "the Casey group," after the Democratic ex-congressman who became its most conspicuous member—had been fired by the vision of Aristotle Onassis, although they evidently remained suspicious of his proposed methods and in due time made their way to Stavros Niarchos, who proved able to assist them in a somewhat different way. The Casey group set up two companies. One, the American Overseas Tanker Corporation, was formed in the United States and legally owned a number of surplus T-2s. The other, a Panamanian corporation especially established for the purpose, chartered the vessels and put them to work for the oil companies. What happened next is mildly complicated—it was meant to be—

but it gives an instructive glimpse of the methods that Niarchos and Onassis, both of them men with a healthy dislike of the tax collector, had developed to mask their activities. The Casey group's American company was next sold to the Delaware Tanker Corporation, yet another American concern in which Stavros Niarchos had an interest. The Panamanian Company, where the actual money was made, was purchased by Greenwich Maritime, a second Panamanian concern whose sole owner was Stavros Niarchos. In the upshot, Casey and the others made a profit of $3,250,000 on an initial investment of $101,000, and Niarchos received a lucrative source of income that was sheltered from all but the most nominal taxes by virtue of the benign business climate of Panama, where he and his brother-in-law would cut many such deals. Meanwhile, the vessels, like the nine T-2s owned by Niarchos's North American Shipping and Trading, flew the American flag. His persistent claim that he did not, in fact, own any of the ships in question—technically that was correct; he merely chartered them—was undermined by his practice of painting a large and conspicuous "N" on their funnels. Even so, the Justice Department was initially by no means certain that it could make a successful prosecution for illegal foreign ownership until the Republicans arrived in Washington, together with their new national agenda. Niarchos was not indicted until April of 1953.

Unlike Onassis, he did not immediately rush to America to confront his tormentors on their own ground. If he was less rich than his brother-in-law, he was also less impulsive, and he always seemed less secure in his fortune. ("This," he once told an associate, surveying his fleet, his yacht, his private island, and his estates, "is for my sons. If anyone tries to take it, shoot them." If Onassis ever made a similiar utterance, it was not recorded.) The indictment had been handed down barely a week after the keel of his record-breaking new tanker, the *World Glory*, was laid in the Bethlehem Steel shipyard in Quincy, Massachusetts, and slipways had been reserved nearby for two sister ships. Each vessel represented a $10 million investment and four million man-hours of labor, a not inconsiderable contribution to the chronically hard-pressed American shipbuilding industry. In an illuminating contrast to the later Onassis tactic of open, courageous, and perhaps foolhardy confrontation with Warren Burger, Niarchos canceled the two ships on which work had not yet begun, single-handedly precipitating a recession in the yards.

The government was not visibly impressed. Nor did Niarchos and his father-in-law appear capable of analyzing the situation with the clarity that was the Onassis trademark in those days. Stavros Livanos dispatched Spyros Skouras, the head of Twentieth Century Fox, to Washington, but Skouras was unable to learn anything of importance. L. E. P. Taylor, the British attorney, met with better luck, but only marginally so. The government would unseal the indictment and enter into discussions, Taylor was told, only when Niarchos returned to America and "submitted himself to United States justice." Taylor decided—rightly—that the charges were criminal, not civil. Aristotle Onassis would later tell the story of his arrest and brief incarceration with relish. Stavros Niarchos appeared to view the prospect with horror. The bludgeon of the ship cancellations had failed. He would have to play his trump.

It was never clear just when, exactly, Niarchos obtained a copy of the document known as the Jiddah Agreement, or by what means he managed to lay hands on it, but there is no doubt that it made for compelling reading. It, too, bore the Onassis trademarks. It was audacious, but it was also simple. And if it was ever implemented, it would make Onassis rich beyond the dreams of avarice.

As he had refined his plans during the typically convoluted negotiations with the Saudi representatives in 1953, Onassis had proposed to construct a fleet of Saudi-flag tankers that would eventually be manned by Saudi crews supervised by Saudi officers trained in a maritime academy he would establish at his own expense. In return, he asked only for exemption from export taxes— and permission to establish a monopoly in the transportation of Saudi Arabian oil. He was prepared, he later explained, to offer the same service to any country that asked for it.

His timing, as always, was impeccable. If the emirates and kingdoms of the Persian Gulf had ever doubted that they were little more than client states that prospered only at the sufferance of the British and the Americans, they had only to look to Iran, where Premier Mohammed Mossadegh, weeping from the bed on which he was carried into parliament, had nationalized the holdings of the British Petroleum Company (and deposed his rightful ruler, the young shah, a practice that was definitely not to be encouraged) but had swiftly fallen in a counterrevolution engineered by the CIA station chief, Kermit Roosevelt, when Mossadegh proved unable to export the country's production. As long as the countries of the Gulf lacked a fleet of tankers—and as long as the British and the Americans possessed the will to enforce their policies, something they would not lose until twenty years later—their rulers were not truly sovereigns in their own lands. Aristotle Onassis was proposing to make them just that. It was an offer that the Saudis, helped along with a few well-placed bribes, had evidently found irresistible.

Onassis and the Saudi finance minister had signed the agreement in January of 1954, just before Onassis's dramatic return to face charges in America. While Tina took tea with the king's four wives, the monarch presented him with two thoroughbred horses and a jeweled sword. His partners, Niarchos learned, were two. The more visible of the pair was Spyridon Catapodis, an excitable Riviera-based deal-maker. The other was Dr. Hjalmar Schacht, the financial wizard of both the Weimar Republic and the Third Reich, who had somehow managed to emerge from the ruins of postwar Germany with his freedom and personal fortune intact. Schacht's precise role in the negotiations was never disclosed and perhaps could not be learned, for the doctor was a man of discretion, but his presence in the deal could be calculated to further alarm an American government that would be rendered highly alert when its benefactor— none other than Stavros Niarchos himself—revealed the contents of the document he now held in his hands. With the Jiddah Agreement as his leverage, or so he believed, Niarchos had the means to free himself from the criminal charges in Washington while simultaneously avenging the betrayal at Monte Carlo. For Onassis's Jiddah Agreement was a clear violation of a pact between the American oil companies and the Saudi Arabian monarchy. Niarchos had found the means to destroy his brother-in-law.

The unsuccessful wiretap had been only one of many strings that Stavros Niarchos had in his bow. With Niarchos's long purse at his disposal, Robert Maheu activated several of the ex-FBI men he had at his disposal, thanks to his close ties to the Society of Former Agents. Maheu set them to work preparing a detailed analysis of the situation. When it was complete, he presented it to Vice President Richard Nixon and, through the vice president's good offices, the National Security Council. Nixon also insisted on regular briefings, and he personally laid down the guidelines of the operation to Maheu and John Gerrity, one of Maheu's operatives. "Nixon gave us the whole bit—you know, the 'Your assignment, John, should you choose to accept it . . .' sort of thing," Gerrity recalled later. "He kept saying that this was top secret, and that if we took the assignment and got caught—well, the government couldn't be of any help. They'd deny all involvement. Well, I told him I thought that was standard procedure, and he said, 'Of course it is, of course it is: I just want to be sure you understand.' " What Nixon had in mind, it seems, was to assign employees of the Central Intelligence Agency to assist Maheu, Gerrity, and their employer, Stavros Niarchos.

In February, a few days after Onassis was arrested in Washington, Maheu and Gerrity published the text of the Jiddah Agreement in an Italian newspaper secretly owned by the CIA. With a liberal disbursement of cash, Gerrity was also able to purchase European newspaper editorials denouncing the agreement, hinting that Saudi Arabia would nationalize the oil fields, and pointing to the sinister involvement of Dr. Schacht, but a second electronic bug, implanted in the Onassis flat on avenue Foch in Paris, evidently produced nothing of value. In New York, the *Daily News* received and published extracts from a 1942 letter written by J. Edgar Hoover to the head of the War Shipping Administration, in which the FBI director charged that Onassis had "expressed sentiments inimical to the United States war effort," and suggested that "his activities and movements while in the United States should be carefully scrutinized." Onassis began to see a little light, although he was still ignorant of the forces that were being mobilized against him. "What I'd like to know," he wondered aloud, "is how my brother-in-law can get such a government document."

Through an intermediary, Robert McCormick, Niarchos informed the State Department that he viewed the situation precipitated by his brother-in-law as "unfortunate," and he volunteered his services in finding a solution. The Onassis oil fleet, McCormick pointed out, was built with money advanced by American insurance companies and banks. It should be a simple matter, then, for the diplomats to advise the financial institutions to refuse to underwrite any vessel that would fly the Saudi flag (which would effectively scuttle the Jiddah Agreement) or to cancel all their outstanding arrangements (which would effectively scuttle Onassis). For a variety of reasons, the diplomats were unable to adopt the proposal, but at McCormick's suggestion the Justice Department was informed of Mr. Niarchos's cooperative attitude.

Maddeningly, Onassis pressed on as though he were invincible; he was always invigorated by a crisis. King Saud ratified the Jiddah Agreement in May. The State Department prepared for a major confrontation. The American ambassador called at the palace to give the monarch a course of instruction in the probable consequences of his act. The consortium that did business as the Arabian American Oil Company—ARAMCO—invoked the wording of its own agreement with the Saudi government and announced that under no circumstances would any Saudi-flag vessel be allowed to take on a cargo of oil at the depot in Ras Tanura. Onassis responded by naming his latest 46,000-ton tanker the *Al Malik Saud Al-Awal*, after the king. The bottle of christening water from the holy well at Zem Zem was swung against the hull three times before it broke, an unlucky occurrence, but Aristotle Onassis did not believe in omens. The *Al Malik* was prepared for the sea.

In August, Maheu was summoned to the Niarchos suite in Claridge's Hotel in London. He found his employer's obsession with his brother-in-law in full cry; the meeting began at breakfast and ended at five o'clock the following morning. Onassis, Niarchos said, would upset the balance of power in the Middle East. Onassis would exclude Niarchos from Saudi Arabia. Onassis, with his scheme producing an estimated cash flow of $17 million in the first year alone, would become unstoppable. Maheu had heard it all before; it was old ground, but then Niarchos introduced something that was new. Because of the carefully constructed interlocks between the ships, their mortgages, and their charters, Niarchos estimated that his rival could lay hands on no more than $5 million, and for this reason a certain recent incident at the Nice airport was of particular interest. There, Spyridon Catapodis, the deal-maker, convinced that Onassis had used disappearing ink to write the agreement between them acknowledging Catapodis's role as go-between (a chemical analysis of the paper, ordered by Maheu, suggested that this was so), and driven berserk by his erstwhile partner's refusal to pay his commission, had seized Onassis by the neck, driven him to his knees, spat in his face, and called him a goddamn Turk. The Greek consul, standing nearby, had refused to intervene. "I would have done exactly the same," he said. Perhaps Niarchos decided that Spyridon Catapodis was a man who bore watching.

In September, Catapodis filed a sixteen-page affidavit and thirty-four exhibits with the British consul. Among other things, he charged that Onassis had paid a million and a quarter dollars in bribes to a Saudi minister and other officials, a commonplace practice but an accusation that the king might find it difficult to ignore in view of the powerful American pressure that was being exerted. In addition, Catapodis charged, Onassis had expressed disdain for his Saudi partners, and had spoken of his determination to disrupt ARAMCO while carving out a major role for himself in the development of the country.

Because Catapodis had nothing but a blank sheet of paper where the all-important contract should have been, his case was unlikely to go far in the courts, but his allegations were a gift beyond price to Niarchos and Maheu. Maheu had previously located Karl Twitchell, the geologist who had negotiated the original 1933 agreement between the late King Ibn Saud and the oil companies that had led to the formation of ARAMCO, and Twitchell, Maheu was interested to discover, was a right-thinking American who could be relied on to talk sense to Ibn Saud's son. Now, with Twitchell in tow, Maheu flew to Jiddah and—through intermediaries—laid the charges before the king.

Maheu's timing, too, was impeccable, although luck had played its role. With the king facing an American suggestion—never stated in so many words, but it was there—that if a revolution could be arranged in Teheran, it might be possible to arrange one elsewhere, it appeared that Maheu and his evidence had arrived at the perfect psychological moment. He was soon able to report complete success to his employer over the confidential CIA communications link that had been placed at his disposal. The Saudi minister accused of taking Onassis's bribe had just been sacked. The Saudis had instructed Onassis to reach a compromise with ARAMCO, an impossible task. Lastly, the royal advisers had given Maheu permission to publish the Catapodis documents in Europe but not in America, where relations at present were in a somewhat delicate condition. (The advisers' notions of modern communications were somewhat primitive.) The Jiddah Agreement was dead and could not be revived.

"You're a lousy businessman," Niarchos told Maheu when they met in Washington at the Mayflower Hotel. (It was now safe for him to return to America.) He had examined Maheu's expenses; they were accurate and, by Niarchos's lights, too small.

Maheu exibited a willingness to benefit from his employer's generosity, if his employer was so inclined. "It's not too late," he said.

"Yes, it is," said Niarchos. "If I gave you the money now, you'd never learn the lesson." However, it was possible that a course of instruction might be arranged. "I don't like the house you live in, I don't like the car you drive," said Niarchos. "If you'll promise you'll get a new house and a new car, I'll send you fifteen hundred dollars a month until you have fifty thousand dollars."

Even in victory, Stavros Niarchos was a stern taskmaster.

And even in defeat, Aristotle Onassis placed his faith in the powers of illusion. The oil companies, determined to make an example of him, imposed a boycott of his fleet that, if continued indefinitely, would achieve Stavros Niarchos's most cherished goal: They would break him. Ships coming off charter could find no new work, chartered ships were delayed in harbor, yet in Monaco Onassis proceeded with his program of rejuvenation as though nothing out of the ordinary were occurring. He floodlighted the casino and regilded its decorations, laid out new beaches that were as swiftly swept away, made plans for a new swimming pool and a helicopter link with Nice, and spoke of creating an artificial island off the tiny coastline.

In the southern Pacific, Peru announced that its sovereignty now extended 200 miles offshore, a move specifically designed to halt the depredations of the Onassis whaling fleet and one that, or so many believed, could not have been taken without the tacit approval of the United States, whose ambassador distinguished himself by his silence on a subject that—in those days—invariably brought forth vigorous American protestations. Onassis ordered his whalers to cross the line. The Peruvians responded by dispatching obsolete warplanes and a pair of aged destroyers to round up the factory ships and killer boats. Shots were fired, and ten thousand miles away Onassis majestically sailed the completed *Christina* into Monte

Carlo harbor and tied up in the preferred berth near the head of
the sea wall. He also let it be known that he had pacified the prince
—who was, in truth, a trifle ruffled at the thought of sharing his
sovereignty with a man who called him "that boy"—by arranging
for Rainier to acquire a 137-foot yacht, the *Deo Juvante*. Unless
asked directly, however, Onassis neglected to make clear that the
prince had paid the $120,000 purchase price himself.

With half his tankers idle by the end of 1955 and his losses mount-
ing toward $20 million, his creditors became watchful, but when
Rainier married the American actress Grace Kelly in April, 1956,
the seaplane from the *Christina* showered the nuptial barge with
red and white carnations, the Grimaldi family colors, and at night
a projector aboard the yacht beamed the prince's coat of arms onto
the escarpment that overlooked the barracklike palace and the
refurbished casino. The prospective Onassis wedding gift was much
discussed and widely expected to be lavish—another yacht, perhaps
his own, or perhaps a trinket costing in the rumored vicinity of $4
million. In any event, it would be something cut to the Onassis
measure. The actual present proved to be a painting by his friend
Ludwig Bemelmans. People were puzzled.

Another man might have battened the hatches of his private life,
laid up his yacht, placed the servants on leave, closed all residences
but one (his most modest), and sought to portray himself (the cliché
recurs at times like these, even if it does not resound) as a simple
David in the field against the Goliath of the petroleum multination-
als. The image, one might think, would appeal to him. Perhaps it
was simple gallantry that prevented him from invoking it, or a
desire to go out—if go out he must—with flair. But there is another
explanation, and it is one that does much to explain the kind of man
he had become—and the kind of man he would shortly prove to be.
His dwindling wealth had been amassed, and amassed with astonishing speed, by his ability to combine insight with an ability to plan,
but many men have insights, just as many men are capable of
making clever plans, and they do not become rich. The other essential ingredients in the rise of Aristotle Onassis were his gambler's
instincts and the ability, so often found in confident men, to persuade other, more stolid individuals of the validity of his dream.
Before the war, and with surprisingly little difficulty, he had persuaded the Swedes to build tankers larger than any others and to

entrust them to a man who had no experience in the trade, a task that was lightened to some degree by Ingse Dedichen's mother, herself the widow of a shipbuilder and a woman of influence, who believed—as no doubt did Onassis himself—in the intensity and permanence of his attachment to her daughter. It was the same in New York just after the war, although his task there was lightened by the newfound venturesomeness of the insurance companies and the fact that all his predictions had come true. And yet—as he himself seemed to realize when he described himself as a poor man —the very success of his plan meant that he had now subjected himself to a form of serfdom, the consequences of which were before him.

It is an axiom of the banking business that the major debtors own the banks, i.e., that they will be supplied with abundant funds, no matter what the condition of their balance sheets, as long as the possibility of repayment exists, and that the spigot will close only when all hope is lost. It was this unhappy latter contingency that Onassis was fast approaching, thanks to an unavoidable flaw in his scheme. He had become rich, but he had done so at the sufferance of others—the oil companies—and these others were not without alternatives. His financial methods were known and copied. There were other independent oil fleets on the seas, among them the fleet of Stavros Niarchos. Onassis was not essential. Onassis could be replaced. His monopoly would have freed him, of course. But his failed monopoly had become the very occasion for his undoing.

At the same time, just as the gambler must believe in his luck and a charlatan must subscribe to the reality of his deception, it became vital for Onassis to believe in the permanence of his limitless wealth, although he knew perfectly well that it was not limitless and the oil companies were in the process of proving that it was not necessarily permanent. In some essential part of his being, he had become identical with his fortune. He could not strike back at his tormentors because the very nature of his situation denied him the necessary weapons. But neither could he turn aside from the course on which he had embarked—the gilded domes of his casino, his great yacht, the cascades of carnations, and the rest of it, though he might cut a corner here and there. Perhaps his luck would return if he pretended he had never lost it; perhaps the illusion would again become reality if he maintained it. If he lost his money, he would cease to exist.

The crisis slowly began to ease, but not by enough. Thanks to an airtight insurance policy, the whaling fleet was released from its Peruvian captivity when its $2.8 million fine was paid by Lloyd's of London, with the British Foreign Office moving discreetly in the background. A formidably well-documented case against its illegal hunting practices was rendered moot when Costa Gratsos sold the vessels to the Japanese for $8.5 million, pocketing a handsome commission for his trouble. There was no more danger from that quarter.

In Washington, the Justice Department had added a $20 million civil suit to the criminal charges, but Burger and his colleagues were by no means confident in the strength of their case. The true villain of the piece appeared to be the federal regulatory apparatus, which had bungled the situation badly. Because of similiar difficulties, the government was already arranging a settlement with the cooperative Mr. Niarchos, a settlement which eventually included the withdrawal of the criminal charges against him. The charges against Casey and his group had been dismissed, and charges against Manuel Kulukundis were dropped after a company affiliated with him was acquitted. On December 21, 1955, Onassis agreed to submit to a $7 million fine, a sum that could easily be paid over an agreed upon span of years if only his cash flow recovered. In exchange for his promise—on which he successfully reneged— to build three new ships, two 46,000 tonners and one 106,000 tonner, in American yards, he was permitted to transfer the disputed surplus vessels to foreign flags of convenience, and his American companies were placed in a trust administered by the Grace National Bank, with a 25 percent beneficial interest going to one of his Panamanian companies and the balance assigned to his children. (By 1958, the trust would earn $20 million. Alexander and Christina would be rich.)

Under normal circumstances, the American settlement—it was even better than the one negotiated by Niarchos—would have been a source of glad rejoicing, but circumstances were not normal. The oil company boycott continued. In Greece, keeping up his image as a plutocrat, he had opened negotiations to buy the national airline, TAE, but almost half his ships remained idle, swinging around their anchor chains or steaming slowly at sea to save fuel. Onassis was reduced to chasing new business, begging for charters (British Shell claimed it helped him here), or seeking cargoes in the volatile spot market, which before 1954 he had played for entertainment and quick killings. There seemed to be no way to take up the slack. His once infallible luck seemed to have taken a holiday. No miracle occurred. The losses mounted. Somewhat later than Niarchos had predicted (there was no indication that Niarchos had a hand in the present catastrophe), Onassis was going broke. "You are really hurting me, you know," he told the British oilmen as he passed through London. "You guys are giving me the worst time of my life." The oilmen knew perfectly well what they were doing. The example they proposed to make of him was to be a salutory one, a valuable object lesson to any other independent tanker owner who might attempt to cut a deal with the producing countries on his own. Onassis was not merely to be punished. Onassis was to be crushed.

In private, the injustice of it all drove him from rage to despair and back again. Unlike all too many Greeks, he paid his crews top dollar and maintained his vessels in accordance with the highest standards. He had never lost a ship. In Saudi Arabia he had only attempted to do something he believed (rightly) to be inevitable. Unlike the American State Department and the major oil companies, he had recognized the peculiar intensity of Arab nationalism, and he had perceived an opportunity there. If he proposed to make an immense profit from his discovery, whose business was that but his? "My mistake was that I woke up too early and disturbed those who were still asleep," he said later, "and as a result I got into the biggest mess of my life."

The end was rapidly approaching, the moment when Stavros Niarchos's revenge would be complete. 1953 had been the year when all Onassis's dreams seemed to come true at once. 1956, the year he celebrated his fiftieth birthday, seemed to be the year when an old Greek truth would once more be demonstrated. After hubris comes nemesis.

And still the miracle did not occur.

CHAPTER FIVE

Maria Callas

On November 1, 1956, as a combined Anglo-French war fleet approached his shores, unopposed RAF bombers cratered his airfields, and the Israeli Defense Force mopped up the shattered remnant of his armies in the northern Sinai, President Gamal Abdel Nasser of Egypt ordered the first of seven blockships sunk in Lake Timsah, roughly halfway along the length of the Suez Canal, and thus saved Aristotle Onassis from almost certain bankruptcy.

Nothing less would have done it. As Onassis was somewhat too pointedly aware, he was no longer as other men were, even in defeat. Rescue could be forthcoming only through the mercy of his tormentors among the oil companies, some of whom were themselves the size of sovereign states—Gulf Oil, to name but one, virtually owned the country of Kuwait—or through the force of history itself, as had in fact just occurred. With the Suez Canal blocked by the spiteful act of a defeated dictator and the short route from the oil fields to Europe severed for months to come, the oil companies could no longer afford the luxury of didactic revenge. As they scrambled to find tanker capacity for the long voyage around the Cape of Good Hope, only one man possessed—thanks to those very oil companies—enough surplus tonnage to take full and satisfying advantage of the bonanza in preferential rates. Onassis later estimated that he made between $60 and $70 million in the six months the canal was closed. It was possible to make as much as $2 million on a single voyage. The boycott was forgotten. He was needed again, and needed badly. Nasser made him rich again. All was forgiven. "After 1956," said George Moore, his banker, "he had the ability to throw money out of the window, but a hard core of caution prevented him from doing it."

And yet, in his business life, he was a changed man. Before the boycott, he had been a brilliant adventurer who seemed to pull ideas out of the air, to act on impulses that had no discernible rational basis but which were almost infallibly correct, to identify and seize opportunities with an uncanny prescience. He was, in short, a genius, but after the boycott he was a genius no more. Perhaps it was the hard core of caution of which George Moore spoke, or perhaps it was fear of losing something more important than money, the image of himself that seemed to be identical with his bank balance, but once his fortune was restored he was quite content to tend his cash flow and obediently follow the market as it was defined by the oil companies. They had, apparently, taught him no end of a lesson. "I wouldn't say there was anything remarkably brilliant about him when we got to know each other," said Sir Frank (later Lord) MacFadzean, a scholarly executive who served as the head of Shell's department of supply and logistics. "As I recall it, Ari was very much middle average in terms of his success at guessing trends." He would never overtake his father-in-law. Unlike Daniel Ludwig, who attempted to carve a personal empire out of the Amazon jungle and later planned to build skyscrapers in New Jersey, he would undertake no bold new commercial ventures. By the best available estimates, he would eventually be worth a good half billion dollars, but Ludwig would far surpass him. He would be overtaken by Y. K. Pao, the Chinese master of the long-term charter, and by a latecomer, Costa Lemos, who was called "the Ghost." In the end, Stavros Niarchos would finally be the richer of the two. The glory days had ended.

To old friends like Basil Mavroleon, he remained much the same as always and would remain so to the end of his life, cracking his bad jokes, playing his old guitar and singing in his strong voice, a man who smoked cigarettes before dinner and cigars after, perspired freely in all seasons, and drank the night away at El Morocco or La Privée or Éléfant Blanc with a telephone always nearby, his battered notebook never far from his hand, and a bewildered petroleum executive somewhere in the vicinity, trying to do business when other sane men were in bed. "He would sit there at his front table at 21," said one such executive, "in a suit that *I* wouldn't wear, put a handkerchief to his brow, and tell me that I was going to ruin him in his old age." Unlike Niarchos, he remained interested in the lives of ordinary people; it was, his friends agreed, one of his finest qualities. "You got the impression that Niarchos never wasted a moment's time on anyone who was of no importance, no use to him," said Sir Frank MacFadzean. "Ari was quite the opposite. He made great friends with my secretary and they got along very well, although she didn't want anything from him and couldn't help him in any way. I think he just loved getting away from the sort of business entertaining he had to do and the crowds of hangers-on who were always after him for something. Niarchos was always surrounded by toadies."

"He always came to the newspaper without telephoning, and he would ask for me in a very modest way," says Helen Vlachos. " 'Eleni,' the doorman would call up and say, 'there's somebody here who says he's Mr. Onassis.' Of course, the doorman didn't believe him, but I knew that it was only the Onassis way of playing the situation. Because I knew that after five minutes, all the newspaper would know that Mr. Onassis had come and the man downstairs had very nearly thrown him out. He would come up and sit here and I would tell him, 'Why don't you ring up like everybody else, why don't you say who you are? You're stupid.' And he would say, 'The one thing, you know, is that at this moment I'm terribly hungry. Do you have any bread and cheese?' So I rang up for some, and five minutes later everybody knew that Mr. Onassis was hungry and wanted bread and cheese. But you know, Onassis was the one rich man I have ever known, and I have known a great many, who was generous with his time. He would sit and talk and wait and never be in a hurry; it was part of his charm. 'Oh,' he would say, 'can I stay a bit longer in your office? You know, it's so fascinating for me to be at a newspaper.' And I would say, 'Come on, Ari, don't be a fool.' 'Oh no,' he would say, 'it's quite true. If you don't mind, I'll just sit here in the corner and watch you work.' And of course all the young people on the newspaper would come up and look at him."

And yet in his business, he allowed himself to go slack. Unlike the royalist Niarchos, whose private secretary was Count George Theodoki and who had a genuine if deposed prince, Alexander of Yugoslavia, in his London office, he continued to surround himself with the cousins and cronies he had brought from Argentina or had encountered on his travels. This was not necessarily a bad thing, but it was time for his company, now named Olympic Maritime, to pass beyond the heroic entrepreneural days of its founding, when the writ of its owner was law and all decisions emanated from his desk. A new corporate structure was called for, with authority delegated and clear lines of communication established. Instead, with Olympic's income again secure and its founder newly obsessed with the villainy of his brother-in-law, it came to resemble a banana republic or a Balkan court of the previous century. "The main characteristics of the organization were spying, intrigue, and accusation," said Professor Georgakis. "Ari was fertile ground; he thirsted for intrigue. If there were two explanations for something, a simple one and a byzantine one, the simple one would not convince him but his ears would start to flap as the more complex hypothesis was put forward. Having someone like him at the top could only encourage that sort of thing. Ari made a mess of everything."

He placed his cousin, Nikos Konialidis, who had been with him in Buenos Aires and had married his half-sister Merope, in charge of the newly acquired airline, renamed Olympic Airways, where some highly creative (but entirely legal) accounting was required to conceal the true state of the company from the revenue-starved Greek government. At Olympic Maritime, Nicos's brother Costa became, in effect, the mayor of the palace by employing a time-honored expedient: He controlled access to the boss. Employees and executives who wanted to speak directly to their chief were sidetracked or, if they persisted, fired. Bids were seldom taken for corporate purchases, with Costa buying where he chose—and creating a constituency, loyal to himself, among the company's suppliers. If possible, bad news was not allowed to reach the Onassis ear unless it served some useful purpose. He was told that a pay raise for the staff had cost only 11 million drachmas when in fact the real figure was 20 million, and as late as 1973 he was completely unaware that aviation fuel had gone up to 44 cents a gallon, adding $17 million to the airline's costs and draining it of cash. Once he had been so proud of his accomplishments and his ships that he displayed elaborate drawings at each of his launchings, depicting the new vessel's specifications in exhaustive detail for all to see. Now he attempted to operate with a secrecy as obsessive as his father-in-law's, without accurate information, sometimes with no information whatever, and occasionally with information that was patently false. Nor were his methods of dealing with his employees calculated to bring him enlightenment.

"You're not doing well," he told his chief engineer one day over the phone.

"What?" asked the man. "What do you mean?"

"Listen, I'm telling you, you're not doing well. Pull your socks up."

Mirto Yannicopoulos, Olympic's chief of security, was in Onassis's office and heard the exchange. After his employer hung up, he asked, "What's he done wrong?"

"Nothing," said Onassis. "I'm just keeping him on his toes."

As long as the oil business continued to thrive, none of it mattered. "After 1959, he didn't need any money; he had to find ways of spending it," said George Moore. "So it became a game: If you don't need the money, you win. You may not even want it, but that in itself enables you to make even more. He would let people come to him; he wouldn't go to them anymore. It's an irony I think he appreciated. He'd spent most of his life hustling for business, and now he was going to sit back and let other people hustle him." He toyed with the idea of going public with a portion of his fleet and selling stock, but he would never have been able to bear the scrutiny bestowed by governments on such enterprises, and the plan went nowhere. He dragged Moore, who knew nothing about minerals, to South Africa, where he examined a possible tin mining venture, spent a bibulous week in Johannesburg, and returned home none the worse for wear but with a hearty dislike of Afrikaaners and a complete disinclination to put his money into tin. He explored another mineral project in Alaska with equally barren results, bought a small bank in Geneva, and speculated modestly in gold. "George," he would say to Moore, "give me some business. You must have some ideas." There were rumors of bizarre acquisitions, a baby food factory in Brazil, a taxi company in Liechtenstein, but they were as groundless as the document that presently began to circulate privately in California, accusing him of kidnaping Howard Hughes, controlling the Mafia, and secretly ruling the world. His casino and his airline were hobbies, and that was precisely what he called them; any other venture would also be such a pastime, but

nothing except his Swiss bank seemed like enough fun. "Olympic
Airways are the leaves of the plant," he once told his son, Alexander,
"but the root of the plant is the shipping business." If nothing
interfered with his ships, he was free to indulge himself.

Obsessed—and enormously entertained—by the supposed wick-
edness of his brother-in-law, he created a private intelligence apparatus and spent hours overseeing its operation. On Yannicopoulos's
advice, he never discussed confidential matters in the office or at
home but reserved them for the street, where eavesdropping was
presumably more difficult. "But he could never keep a secret anyway," complained his security chief. "After ten days it would be too
much for him and he would tell everyone himself." Yannicopoulos
hinted of bugging devices on the Niarchos premises; where possible, Niarchos's domestic staff and the crew of his yacht were sub-
verted. "If we heard that Niarchos was looking for a new maid, she
would be ours before she arrived," said Yannicopoulos. "It would
not cost much, but it would be a sum she would never have
dreamed about." His own crew and staff were carefully scrutinized,
but he could no more abide by his own precautions than he could
keep a secret; he hired at least one crew member, young Yorgos
Zakarias, who became Alexander's particular (and for a while, only)
friend, on sheer impulse. Still, he believed he detected leaks in his
organization and he suspected there were more. People were peri-
odically dismissed. Misinformation was deliberately planted, usually by the transparent expedient of discussing it in an unnaturally
loud voice in the presence of the hired help. Watch was then kept
to see if it surfaced in the enemy camp, but Niarchos proved an
elusive foe. "All we could get on him," lamented Yannicopoulos,
"was his womanizing."

Even so, Onassis was unable to listen to the voice of reason. Over
dinner one evening at Monte Carlo, Stavros Livanos reduced the
now celebrated rivals to shamefaced silence as he recounted their
sins of the past and present, but not even the displeasure of their
formidable father-in-law was enough to make them stop. Yannicopoulos himself, who maintained a shadowy connection with
Niarchos while simultaneously plotting against him, came to believe that the battle had gone on too long and that it was being
deliberately fomented by underlings in the respective camps. "I

used to say to both of them, 'Why do you let third parties inflame you, why not get together and bury the hatchet?' But they never would."

For Onassis, at least, the rivalry was a congenial game that passed the time, but perhaps it was also more than that. Professor Georgakis, who joined his entourage later, immediately noticed that his new friend and employer possessed an unusually mutable identity for a man so rich, and the professor came to regard the Onassis changeability—his acting, the professor called it—as his single most distinguishing characteristic. "In Greece, he was a Greek," Georgakis remarked. "In England, he was an Englishman. In an international forum, among international ethics, he was superb." (Jacqueline Kennedy, when she was married to him, remarked on the same thing.) But on television, where he was required to project himself for the benefit of the cameras, he was a disaster. It may not be too much to say that the existence of his brother-in-law provided invaluable assistance in his persistent attempts to define himself. As long as he was the enemy of Stavros Niarchos, he knew exactly who he was.

He was also—belatedly, because of the oil company boycott—a host of international renown. Like many another self-made man, he collected celebrities for his table, and no doubt he did so for the same reason: The presence of famous laps beneath his napery confirmed his status and told him that he had arrived at last. As long as Manuel Kulukundis lived, he would never be a bona fide member of the shipping aristocracy, but it proved astonishingly simple for him to become a playboy.

"Tina told me he wanted only important people around him," says one of his wife's friends, but his notions of importance were somewhat peculiar. Intellectuals and politicians interested him as little as the artists he neglected to patronize. He paid $200,000 for El Greco's *Madonna and Angel* and hung it in his yacht only because Niarchos had paid $100,000 for a similar painting, and because his friends called him "el Greco." His notion of fame was shaped by the periodicals he skimmed rather than by the books he utterly failed to read. He was drawn to the synthetic glamour of Hollywood stardom, to deposed royalty, to people who were famous for being famous, and with his newfound caution as his watchword in his business dealings, he focused all his enormous energies on the acquisition of such worthies, especially if they had previously been collected by Stavros Niarchos. The elusive Greta Garbo he knew from New York, although the precise nature of their relationship and the manner of their original meeting remained a mystery to the end. He knew Dame Margot Fonteyn because she was married to his Panamanian lawyer, Roberto Arias. Now, using his yacht, his casino, and his bankroll as bait, he attracted Farouk of Egypt, ex-King Peter of Yugoslavia, Marlene Dietrich, Cary Grant, and Ava Gardner, and he hired a young New Zealander, Nigel Neilson, to make certain that his social exploits appeared in the better sort of paper and in a manner that reflected credit on him. He staged fireworks displays above Monte Carlo and presided over cruises to the islands and lavish dinners both ashore and afloat. For him to take a meal alone with his family was a rare event. The *Christina* shipped two chefs who prepared both French and Greek specialties, with most guests choosing the latter in deference to their host, whose own favorite dishes were raw onions liberally doused with olive oil, stuffed tomatoes, and baked eggplant, all washed down with Dom Perignon champagne.

His consideration became legendary. Sailing time was usually delayed until late in the morning to accommodate his guests' hangovers. Because the *Christina* had a bad pitch and an equally bad yaw, the actual journeys were accomplished in short hops, with the majority of the time devoted to amusements ashore. He would hire whole bands and bring them aboard, dispatch his seaplane to fetch delicacies, and if they happened to be anchored in Greece, he would initiate his guests into one of his favorite recreations, breaking every plate in the local taverna by hurling them into a handy fireplace.

Two ladies' maids and a valet were on constant call, and a touch of a button summoned the barman, an essential feature since the host himself now avoided the bar, whose fittings were painful reminders of his lost whaling fleet. He was rarely in evidence during the day, either sleeping late or monitoring the movements of his ships on one of the forty-two radiotelephones, and it was only in the evening that he emerged to play his guitar and tell his stories and preside over the entertainment, although he invariably found time to swim his daily mile—the one time, he said, when he was able to be alone with his thoughts. If he experienced any second thoughts about his new friends—"They are all shits!" he exclaimed to an old friend from the German days, and he spent a long boozy evening lamenting his fate and remembering happier times, when he was launching his first ships and life was good—he did not share his disillusionment with his family. Indeed, it is difficult to discover anything, other than his fortune, that he shared with them. With his actorly instincts, he had changed the story of his life from the high drama of shipbuilding and commercial warfare to a drawing room comedy of social nuance, shipboard romances, and cocktails in the afternoon, but he could still find no very prominent place in the tale he had spun for his wife and children. He had assigned himself the role of host only to the small degree required to flesh out his impersonation as he, and he alone, continued to star in what he seemed to regard as the movie of his life. And he was after bigger game.

In the summer of 1958, Randolph Churchill introduced him to his famous father, and Onassis immediately set out on a campaign of conquest. The old warrior was only occasionally himself in the twilight of his years. Onassis invited him on a cruise, on many cruises. In an unprecedented step, he actually read Sir Winston's books and vainly attempted to discuss them with him, and on one memorable if poignant occasion, he fed him caviar with a spoon. He saw to it that Sir Winston's glass of whiskey was always on his breakfast tray; when Sir Winston's beloved canary escaped in Monte Carlo, he organized search parties that eventually located the bird (or, more probably, a reasonable facsimile) in Nice. He never gambled at his own tables. He found the stakes uninteresting, he said, and he was unwilling to set what he regarded as a bad example. One of the major bones of contention between Onassis and Rainier was the prince's dream of attracting a middle-class clientele that, Onassis felt, could not afford the inevitable losses. But he made an exception for the sake of his newest and most illustrious guest, who was a keen fan. He quoted the old man tirelessly, especially if there was a journalist or a social lion in the vicinity, took him to America on the *Christina* and entered New York harbor in triumph, and if he had been permitted, he would no doubt have made the former prime minister a permanent fixture in his establishment. He seemed to have no idea of how the two of them looked together, or of the things that were being said behind his back. Having acquired

*Aristotle Onassis with his wife, Tina, and their children,
Alexander and Christina, at a ship launching in Germany
during the winter of 1954. Tina had broken her leg "standing
up" while skiing in Switzerland. Onassis was said to dye his
hair black for social occasions, gray for business meetings.*
(UPI/Bettman Newsphotos)

Aristotle Onassis in 1954 with his children and Sheik Mohammad Abdullah Alireza of Saudi Arabia. The Arabian scheme had already gone awry, but Onassis was determined to play out a losing hand. (UPI/Bettman Newsphotos)

Tina Onassis and her husband arrive at the opera in Monaco, 1956. In a few short years, he would become an expert on the subject. When they had married, ten years earlier, he was forty; Tina was sixteen.

(UPI/Bettman Newsphotos)

Christina in Monte Carlo, at thirteen, before plastic surgery to her nose and under her eyes. (Publifoto/Black Star)

*Actor Glenn Ford sunbathes on a Monaco jetty in 1962
with Onassis's yacht* Christina *in the background. The vessel's
bar stools were upholstered with whale scrotums, and the music
box in the children's nursery was disguised as a slot machine.*
(UPI/Bettman Newsphotos)

*The battle of Skorpios. Onassis bodyguards and the press
grapple on the day before he married Jacqueline Kennedy.*
(UPI/Bettman Newsphotos)

Onassis with Maria Callas in 1960, a year after the breakup of his marriage to Tina. "It was not," says one of his intimates, "a very interesting affair." (UPI/Bettman Newsphotos)

Left: Onassis at the Glyfada villa with Prince Rainier, Princess Grace, and Princess Caroline (right) during a royal visit in 1961. "He never bore grudges," the prince remarked after he expelled his former host from Monte Carlo in 1963. "It was a very fine trait." The child with the hat is not identified. (UPI/Bettman Newsphotos)

Below: Onassis with the aged Sir Winston Churchill in New York, 1961. Tina regarded the old warrior as a hopeless bore. (UPI/Bettman Newsphotos)

Aristotle and Jackie on the yacht Christina *following their wedding in 1968. The press was invited for a glimpse of the nervous couple.* (UPI/Bettman Newsphotos)

Churchill the way he might have acquired a floor lamp, he seemed to have no concept of dignity.

James Cameron, the British journalist, encountered the unlikely pair at Lord Beaverbrook's house during a visit to the Riviera. "A sudden confusion arose," Cameron wrote in his memoirs.

The outer door of the house opened to admit several manservants, bearing among them the recumbent form of—observing the famous countenance for the first time—what could be none other than, of course, Sir Winston Churchill.

It was a strange and uncomely way in which to see for the first time a human being of such reknown and consideration, the man who, by an association of so many adventitious qualities and chances, had been for a large part of my adult life the most significant figure in Anglo-Saxon politics, and for some five years of history at least the most celebrated public figure in the world. And here he was being borne in to dinner by footmen. . . . For a moment it seemed to me that Sir Winston Churchill, ripe and full of years, had fulfilled Mr. Macmillan's curious prophecy to the editors by passing away immediately on Lord Beaverbrook's doorstep. . . .

While these considerations passed through my mind, standing helplessly in the hall, the crisis was abruptly resolved: The prostrate figure of Sir Winston Churchill came emphatically into being, gesticulating and muttering in a fashion most indicative of life, and within a few minutes was established in a drawing-room chair and manifestly the man who came to dinner. . . .

Having been deposited in his chair, the old gentleman was clearly content to let circumstances take their course, and by and by fell into a doze. He continued in a light sleep throughout the meal. . . . I observed that our host addressed Mr. Onassis as "Harry": it had never before occurred to me that such was the comradely diminutive of 'Aristotle.' I reflected with some pleasure on that discovery, while the newspaper baron and the millionaire shipowner debated in the mysterious language of money, and the former prime minister of Britain slumbered away in his own private dreamland, as remote from the gathering as myself. . . .

For one brief moment in the course of this strange party did Sir Winston Churchill suddenly surface from his private considerations and join, albeit momentarily, in the convivial scene. In the middle of some complex discussion about investments Sir Winston opened his pale blue eyes and said, apropos of nothing whatever: "Max, did you ever go to Russia?"

Lord Beaverbrook turned to him in surprise and said, with a sort
of affectionate acerbity: "Come now, of course I did; you sent me
there yourself; I had the ministry; you gave the mission to Stalin; do
you not remember sending me to Moscow?"

"Ah yes," said Sir Winston in a faraway voice. "But did you ever
go?" And with contentment he settled himself at ease, and no more
was heard from him that night.

After dinner somebody put a cigar in his mouth and lit it; it seemed
a ritual gesture without dignity; the completion of an effigy. Already
I had begun to find this a profoundly melancholy occasion. My own
admiration of the old gentleman's vigorous and abrasive qualities had
been qualified by opposition to almost every one of his public atti-
tudes; nevertheless, he had been a hundred times the person I could
ever hope to be, and it was sad to see him, for the first and last time,
diminished to a totem, part of the social image of a rich Greek patron.
Of course the old man's achievements had secured him sufficient
place in the records of history to transcend the ignominy of a nursery
party at Cap d'Ail. I could have wished, however, not to have been
present as the footmen bore the old man out in his chair like a small
statue, just still enough aware of his exit to raise his hand in his reflex
gesture of the separated fingers.

At the same time, and in fairness, there is little doubt that the
Greek millionaire did much to make his elderly friend's last years
happy ones. "I enjoy living on your yacht," said Sir Winston.

Tina could not say the same. Onassis had given her many things,
but he had never given her much in the way of a marriage. It was
almost as though they were going steady, and Tina, a woman with
very little endurance or character, was about played out. In truth,
she found that her husband's style left something to be desired.
"After a certain point, valuable possessions become a bore," she
once remarked with as much philosophy as she could muster.
"There really isn't much difference between being married to a
medium rich man and a very rich man." (She would soon find that
she was wrong about that.) Monte Carlo bored her and so did Sir
Winston Churchill. "All that Monte Carlo stuff!" she told William
Hickey of the London *Daily Express.* "Buying up the place! I can't
tell you how much I dislike Monte Carlo. . . . He had his friends, and
I started to find mine." It was obvious to almost everyone but her
husband that her mood was becoming dangerous. She was no
longer amused by their life together. And Tina was a woman who

required a great deal of amusement. "She told me that Churchill was quite gaga," says one of her friends. "There was just one day that he was not, when they went on an excursion to Marrakesh by jeep. Tina told Ari that the trip would kill the old man, but when they got back to the yacht that day, Churchill was absolutely brilliant and spoke for hours of his experiences in the war. And Tina said that he was so interesting. But it was the only time." She was tired of her husband's protracted absences and she was tired of the pomp he maintained at home; the yacht bored her too, and so did Monte Carlo. Her husband was neglectful, but he was also possessive, and he could be spiteful. Once, when she wanted to dance with another man at the Éléfant Blanc, he deliberately burned her on the shoulder with his cigar. "He is a wonderful person," she told Jimmy Stewart, the fleet's insurance broker and an old family friend, "but I am a very simple one. I don't like dining with something between twenty and eighty people a night. This life is killing me."

When her daughter became old enough to enroll in classes at the Cours Victor Hugo in Paris, Tina sometimes tried to behave as other mothers did, waiting for Christina after school and walking her home to the flat on avenue Foch. (Perhaps Stavros Livanos, the dedicated family man, had a hand in this.) There were no bodyguards—none would be engaged until Christina's father married Jacqueline Kennedy many years later—and with the disposal of the Chateau de la Cröe, which had immediately been bought by Niarchos, there were few on-shore retainers. Forever afterward, Christina would remember the period as the happiest in her life, but Tina was not a woman to seek distraction from a failed marriage in the absorbing tasks of parenthood. In later years, friends would search their memories in vain for motherly exploits, nor could they furnish Christina's childhood with the adventures that are commonplace in the early years of other children. With neither of her parents particularly interested in her development, Christina seemed almost devoid of qualities except for the tantrums that still occasionally rent the air, as they would continue to do for much of her life. She was happy, but she remained withdrawn. When asked to name a quality that might set her apart from other children of her age, Christina's contemporaries could only remember that she drank enormous quantities of Coca Cola.

Her brother, Alexander, fared little better. His chief interests were the miniature electric cars his father had bought for his entertainment and the electric boats he was allowed to sail in the yacht's pool. Both then and afterward, he seemed to have an intuitive knowledge of engines of all sorts, instinctively sensing when something was wrong, and why. Like the equally unfortunate Louis XVI of France, he might have made an excellent mechanic, given a different sort of life.

In 1956, when Alexander was eight, his father made a few attempts to teach him to swim, after which the task was left to the crew, who became the closest thing to a family that Alexander would ever know. Despite the feud between his father and his uncle, he was occasionally allowed to play with his Niarchos cousins when the two yachts were anchored together at Vougliameni or Monte Carlo. He was also friendly with the son of a Piraeus drydock owner, and his companion and henchman on the yacht was young Yorgos Zakarias, the most junior member of the crew. The list of Alexander's childhood associates was a small one, although it was longer than his sister's. He was a slight boy with huge dark eyes and the Onassis nose that, like Christina, he would have bobbed. He was also an extremely dangerous young man to have around.

He cracked up his first full-sized speedboat at the age of nine, an Albatross that he somersaulted at Vougliameni when he opened the throttles full blast to see what would happen. He and his passenger, a member of the yacht's crew, were thrown clear. At ten he cracked up another speedboat by driving it into one of the *Christina*'s metal lifeboats, putting a ship's officer in the hospital where he was dutifully visited by a saddened but unrepentant Alexander, who often looked in on sick or injured members of the crew and sometimes fed them their meals. His father yelled but did nothing. Onassis had led a fairly wild boyhood himself, messing about Smyrna in boats, and he seemed to detect no difference between his own youthful experiences and Alexander's almost suicidal exploits. It also did not seem to occur to him that his son might be trying to attract his attention, or to learn where the limits of his world were, or to alleviate the immense boredom that the Onassis life-style seemed to inflict upon every member of the family circle with the possible exception of Onassis himself. "Whatever Alexander got his hands on," said Yorgos Zakarias, "he would drive flat out and see how many dangerous and difficult things he could do with it."

At the age of twelve, Alexander succeeded in luring his father onto the water for a spin. "You're driving like a madman!" his father shouted, the parental attention finally having been engaged. Alexander explained that the boat was out of control. "It's not the boat, there's nothing wrong with it!" his father shouted. "You're driving like a lunatic, don't you hear me?" Clearly, something would have to be done, and the Onassis solution was typical of the man and father. He turned the boy over to Costa Koutsouvelis, the brother of his chief captain, who was supposed to become Alexander's escort, guardian, and, it was hoped, moral tutor—everything, in short, that his father was not and had no intention of becoming.

At the age of sixteen, the same year he failed the lycée in Paris, Alexander took up shoplifting.

Still, there was no reason the situation couldn't have lasted for years, with Alexander wrecking his boats and stealing watches at Orly airport, Christina drinking her soft drinks and shrinking deeper into her shell, and Tina wearily presiding as her husband's hostess, escaping to Paris when the pace overwhelmed her. Among the rich and the deliberately famous—especially the latter—it would not have been an unusual life. The chronicles of wealth and renown are littered with the names of victimized wives, sons, and daughters, of spouses and children beaten to the earth by the shower of God's blessings as those blessings descend on the head of the household. There was only one problem.

"Tina fell in love," says one of her friends. The object of her affections was Reynaldo Herrera, a handsome Venezuelan oilman, younger than she, who, though well connected and accepted in New York society, was a relative pauper when compared to her husband. Perhaps that was part of his appeal. (Christina would later expend an enormous amount of emotional capital on two doomed attempts to remain married to men who numbered among their virtues the fact that they were nowhere as rich as her father.) There was nothing particularly secret about the relationship. Photographs of the happy couple appeared in the gossip press, where they inevitably attracted the attention of the interested husband as he scanned the pages for news of his own doings.

Ski instructors were one thing and, as Onassis was the first to admit, anticipated; so was the occasional dalliance and even the long-term affair. Public betrayal in the newspapers was quite another matter. Exposure in the press, thanks to Tina's imprudence, would subject him to the concealed amusement and, worse, the patronizing sympathy of his new friends. But it was possible that his wife's crime was even greater in magnitude, and for a reason that was specific to the peculiar character of Aristotle Onassis. If, as seems likely, he possessed an uncertain sense of his own identity, it was in newspapers and periodicals, rather than in his shaving mirror, that he encountered himself in his most solid and comprehensible form. He had an almost primitive sense of the mystical power of images and words; the fact that he had scattered happy portraits and photographs of his children throughout his yacht seemed to do much to convince him that they were, in fact, happy. Most rich capitalists engaged press agents when they became rather too well known for activities and sharp practices that were better kept under wraps—John D. Rockefeller, Sr. was the pioneer in this regard—but Onassis had laid on expert assistance in the publicity department when he was almost totally unknown, with the object of becoming famous. His money and his rivalry with Niarchos were important elements in his struggle to define himself, but money and adversity were not enough. He needed an audience; more than that, he needed to know that he had an audience, and he needed to see himself through that audience's eyes. Unlike most rich men, he boasted openly about his fortune and named a fairly precise figure, $350 million. Before the oil company boycott, he had declared himself the lone wolf of the sea lanes, spoken openly to reporters, and all but challenged the governments of the world to bring him under control. After the boycott, with the details of his operations shrouded in secrecy, he encouraged the press to regard him in a new light, as a sort of Croesus surrounded by a court of notables—and the personal friend of the great Sir Winston Churchill. The very existence of the court did much to confirm the status that, to Aristotle Onassis, was simultaneously his identity, but it was as though his grasp of the reality he had created was incomplete without the magical confirmation of the printed page. For Tina to have visibly betrayed him in the press, therefore, was an unforgivable act. In a way that he probably could not have explained but that he nonetheless felt as powerfully as anything he had experienced in his life, Tina's treason had become real. (Alexander and Christina, when they became old enough to read of their parents' infidelities in the papers, reacted rather differently. They were simply ashamed.)

There was nothing in his new life-style that equipped him to meet the emergency. "Every Greek, and there are no exceptions, beats his wife," he had told his prewar mistress, Ingse Dedichen, but that was another Ari, a man he had left behind. ("He knew how to hit like an expert," Dedichen agreed.) His father-in-law might have actually approved of such a course, but among his polished new friends wife-beating was a sport rather than an instrument of policy. He needed time to think, to mature his plans. In the meantime, he could only indulge in helpless rage. "Imagine," he told Basil Mavroleon, fastening on what he regarded as the ultimate insult, "I had to accept that bastard on a cruise!"

It would be important for him to leave her before she left him, that much was clear, just as he had been the first to violate the marriage vows. Either that, or he had to humiliate Tina in a way that would bring her to her senses. It was true that the marriage had failed in most respects, but she was his wife in the eyes of the world, an important part of the legend he had created, and the mother of his children. He was still conventional enough, and Greek enough, that these matters had weight. There was only one thing to do. He had to find another woman.

It could not be any woman. Not only must she be capable of eclipsing the image of Tina that Onassis and his public relations expert had carefully fostered—the beautiful young wife of the man who allowed himself to be called the Golden Greek—but she would be the equal of the Golden Greek himself, someone who would contribute to his grandeur. As usual, he was thinking only of himself, or rather of his image; he did not turn his mind in the direction of his children, nor did he consider their needs. (Alexander was entering adolescence, always a difficult time.) In his search, he would be guided by his luck and his intuition, and he would rely on his charm—faculties that, as it happened, were working overtime that summer of 1959, at the annual ball of the Countess Castelbarco in Venice.

It was the sort of occasion he expected to dominate. The *Chris-*

tina, with his family aboard, was anchored at the mouth of the Grand Canal; he had boarded her only a few days previously with one of the grand entrances that always followed an extended business trip. He entered the ballroom with Tina on his arm, looking much as she had appeared on the recent cover of *Town & Country* magazine. She wore a gown by his favorite designer, Jean Desses; her throat was encircled with diamonds and emeralds, his favorite jewels, and an antique Russian bracelet of diamonds and rubies wound up her forearm. It was one of those moments when it seemed that she might be young forever, rich and fortunate amid the lights, secure in a world where everything was, as she might have said, divine—until her husband looked across the room, and there was Maria Callas.

It was the sort of moment the old novelists loved, the kind of drama in which the world indulges: the glittering company and the lofty room, the massed flowers, the orchestra in evening dress, and the eyes that met, and all the lives that would never be the same again. In the end, when only Christina and Stavros Niarchos were left, it would seem that the last act in the drama of Aristotle Onassis had begun here, that he took the irreversible step and made his world anew, and made it wrong.

After what seemed to be a strategically decent interval, he slipped away from Tina's side, only to reappear in the vicinity of the diva. Alert to the development and sensing trouble, Tina and Callas's husband-manager, the sixty-year-old Italian industrialist Giovanni Meneghini, immediately converged on the pair, but Onassis was already launched on his campaign of conquest. He claimed a previous acquaintence (he was delighted to meet Meneghini, of course); he believed that Callas had been a classmate of one of his nieces in New York, twenty years ago. And he was struck by a happy inspiration. Nothing would please him more than if the Meneghinis would join him on a planned cruise. He added that Winston Churchill would be aboard. But Callas was compelled to refuse. She was reviving difficult and little known works that were suitable to her remarkable voice and her gift, unusual in a soprano, for dramatic acting, and she was opening *Medea* in London. It would be the first time the opera had been performed there since 1870. Onassis, who hated opera, immediately announced that he would attend.

Later, there were those among Tina's circle who professed to believe that her husband's involvement with Maria Callas would be no bad thing. Tina, after all, was British by birth and Mayfair bred, with the right schools in her background and the right sort of friends. There were those who knew that the marriage had become a sham, although they had expected nothing less. The story still circulated that Tina had been bought, and in any event it was clear that her husband could not escape his origins; his very excesses were ample proof of that. The man was a peasant. "Callas was perfect for him," says one of Tina's friends. "They were both Greek, of simple origin, and tough. They had lots of things in common. Yes, she was the woman for him." More to the point, she exactly matched his requirements of the moment. The tough Greek woman of simple origin was also the temperamental long-lost universal soprano, an artist who could sing virtually anything written in her range for the human voice. An American citizen, born Maria Kalogeropoulos in Manhattan and raised above a pharmacy in Brooklyn, she lived with her aging husband in a villa on Italy's Lake Garda and sang, when it suited her to do so—she had once walked out on a performance for the president of Italy—in Milan, Rome, Paris, London, Barcelona, and New York. Like the man who proposed to become her lover, she had lived adventurously, surviving both the German occupation of Greece (where she had gone with her mother) and the civil war that followed. Like him, she had a hated rival, Renata Tebaldi. Like him, she had made a marriage of convenience, although Meneghini, who had saved her career, loved her dearly. At the time she met Onassis, they were the two most famous Greeks then living. "She was the greatest artist we have produced since the age of Pericles," says Manuel Kulukundis, seated amidst his watercolors in the office he still maintains in his New York townhouse. He is a courtly man, grown old but still vigorous, with a soft voice obscured by a pipe he lights incessantly. ("I smoke mostly matches," he once said.) At the thought of Maria Callas and his old enemy, his hands clench and unclench on the desk, and his words come in a fierce whisper. "And he ruined her! *He ruined her!*"

To ensure that his homage would be the event of the London season, Onassis purchased forty tickets to the performance, most of them from scalpers at ruinous prices, and personally distributed them to assorted Churchills (but not to Sir Winston, who was rarely up to that sort of thing anymore), various royalty, and the usual celebrities. He laid on an after-theater supper for 160 guests at the Hotel Dorchester. He and Meneghini were photographed embracing an exhausted Callas (out of camera range, a subdued Tina looked on), and before the party broke up at three in the morning, he repeated his invitation to the cruise. No definite answer was forthcoming, but in the weeks that followed, telephoning incessantly to the villa on Lake Garda, he renewed the invitation again and again until Meneghini's resistance was worn down; Callas's husband was not in the best of health, and he was not a resourceful man.

The holiday began, as so many of them did, at Monte Carlo. Prince Rainier saw them off in person and spoke of establishing an opera house where Callas would reign supreme. The Churchills— Sir Winston, his wife, and his daughter Diana—greeted the new arrivals at the head of the gangway. Garbo had declined an invitation, but Umberto Agnelli, the head of Fiat, the giant Italian automobile company, had not. The host's favorite sister, Artemis, was aboard with her husband, Professor Theodore Garofalidis, and so were Tina and the children. Whatever Onassis proposed to do—and it is possible that he had no very clear idea—he proposed to do in the midst of his family, and accompanied by witnesses.

A leisurely three weeks were planned, with a stopover at Delphi, a visit to the Onassis birthplace, renamed Izmir by the Turks, and a cruise up the Dardanelles to Istanbul with a pause, if Sir Winston's health permitted it (it did not) at the Gallipoli Peninsula, where as First Lord of the Admiralty during World War I the old man had presided over the slaughter of the Australian and New Zealand expeditionary force that attempted to take the straits. The weather turned rough shortly after the start of the voyage; most of the party was confined to staterooms with seasickness, and the Meneghinis began to bicker. Callas's husband felt out of his depth. He was a millionaire himself but a comparatively small one. He placed no trust in his host, and he was worried about his aged mother. Callas and Onassis, uneffected by the general malaise, spent long, late hours in the yacht's saloon—discussing the diva's business affairs, Onassis said. At Istanbul, they went ashore together and remained for several hours, causing Meneghini to create a scene that none of those present were willing to relate in detail. He locked himself in his stateroom and refused to emerge even after the missing couple returned. When he finally opened the door, his wife told him what he already knew. "It's all over," she said. "I love Ari."

There seemed hardly any point in continuing with the itinerary. The yacht returned to Monte Carlo, where the debarking guests put on brave faces for the waiting press and pretended that a good time was had by all, except that poor Mr. Onassis had injured his back in the swimming pool. The Meneghinis returned to Lake Garda. Onassis sent the vessel to Venice with Tina and the children and sat down to ponder his next move.

Only with difficulty could it be said that he behaved like a man besotted with passion during the next few days; he more closely resembled a man goading his wife beyond endurance. He dined twice with Callas in Milan, returned with her to Monte Carlo, flew her back to Milan, and continued on to Venice alone. With exquisite timing, his Piaggio seaplane touched down next to the *Christina* just as the yacht was making port. Apparently he discovered that the desired effect had not been created; the next day, he dined with Callas in Milan, this time with photographers present. His children, kept in their own quarters aboard the vessel, suspected nothing.

Tina, unwisely choosing to fight on her husband's chosen battle-ground in the international press, turned for support to Elsa Maxwell, the celebrated (and vastly overweight) society hostess then resident in Venice, who had previously been a great patroness of Callas. Onassis stepped up his campaign. While reporters eagerly awaited him in Milan, he picked up the diva in Turin and disappeared with her for the weekend. On Monday, Callas and her husband announced that they were separating. As a resentful Meneghini understood the situation, his enemy proposed something in the nature of a business deal, wherein Tina would console herself with Herrera, Onassis would marry Callas, and Meneghini was left free to pick his way out of the wreckage as best he could. "Onassis wants to glamorize his grimy tankers with the name of a great diva," he told the waiting reporters. "They are in love like children."

"I am a sailor," Onassis remarked when he allowed himself to be cornered in his hotel, "and these are things that may happen to a sailor."

"That man has an ambition like Hitler," raved Meneghini, "who wants to own everything, with his accursed millions and his accursed cruise and his accursed yacht!"

This time, when Onassis returned to Venice, Tina was gone; she and the children had decamped suddenly, under cover of darkness. "That night was confused—daddy wasn't there," Christina recalled later. "I imagined that I was losing something important. I didn't know what. Mother only said we had to leave, and she was sure we were not coming back."

Her husband soon traced her to her parents' home in Paris, where Stavros Livanos was observed pacing the rug, muttering "I knew it, I knew it." Onassis soon presented himself on the Livanos threshold, disingenuously protesting that he was only advising Callas on her business affairs; his father-in-law's response to this astonishing statement has apparently been lost. At the same time, Onassis took steps to ensure that there would be no doubt about who was leaving whom. On September 11, in a blaze of publicity that was spectacular even by his own elevated standards, he sailed back to the Aegean with his new mistress. Tina resumed the use of her maiden name and fled to New York with the children.

Her husband, the picture of baffled innocence, repeatedly denied that he was seeking a divorce. A reconciliation, he said, would please Sir Winston very much. Simultaneously, he attempted to plant a story that Tina had kidnaped his offspring and was holding them for $20 million in ransom.

On November 25, looking pale, Tina summoned the press to the house on Sutton Square and read a prepared statement.

> It is almost thirteen years since Mr. Onassis and I were married in New York City. Since then he has become one of the world's richest men, but his great wealth has not brought me happiness with him nor, as the world knows, has it brought him happiness with me. After we parted this summer in Venice, I had hoped that Mr. Onassis loved our children enough and respected our privacy sufficiently to meet with me—or, through lawyers, with my lawyer—to straighten out our problems. But that was not to be.
>
> Mr. Onassis knows positively that I want none of his wealth and that I am solely concerned for the welfare of our children.
>
> I deeply regret that Mr. Onassis leaves me no alternative other than a New York suit for divorce.
>
> For my part, I will always wish Mr. Onassis well, and I expect that

after this action is concluded he will continue to enjoy the kind of life which he apparently desires to live, but in which I have played no real part. I shall have nothing more to say and I hope that I shall be left with my children in peace.

The grounds were adultery, the only ones then admissible in the state of New York. Attempting to deny her husband a complete victory and at the same time to settle an old score, Tina named a certain "Mrs. J. R." whom she accused of having an affair with her husband "by land and sea." It was soon discovered that the initials referred to Tina's old classmate and former neighbor at Cap d'Antibes, Jeanne Rhinelander, who denied everything. Callas was never mentioned.

In the end, with the appropriate gestures having been made by both parties, it was all settled amicably. Herrera tidied up the landscape considerably by the simple expedient of removing himself. ("Naturally, he ran," says one of Tina's circle. "He was delighted to have an affair with Mrs. Onassis, but when she asked for a divorce he rushed back to Venezuela.") Further scandal was avoided, to Stavros Livanos's huge relief, by moving the divorce petition to Alabama, where the marriage was dissolved in June, 1960 on the harmless grounds of mental cruelty. Tina waived alimony and kept the children, Onassis received generous visitation rights, and the Greek maritime community was left in no doubt that it had done the right thing when it assigned him to role of parvenu and outsider. "I hate to say it, but I suspect his motive was publicity," said Basil Mavroleon. "Callas was no beauty to start with. Would you exchange a young girl for an old hag?" Tina had her freedom, Onassis had his soprano, the Greeks had their opinions, and everybody was happy but the children.

"It was probably the first taste of ordinary hurt, the pains of everyday life, that Christina had ever experienced," one of her classmates recalled. "She once told me she cried every night for a year after her parents broke up. And when you looked at that small, strained, haunted face of hers, you had to believe it." Perhaps it was then that she formed the fantasy of dwelling alone in a small house, perhaps by the sea, where she would live as she believed other people lived and pass the time by playing board games with children her own age.

Shortly after the divorce, her mother took her to her uncle's private island of Spetsopoula in the Saronic Gulf south of Athens. The family was in residence: Stavros Niarchos, whom—on very little evidence but her father's word—she had come to hate and fear; her aunt Eugenie, quiet and thoughtful, whom she loved; and her cousins, the older ones already in thrall to their demanding father. Stealing a considerable march on his rival, Niarchos had improved the island, built houses and a harbor, laid down roads, constructed a village for the widows and orphans of the seamen he had lost while laying the basis of his fortune in the wartime convoys, and stocked the fields with pheasants that the farmers of the vicinity gleefully blasted out of the sky with ancient fowling pieces whenever the birds ventured overhead. There was a go-cart track that the cousins negotiated with suicidal abandon, much like Alexander and his speedboats. During the summer, other children were imported as companions; Christina was sent to join them while the adults talked. "We'd just finished a dirt fight when she showed up," recalls one. "She had on a red bikini bottom, I remember, and no top, and she stood off to one side, watching us. She had these deep lines under her eyes, not ugly I thought, but striking and sad. She refused to speak to anyone all day." She was the child her parents had made. She was nine years old.

CHAPTER SIX

The Greatest
Social Climber
of All Time

In the curious architecture of Aristotle Onassis's life, it was always a thing—an object—that marked the transition from one phase to another. No one ever pretended that he was either a very profound or—after the failure of the Saudi Arabian initiative—a very original thinker, nor was he renowned for the pungency of his utterance or the penetration of his insight. He was, by all accounts, a deplorable father and he had been a faithless husband. As a businessman, he had been saved from certain ruin only by luck and the RAF. His enemies, of whom, in addition to Stavros Niarchos, he had a few, regarded him as a peasant, with a peasant's circumscribed and egocentric view of the world, and while it was true that he was considerably more of a personage than that, it was equally true that he did not trouble himself with abstractions nor torture himself with the contemplation of the probable consequences of his acts. Like his primitive Greek forebearers, he objectified his surroundings and thus rendered them comprehensible or controllable, but unlike the ancient Greeks, he preferred to transform these surroundings into possessions rather than gods. His tankers were such malleable objects, and so was the fortune they had bestowed on him. His yacht was also such an object and a potent symbol as well, his wealth made tangible both to its owner and to the larger audi-

ence he wished to impress. That the celebrities he thereby attracted proved disappointing suggested nothing to him.

Tina had been such an object and so had Sir Winston Churchill.
So, in somewhat different fashion, were his children. (After all, he
had created them. It did not occur to him that they would behave
in any way other than exactly as he wished, and as Professor Georgakis later remarked, he had no "system" for dealing with them
when, inevitably, they refused to do so.) The near senile Churchill,
dreaming away his days after a long and adventurous life, was
content with his lot. Tina had been discarded not when she had her
first affair (affairs were expected) but when she entered into one
that was not part of the plan. And on the autumn day in 1964, when
the yacht *Christina* raised the tiny Ionian island of Skorpios and
tied up at a new buoy offshore, Maria Callas seemed, like Sir Winston, to be perfectly happy to live out her days as a possession of
Aristotle Onassis. That, perhaps, was part of the problem.

The island supported a permanent population of two, who
tended the olive grove that produced an annual fifteen thousand
kilos of oil. It was otherwise barren and unimproved, and it had
been a bargain at $110,000. Its four hundred acres made it considera-
bly smaller than Niachos's five-thousand-acre Spetsopoula, but unlike Niarchos, Onassis did not propose to preserve game or create
playgrounds for his children, and he did not have a significant number of dependents. The NATO airbase at Aktion, on the nearby
mainland, would provide a landing strip for his Lear jet and for
planes borrowed from Olympic Airways, but on relatively remote
Skorpios, the Onassis style would not be cramped by the proximity
of Athens, the presence of other wealthy men, or the none too
refreshing indifference of the metropolitan population, so unlike
that of London or Paris or New York, to his status and power. "It's
rather strange, you know," said Helen Vlachos one morning in a
concrete city that smelled of gasoline, while the Parthenon melted
in the polluted air and sleek gray men in sleek gray suits gathered
in the coffee shop of the Hotel Grande Bretagne to drink bottled
water and talk of money. "In Athens, we know that we have thirty
or fifty people who are just as important as Onassis and Niarchos—
the Livanoses, the Kulukundises, the Embiricoses—and the two big
names that have somehow emerged internationally are not so important here. I remember going out in the evening to a bistro or

someplace with Stavros or Onassis, and people wouldn't even turn around." On Skorpios, far away, Onassis would be a king. Moreover, he could see the mountains of Ithaca from there. Costa Gratsos was from Ithaca, and there were always a large number of Ithacans working in the Onassis fleet. And of course, it was on Ithaca that the wandering Odysseus had ruled.

It was only with the benefit of hindsight that the acquisition of the island would seem like another milestone in his life, an event that made change inevitable and chaos likely. The purchase of his yacht had marked another such moment of transition, the moment when he ceased to be the agreeable young shipowner and began to confuse himself with a force of nature. It was always the things that he bought rather than the things that he did with them that shaped his personal history. They defined his boundaries and dictated his purposes, much as the newspapers defined his daily life.

Maria Callas first saw Skorpios that autumn of 1964. A year earlier, he had shown it to another woman, the young and beautiful wife of the president of the United States, who would later play such a prominent and destructive role in his life.

For a man whose existence had been as much characterized by its turbulence as it was by his checkbook, the past five years had been a relatively quiet time; the ball, as the saying goes, had bounced into Tina's court. A year after the divorce, without confiding in her children, she married the thirty-five-year-old John George Vanderbilt Henry Spencer Churchill, a man known as "Sonny" to his American friends and "Sunny" to his English ones. He was also the marquess of Blandford and the eldest son of the tenth Duke of Marlborough. Alexander, who learned of his mother's remarriage by reading about it in a newspaper, refused to speak to her unless he was absolutely forced to, and he was not alone in his disapproval. The marquess was adequately wealthy by contemporary British standards and he was well enough liked in his own set, but the Greeks did not particularly take to him and there were members of Tina's circle who found, perhaps to their surprise, that they rather missed Aristotle Onassis.

"Blandford was such a bore," says Helen Vlachos. "You couldn't bear him, poor man, unless you were drunk from morning to night. I remember meeting them on Spetsopoula, and I was bored to death. But of course, I was not Tina. I suppose you couldn't get a greater contrast to an Anatolian carpet vendor, full of charm and with beautiful eyes, which was Aris Onassis, than an Etonian aristocrat like Sonny Blandford. The maximum, the farthest away from Onassis, was Blandford."

Nor did Blandford appear to be the solid father-figure that the children needed at a difficult time in their lives; he once told a friend of Christina's that he had avoided higher education because it would have made him too practical, and practicality was a thing that the thirteen-year-old Alexander and the eleven-year-old Christina badly needed in sizable dosages. "Very dull fellow," says a friend of Tina's. "Very, very dull, very British. The sort of joke he and Tina liked at St. Moritz was throwing pies at each other in the club. They did stupid things like that, like a couple of kids. I don't think she was in love with him, but she was very fond of him. It amused her to be Lady Blandford. It amused her for quite a long time."

If the children remained unamused, they also remained almost totally unprepared for life as it is normally lived on earth. Their mother's British marriage did nothing to introduce them to an invigorating British sense of self-discipline, nor did it help to train them in the use of their minds. In New York, while her mother waited out the divorce, Christina had been placed in the Hewitt School, where her Aunt Eugenie had gone. Later, in England, she was sent to board at Heathfield, her mother's old school in Oxfordshire near Lee Place, the traditional country residence of the Marlborough heirs, but once Tina had purchased her daughter a suitable and expensive education, she did nothing to see that it was absorbed. "I find that Christina is an intelligent girl," says one of Tina's friends, "but she didn't get a literary education, she didn't get a musical education. She is not well educated at all." (In Paris, Alexander was having his own difficulties at the lycée.) Having secured herself a title, the expectation of a dukedom, and a husband whose idea of a quiet evening at home did not include fifty guests at dinner, Tina carried on much as always. The children, as always, were left to the servants. Their father, as always, was otherwise engaged.

There were rumors, duly circulated (that, too, was as usual) of tempestuous passions and memorable rows aboard the yacht where he and Callas were now sporadically in residence, but in fact Onassis had settled down to what was, for him, a distinctly suburban existence. "It was not," Professor Georgakis observed, "a very interesting relationship." Apparently Callas wanted nothing so much in the world as to retire from the stage altogether. Her voice, though increasingly shaky in the upper register, was still a remarkable instrument, but it was heard less and less as her public performances became rarer and finally ceased altogether, as did her recording dates; she even refused to sing privately for Churchill. She was only 41, hardly an advanced age for a member of her profession. If her health remained good, she could look forward to many years of continued fame and professional eminence; her services were as much in demand as they had ever been. Yet Callas was no longer inclined to offer them to the public. She spent her time in the yacht's "Ithaca" stateroom, playing records. When the vessel was docked, she walked her dogs on the quay. Of her celebrated temperament, there was only the faintest shadow, and then principally when her lover was late to dinner, an event that made her fretful —as though, said one of his associates, she had cooked the meal herself. She no longer seemed to want very much: a measure of peace, an end to the tyranny of her art, and a man she could love. He would slip, nude, into her bedroom before flying off on one of his interminable business trips; he would find her waiting patiently when he returned.

They were comfortable together; just as Tina's friend remarked, Maria Callas really did appear to be the woman for Aristotle Onassis. Unlike Tina, she took an active and intelligent interest in his business affairs, and she shared (or convincingly seemed to share, which amounted to the same thing) his taste for night life. With Callas at his side, he felt less of a need to display his wealth; perhaps the answer was that he simply felt more secure. In any event, Callas wanted very little, and in truth there were few new worlds left to conquer with his money, although with the acquisition of Skorpios he would soon begin to think of one or two. For the moment however, he seemed content to play at spies with Stavros Niarchos, tend to his charters with the tameness that had marked all his nautical enterprises since the ARAMCO boycott, and keep a wary eye on his investment in Monte Carlo, where the prince, strangely invigorated by his marriage to the American actress Grace Kelly, exhibited signs of giving way to a mania for real estate speculation.

Otherwise, it was a time of pause, one of the few relatively placid interludes he had ever known.

Displaying a mouth in which a pat of butter was conspicuously not melting, he insisted that his divorce and Callas's separation were the merest coincidence. At the same time, they publicly stated that they were free to marry in any country but Italy, and yet no marriage took place, although Callas would not exactly have been opposed to one. It was the same pattern he imposed on all his women, Ingse Dedichen, Tina, and now Maria Callas: his purposes, not hers, dominated the proceedings, and for the moment he preferred to keep his options open. When she became pregnant he persuaded her to have an abortion. Although she wanted a child and he had once wished for a second son (and would do so again); he wanted no bastard heirs cluttering up the landscape of his future. With Alexander and Christina, he deliberately fostered the notion that he and Tina would miraculously reunite, or at least he did so at the beginning, before Tina married Blandford. It was a cruel deception and his motives were unclear—perhaps it was only a misguided attempt to soften the blow of the divorce—but it, too, served his purposes. His children remained openly and irreconcilably hostile to their father's new lover, refusing to open her presents and roaring around the yacht in one of the speedboats, Alexander's weapon of choice, trying to disrupt her naps. Marriage was obviously impossible, their father explained when Callas broached the subject, as long as the children refused to accept it, and the newly passive Callas made no sustained attempt to win their friendship. She would presently discover that her failure to do so was the greatest mistake of her life.

Meanwhile, there was the pleasurable distraction of Skorpios, the bothersome situation in Monte Carlo, and the seemingly intractable problem of Alexander. On the island, Onassis set about building a house and chapel, a harbor, and sixteen guest chalets. He brought in fresh water and electricity, laid out roads and gardens, and imported a forest of walnut, almond, cypress, and bougainvillea, while his far-flung tankers brought him English roses and South American jungle plants, enabling him to create a riot of mingled scents and exquisite microenvironments that some of his guests found almost erotically stimulating. All of this was hardly the work of a moment. Indeed, the creation of his island kingdom would take years—almost exactly the amount of time, as it happened, that it took Prince Rainier to boot the island kingdom's owner out of the legitimate royal domain that he believed, mistakenly, that he had bought.

In Monaco, a curious reversal of stereotypes had occurred. Onassis, the parvenu, found himself representing the forces of social conservatism, while the prince, whose family had ruled the place since 1297, led the armies of progress. Seemingly galvanized by his marriage, Rainier began by dissolving the minuscule parliament and announcing that he would henceforth rule by divine right, an experiment that was abandoned in 1962 when President de Gaulle of France, who had his own ideas about the intentions of the deity, threatened to shut off the electricity and forced the prince to sign a convention that nearly wrecked the Monégasque economy. Not conspicuously daunted by this turn of events, Rainier pressed on with his plans to modernize his thumbnail-sized country by turning it into what Onassis disdainfully termed "another Brighton." The prince's recent visits to America with his famous and well-connected new wife had worked profoundly on his mind; he foresaw a bright new future based on the middle classes, which he proposed to attract with package tours, inexpensive hotels, and a convention center. Under his enlightened (if no longer divinely inspired) leadership, the principality would become a Mediterranean boomtown, its landscape punctuated with sleek apartment buildings that resembled enormous refrigerators. The railroad tracks that bisected the enclave would be walled in, the beaches would be extended (again), and the highways would be placed on concrete pilings. The plan required only the cooperation of Mr. Onassis, who had quietly expanded his holdings in the SBM to a majority of the shares and whose money would naturally play an important role in transforming the royal scheme into reality. Unfortunately, Mr. Onassis disagreed.

Like many men who had started with nothing and made the bulk of their money very suddenly, Onassis had a clear and fixed idea of what constituted the trappings of wealth, and at the center of that fixed idea, embedded like a fly in amber, lay a Monte Carlo forever bathed in the opulent light of another century. (Needless to say, this was not a vision that the revitalized prince shared. A later project on the slope below the ornate old gambling hall involved a new casino run by an American theatrical concern, creating an architectural ensemble that one British visitor characterized as "a railway station sandwiched beneath a wedding cake.") As far as the middle class was concerned, Onassis suggested that they should be prevented from gambling altogether, lest they be corrupted. He seemed unable to contemplate the possibility that Monte Carlo could ever change, that he might no longer preside over the operas and regattas that had given the principality a renewed if anachronistic life.

When the prince pressed him for his own modernization plans, he responded with a mixture of conciliation and bluster, offering to cooperate (within reason) while threatening to eliminate or curtail events that everyone knew were as close to his heart as they were to the prince's pocketbook, since they attracted the vital tourist trade. The prince began to drop hints that Mr. Onassis was no longer as welcome as he had once been; the French began to refer to him as an "undesirable presence." In the end, following a terrific to-do over Onassis's refusal to install lights in the tennis courts (after all, one could hardly kick the man out over nothing), Rainier watered the stock of the SBM, assigned the new shares to the nation, and in 1967 eradicated the Onassis holding with a $10 million settlement. The royal real estate boom resumed along lines more satisfactory to the prince; Onassis, stung and protesting that he had been gypped, took his departure with as much grace as he could muster. He continued to maintain the office on the avenue d'Ostende (Alexander would turn it into a private refuge), but he returned only once, on his last cruise in the final months of his life, a dying man accompanied by the final but uncertain repository of his hopes, his daughter Christina. "He never bore grudges," said the prince of their last meeting. "It was a very fine trait."

Monte Carlo had been his monument—typically, it had been a purchased one—but Skorpios would replace it, a Skorpios enhanced by yet another new acquisition, just as Monte Carlo had been perfected (and the world astonished) by the magnificent length of the *Christina* at rest in its harbor. And in truth, it is likely that he felt a compelling need to astonish the world just then. Not only had he lost Monte Carlo, but for all intents and purposes, he had lost his son.

It was not that Alexander was a particularly disobedient or wild lad—unless, that is, he was placed in the vicinity of a moving vehicle. (After Alexander discovered automobiles, Yorgos Zakarias flatly refused to ride with him. For one thing, Alexander declined to slow down for curves). The problem, according to all reports, was the intensity of his father's reaction on those occasions when Alexander's fractiousness engaged his attention; it was as though he were disciplining a recalcitrant part of himself. In 1962, when Alexander was fourteen, he spent a weekend away from home without permission. His father threw him out of the flat on avenue Foch, and he lived with his Livanos grandparents for the next six months. When he refused to continue with his education two years later, the eloquent and persuasive Professor Georgakis, one of the few men his father admired solely for his intellect, was dispatched to reason with him, but the mission was not a success. Alexander and his sister had long since learned never to reveal their thoughts and feelings in the presence of either of their parents—for fear, Alexander later explained, that his parents would use the information to "hit [the children] over the head"—but the professor learned that Alexander, at least, had made a close study of his father. "I was surprised at the maturity and subtlety of judgment of this young man whom I was really meeting for the first time," he recalled. "He knew his father like a coin collector knows the two faces of an old, battered, and treasured coin. In those days he was very bitter toward his father, who had neither time nor system for the boy. But he possessed all the elements necessary to analyze his father and in the end the account was positive. Alexander could penetrate the tycoon facade and understand all the dreams and paranoia of the man. You can neither love nor respect a man who has no center. Alexander could see that center. Aristotle was a terrible father, but a passionate one. Their relationship became almost erotic. A nice boy," the professor added, with the clairvoyance of hindsight, "but with an early death written on his face."

But if Alexander could see his father's center, he was perilously close to having no center at all himself. He believed, as his father had told him, that it was unnecessary to have friends, and in fact he had very few. He also believed that he was the most eligible young man in the world, but beyond bringing an occasional girl to admire the wonders of the yacht, he did little in the way of placing himself on the marriage market or broadening his horizons. His energies, and they were not great, were largely devoted to avoiding his father.

At first, he was delighted by the victory he believed he had achieved by abandoning his schooling, but in 1964 it became clear that he had walked into a trap of his own devising. His father did not press the issue; after all, he himself had received no formal education after his sixteenth year. He had made his own way and taught himself the tricks of his trade, and he expected Alexander to do the same, although the son was to follow strictly in the father's footsteps and no deviation from the path was to be tolerated. Alexander was placed on an allowance of $12,000 a year, a pittance that would cease altogether if he exhibited the faintest sign of further rebellion. He was to learn the shipping business. He was expected to attend meetings, to perform minor but instructive tasks, to keep himself on constant call for his father's summons, to become aggressive and bold, and in general to temper himself in the crucible of commerce. If he did something right, he was never praised; if he made a mistake it seemed as if the ensuing tirade would never end. And yet he learned next to nothing. "I don't know how it all fits together," he confessed forlornly in the last year of his life, after eight years of supposed training. "I hope my father does, anyway."

Desperately, he devised stratagems of concealment and avoidance. His father came often to the villa in the Athens suburb of Glyfada; Alexander stayed at the Hilton or put up with his Aunt Artemis. Providentially, he was required to spend a great deal of time in the offices on the avenue d'Ostende in Monaco, where his father of course now never came, although there were constant telephone calls to dictate his every move. (Alexander trained the switchboard operator to route the calls in such a way that it was impossible for his father to tell whether he was working at his desk or catching a few moments of rest in the private quarters on the top floor.) When his father demanded his physical presence, he persuaded doctors to write notes saying he was too sick to attend. Once, snatching a rare two weeks' vacation, he insisted on his father's written permission, and he was surprised when his father failed to renege.

He rose between six and six-thirty and was at his desk by half past eight. He lunched between one-thirty and two, took a nap, and waterskied for a couple of hours behind a speedboat piloted by the young *Christina* crewman, Yorgos Zakarias, his loyal (and virtually only) friend in those days. He showed no interest in nightlife, parties, books, television, movies, serious music of any kind, or most other people. He had taken up smoking—Winston filter kings—but he never drank alcohol; he preferred lemonade or Coke, his sister's favorite beverage, and when his father sent him to Russia to observe the closing of a deal, he had to take lessons in holding his liquor. He went to bed every night at eleven.

"You are young, you have everything, why do you live like this?" asked Yorgos. "Why not have some parties, invite some friends along, enjoy yourself?"

"I can't be bothered with all that," Alexander snapped.

Aside from his waterskiing, his only recreations were his car—he owned a Ferrari—and the boats for which he seemed to reserve a special destructiveness. "I remember once," says a friend of the family, "I was having lunch with about twenty other people at Mrs. Livanos's house in the south of France, and Alexander came in with a small yacht he had. He jumped out while it was still going and it smashed directly into the mole. The bow was ruined."

He had never been close to his sister. The fault was partly hers. Always a withdrawn child, she had avoided him even on the *Christina*—not an easy thing to do. But now he believed that he had reason to resent her. While he had to scrape by on a beggarly thousand a month, her expenses were paid by their mother. "Sucking up to mother" became, in Alexander's eyes, one of his sister's graver sins. Even worse, she had learned that she could manipulate their impossible father by flirting with him ("In public," says a friend of the family, "she positively clung to him."), and she was free of the forced labor that now characterized Alexander's waking life. (In the summer when she was sixteen, her father allowed her to work in the advertising office at Olympic Airways. She was painfully shy and somewhat out of her depth, and her command of spoken Greek was poor—she had, after all, been schooled in America, France, and England. But her father was well pleased by her performance.) And unlike Alexander, she seemed genuinely interested in the shipping business, keeping a close watch on the vessels in her trust, a circumstance that did not escape her father's attention. "Onassis used to say, 'My son should have been my daughter and my daughter my son,' " says one of Christina's friends. " 'He would

say, 'The man should be Christina and the woman should be Alexander.' " It was hardly a statement calculated to inspire brotherly
affection, but his father's complaints were more general than that,
and he was not cautious about airing them—he also told Michael
Thomas, the American investment banker who later became a popular novelist, that he wished Thomas were his son. Indeed, it sometimes seemed that almost any reasonably competent person would
do.

It was in this turbulent and contradictory state of mind—believing everything his father said, while hiding from him at the same
time—that Alexander first met Fiona Campbell Thyssen in the winter of 1967. He was nineteen. She was thirty-five, divorced, the
mother of two teenaged children, rich, and the daughter of a British
admiral. "I'll come and get you in my Ferrari," he said, setting up
their first date. "Listen, my dear," she replied, "I had ten houses,
two yachts, and a jet plane when you were in diapers. You'll have
to do better than that to impress me. You'll have to impress me as
a human being." He had, she discovered, a single conversational
topic: machinery.

Alexander was staggered but he was also intrigued; he was accustomed to being reprimanded, but not like that. Fiona Thyssen was
beautiful and gentle, the sort of person who would one day take an
interest in the occult, but she was also levelheaded, at least as far
as Alexander was concerned. She knew they would never marry;
Alexander was destined, she knew, for the inevitable sixteen-year-
old Greek virgin of good family, and there were her own children's
feelings to consider. Still, on the surface, there was nothing particularly unusual about the understanding they eventually reached. An
affair between an older woman and a younger man was not exactly
unheard of among people of their class; the advantages to both
parties were fairly obvious, provided events did not take a serious
turn. Making the necessary arrangements, Fiona called Eugenie
Niarchos. Alexander had grown fond of his Niarchos cousins, Philip
and Spiros, but he was extremely literal-minded in the subject of his
father's rivalry with his uncle. Fiona had summered on Spetsopoula
and counted herself a Niarchos friend; now she explained to Eugenie that Alexander had insisted that she choose between them, and
she had chosen Alexander. This, too, was in the usual course of such
things. Young men were often headstrong, and they were all people

of the world. There was only one circumstance that was out of the ordinary: Fiona Thyssen had decided to give Alexander a life and a personality of his own.

"If there was one thing that gives me great satisfaction," she said three years after Alexander's death, "it was that I proved Aristotle wrong, that not everyone can be bought. Had I not been very wealthy I could not have afforded five years with Alexander. But money, his money, made no difference to either of us." First she tackled the relatively tractable problem of Christina; a successful reconciliation between the siblings was effected in Fiona's London home. Alexander's relations with his mother were quite another matter. He had never forgiven Tina for her marriage to Blandford, and he was not inclined to relent now that Tina had discovered that it no longer amused her to be a marchioness. Blandford's fortune, though large, was not as large as the ones Tina had been accustomed to, and the old duke's longevity, while doubtless heartening to the duke himself, effectively blocked her access to the title. Tina seemed to be quietly disintegrating, although many of her friends had not yet noticed. She had phlebitis, and she was taking five sleeping pills a night. When he visited her in the south of France, Alexander made it his habit to empty out her medicine chest, but it did no good. She always obtained more. None of them expected her to live much longer. "She was not a normal woman," said Fiona. "She was neurotic and unbalanced." There was little hope in that direction.

Fiona had never met Aristotle Onassis. She knew him only through his handiwork in the form of his son, a deeply troubled young man with neither a mind nor a will of his own, haunted by the thought that his parents had rejected him and unable to shake the conviction that his father was a great man. Alexander was unable—to the point of incoherence—to explain the effect his father had on him. Desperate to show Fiona the exact nature of his plight, he began taping his father's phone calls: Onassis warbling "Singin' in the Rain" for five minutes, interrupting himself with mocking questions ("How's the weather on your end?") to which no answer was expected, then resuming his song, only to conclude his performance with a screaming tirade, demanding and demanding and demanding, while Alexander responded with helpless grunts and monosyllables, his face a mask of defeat.

After listening to a few of these exchanges, Fiona thought she had the answer. It seemed clear that Alexander's father was trying to goad him into making a response, to hector and humiliate him to the point where he would stand up and fight back like an Onassis. Fiona even came to believe that Onassis would have been delighted if she and Alexander had gotten married in the teeth of repeated paternal prohibitions, if only because it would have demonstrated that his son had finally developed a spine. Onassis seemed to want nothing so much in the world as a son he could confide in, the way he confided in Gratsos and Professor Georgakis and even, on occasion, a comparative outsider like Basil Mavroleon.

Gradually, under Fiona's patient prodding, Alexander began to talk back. He spoke to his father in complete sentences. He learned to give as good as he got, although without the same overwhelming lung-power. As Fiona had predicted, the ensuing transformation was remarkable. Alexander and his father discovered that they seldom agreed about anything, but they began to have conversations like normal men and Alexander drew strength and belated insight from their talks. He found that his father was not, after all, a wrathful god. He was mortal and fallible, he occasionally talked through his hat, and he made mistakes. And, as Fiona had foreseen and intended, Alexander became the recipient of his confidences.

Unfortunately, one of the very first of these confidences was also one of the least welcome. Alexander's father announced that he proposed to remarry. Needless to say, the lucky woman would not be Maria Callas. Other than the Queen of England (who was not available) there was only one possible candidate, and Christina, as it happened, had already made the lady's acquaintence.

"I would guess that Christina first met Jackie Kennedy in 1967," says a man who was a friend of the family, "because that was the year I went to Skorpios with Johnny Agnelli. It was August. We came suddenly, Johnny, David Somerset, and I; we were cruising down to Greece in Johnny's boat, pulled up at the island, dropped anchor, and sent a message that we were there. Down came Onassis with his car, and just as he arrived we saw Jackie waterskiing; she never even stopped to say hello. Later, when she was finished, we all had lunch. In those days she was extremely friendly, extremely nice to me, and she spoke to Johnny in that whispery voice: 'Oh,

Johnny.' Typical Jackie. Onassis drove us around in his car; he was just building Skorpios then, and I remember that once he backed up and we nearly went off a cliff. He was sweating, and he wore a lot of cologne. I remember it well; it was August, 1967. Jackie, not married, spent the summer on Skorpios, the colonels were in power in Greece, my wife was trying to leave me, and I got back together with her and we had a good time—it was a magical summer. Christina was insignificant in the scheme of things; in the presence of her father she was often silent. In those days, in a Greek household, a talkative child was not tolerated, and she was—what?—sixteen then. I'm ninety-nine percent certain that there was another Kennedy on Skorpios that summer as well, either Bobby or Teddy, although I would assume it was Teddy; Bobby was always pulling Onassis's leg, trying to get money out of him. Onassis didn't like the Kennedys, but he was a businessman; he got along with them fine. He would have gone to bed with the devil if it meant getting close to power."

Other friends speculated that the Callas affair had shot its bolt—some of them went so far as to suggest, perhaps uncharitably, that because no fresh publicity could be wrung from the association, her usefulness was at an end. Perhaps, too, the loss of Monte Carlo was preying on his mind, together with his failure to transform Alexander into a miniature facsimile of himself. (Then, too, there was the colorless Alexander's improbable alliance with the beautiful Fiona Thyssen. Could it have been that his father, for the merest moment, had suddenly felt his age?) In addition, Tina was on the prowl again, or soon would be—the only woman who had ever left him, no matter how cunningly he had tried to disguise the fact. No doubt his ex-wife would seek to make a brilliant new match, another factor that would have worked powerfully on his mind. Tina's activities were always of keen interest to him, and his interest was not always friendly. (As it happened, when Tina visited Skorpios herself the following summer, rumors began to circulate that a brilliant new match was indeed imminent—a brilliant new match with her first husband. In the closely connected matters of personal ambition and a choice of marriage partners, Tina's dilemma was identical to his. It was a question, finally, of not appearing to have come down in the world.)

Or perhaps, after all, it was nothing more than the crisis certain

men experience at a certain time in their lives, and it was here that
some observers believed that Stavros Niarchos had once again led
the way. In late 1965, almost two years before the members of
Johnny Agnelli's yachting party politely concealed their astonish-
ment on Skorpios, Christina had met Charlotte Ford, the twenty-
four-year-old daughter of Henry Ford II, at a luncheon in New
York. Christina was, however, unaware that Miss Ford was carrying
the baby of her uncle, Stavros Niarchos. On December 14 of that
year, her Aunt Eugenie obtained a Mexican divorce; two days later,
also in Mexico and in a civil ceremony, Stavros Niarchos married
Charlotte Ford. He was eight years older than his new father-in-
law. The newlyweds set up housekeeping in the Palace Hotel in St.
Moritz while Eugenie ("a saint," said more than one of her friends)
continued to live nearby at the Niarchos chalet. The three of them
were frequently seen lunching together at the Corviglia Club. The
baby was born in New York in May and christened Elena, for Niarchos's good (and soon to be former) friend, Helen Vlachos. In
March, 1967, Charlotte Niarchos returned to Mexico and arranged
for a divorce. "He drove me nuts," she explained to Booton Hern-
don, her father's biographer. "My ex-husband is not a happy man.
He can't relax. He has no office, his office is with him wherever he
goes. I found out that he was married to his telex machine. It's as
simple as that." Niarchos returned to Eugenie. In the eyes of the
Greek Orthodox Church, their marriage had never ended.

Now Aristotle Onassis was apparently in full cry after the widow
of the martyred American president. Perhaps, mused one of his
friends, it was simply inevitable, no matter what other factors were
at work. "The Jackie affair was a classic case of the greatest social
climber of all time meeting the greediest woman of all time, but he
didn't lack for warnings," says this man. "Costa Gratsos was his best
friend, a man who really grieved when Onassis died, a man who
loved him, and he was the only man Onassis did not get angry with
when he told him, 'You cannot do this with this woman.' To his face,
Gratsos described her with a phrase in Greek that is not polite—it
is obscene—but which meant that she was poisonous. And he pro-
phesied that she would bring bad luck."

To give him credit, Onassis seemed to recognize that his obsession with celebrities, very few of whom he actually liked, had become something in the nature of an addiction, not unlike a form of

alcoholism. It was a compulsion followed by a hangover that arrived in the form of one of his fits of melancholy, accompanied by a resolve to go cold turkey and never touch the stuff again. His solution was typical of the man. Just as an alcoholic, fearful of what he might learn from a doctor, might pack himself in wet sheets or take long, boiling baths, Aristotle Onassis took a cruise. "Do you know," says Professor Georgakis, "that he used to bring his yacht across the Atlantic *alone*? Alone for days with only his crew for company when he could have flown the distance in a matter of hours. At night, in the grip of his insomnia, he would prowl the deck for hours, his eyes shining in the light from the portholes. How many other rich men do you know who would have done such a thing, not once but many times?" It never worked; he always came back. And in the case of Jacqueline Kennedy, he came back not once, but many times.

He had met the young junior senator from Massachusetts and his wife on the Riviera in the 1950s, introduced them to Sir Winston Churchill, (who may or may not have remembered by then that the young senator's father had once been a none too friendly ambassador to the Court of St. James), and according to some stories, lent them his yacht. After his former guest was elected president of the United States in 1960, Onassis was soon observed in suspicious proximity to the new chief executive's sister-in-law, Princess Lee Radziwill, the wife of Polish emigré prince Stanislas ("Stas") Radziwill, who had made a modest killing in British real estate. There were some observers who, believing what they did about the Bouvier sisters, Lee and Jackie, regarded the relationship with no very great surprise, although it is also possible that they did not regard the sisters without a certain amount of bias. "They'd been brought up to be adventuresses," said Gore Vidal, the author whose mother was once briefly married to Jackie's and Lee's stepfather. "Their father had it in mind for them."

There was nothing particularly secret about the friendship, nor was it marked by the discretion that might have been expected in view of the fact that one of the principals was related by marriage to the elected (narrowly) leader of the most powerful democracy in the world. "I was opening in Chicago once, and Lee Radziwill was also playing there," says a friend of the Onassis family. "I can't tell you what a terrible actress she is. Everytime I go to Chicago, I

always get the same suite at the Ambassador East Hotel. They told
me this time I couldn't have it because Mr. Onassis was keeping it
for Lee Radziwill. I once heard Alexander make a terrible remark.
He said, 'My father is in love with two . . . ' I won't say the word
because you might write it down, a terrible, terrible word. 'One is
Maria Callas,' he said, 'and the other is Lee Radziwill.' " As the
stories spread, President Kennedy became understandably alarmed
and ordered Jackie to intervene. Apparently the intervention was
not effective; soon more stories began to circulate, to the effect that
Lee was negotiating with the Vatican for a divorce. Given the
nature of things, it was not long before Onassis encountered her
formidable mother, Janet Auchincloss.

Mrs. Auchincloss, visiting London in the early 1960s and staying
at Claridge's, the celebrated hotel (although it is never called one),
was seized by a perfectly natural desire to see her younger daughter. "She was told that Lee, who was still married to Stas at that
time, was in Onassis's suite at the hotel," Jamie Auchincloss, Lee's
half-brother, told the writer Kitty Kelley. "Mummy went up there
and knocked and knocked and knocked. But no one answered. She
banged and hollered and finally noticed that the door was ajar.

"Now, mummy is the kind of person who opens other people's
mail and walks through doors she's not supposed to. She's so snoopy
that I once said to her after she opened some of my mail, 'If I ever
catch you doing that again, and I'm of such a mind, I may just take
you to court because there are laws against people who pry like you
do.'

"Anyway, the door was open, so mummy barged right in and
walked down a long hall with a raised platform at one end. Sitting
there at a Napoleonic desk in his silk bathrobe and wearing sun-
glasses was Aristotle Onassis with his feet up on the desk, talking on
the phone.

"My mother took one look at him and shrieked. 'Where's my
daughter?' she screamed.

"Onassis looked up, quite puzzled by this distraught woman
standing in the middle of his private suite. 'Pardon me, ma'am,' he
said, 'but just exactly *who* is your daughter?'

" 'My daughter is Princess Radziwill,' screamed mummy.

" 'Oh, I see,' said Onassis. 'Well, she left here half an hour ago.'

"Onassis went back to his phone conversation and mummy

stormed out of the suite without even saying pardon me or thank you or anything. Knowing Onassis was a name hunter and Lee a fortune hunter, mummy suspected trouble and a lot of it. She never got along with him well afterward because of that one incident. She always treated him in a contemptible fashion."

Mrs. Auchincloss was indeed to have her trouble and there was indeed to be rather a lot of it, but not then and not in the way she may have anticipated. Although Drew Pearson reported that the recently notorious Mr. Onassis proposed to become the brother-in-law of the president of the United States and Meneghini, in Italy, suggested that Maria Callas had already been put aside, Mr. Onassis did not, in fact, do any such thing. He did something else instead.

Dining in Athens with the Radziwills in the summer of 1963, he learned that Lee's sister had fallen into a deep depression following the death of her infant son, Patrick. Onassis immediately had a happy inspiration: Jackie should take a restorative cruise on the *Christina.* Jackie, contacted by phone in Washington, quickly accepted and the president reluctantly gave his consent, provided his undersecretary of commerce, Franklin D. Roosevelt, Jr., accompany the party as chaperone. With much of the country gripped by a mania for all things Kennedy, the political fallout was unlikely to be great, and Roosevelt would not be intimidated by the Onassis milieu. Kennedy's relations with his wife—complicated as they were by her personal extravagance and lack of political sophistication and also by his own recent infidelities—were delicate and complex. And it was true that Jackie was not in good shape. Perhaps, after all, a cruise in the company of people with whom she felt comfortable—as she did not feel comfortable in the White House —would be just the thing.

When the moment came to weigh anchor, Onassis gallantly offered to remain ashore. Jackie would have none of it; of course he would accompany them, as host. Afloat, he attempted to remain in the background, or seemed to do so. His social life was nocturnal at the best of times, but perhaps he had learned that the First Lady was seldom at ease when men of affairs conducted their business in her presence, and like Niarchos, he maintained his office wherever he happened to be at any given moment. Jackie insisted again, and he consented to become her guide. Retracing a path it had followed many times—most memorably, on the occasion when he extracted

Callas from her marriage—the *Christina* touched at Delphi, at Lesbos, at Istanbul, and then circumnavigated the Peloponnesus. Anchored off Skorpios, purchased the previous year and still undeveloped, Onassis confided that he planned to build a 180-room replica of the palace of Knossos on Crete. "Perhaps," he said to Jackie, "you'll advise me on redecorating Knossos when it is finished."

On the last night of the cruise, he distributed the gifts that had become customary on such occasions. "Ari has showered Jackie with so many presents I can't stand it," Lee complained to the president in a letter. "All I've gotten is three dinky bracelets that Carolyn wouldn't even wear to her own birthday party." The president's immediate reaction was not recorded. It was decided, however, that Jackie would definitely accompany him on the trip to Texas he planned for that fall.

Onassis was in Germany when he learned of the assassination in Dallas. Apparently on impulse, he immediately flew to Washington, presented his passport at the gate of the White House, and—rather astonishingly—was admitted. No less astonishing was the sight that met his eyes when he encountered the party of mourners: Ted Kennedy, drunk and doing imitations, Robert McNamara, the secretary of defense, in one of Ethel Kennedy's wigs. At some point, they all piled into cars for a wild ride out to Arlington National Cemetery and back. After dinner, Attorney General Robert F. Kennedy drew up a document in which Onassis agreed to give half his fortune to the poor of Latin America. Onassis, joining into what, to him (on most occasions when his obsessions were not involved, he had a highly developed sense of appropriate behavior) must have been the perplexing spirit of the occasion, signed it in Greek. Jackie remained upstairs, in seclusion.

In the months and years that followed, he became her sympathetic and attentive friend. The press was not informed and, miraculously, did not detect him on his visits to her cooperative apartment at 1040 Fifth Avenue in New York, bringing presents for the children and later for Jackie, too—lavish ones, such as the roses he presented one day, their stems clasped in a diamond bracelet. Lee was quietly dropped, but not in a way that would encourage her to talk in public or embarrass her sister, among whose public escorts he did not number himself once the mourning period was over. (Of these, Lord Harlech, the British ambassador, was frequently mentioned as a possible candidate for her hand, not merely because Harlech was elegant, charming, and titled but because he was also one of the very few such escorts who was neither elderly, married, or homosexual.) If Onassis was indeed biding his time and waiting for his moment, he did it well. Until Jackie sailed past Johnny Agnelli's party on waterskis in August of 1967, not even his friends suspected that something might be afoot. The ground was unfamiliar, the territory was potentially hostile, and Robert Kennedy, the new head of the family and Jackie's protector, was no Meneghini. If an opportunity arose—and of course, it might not— and if Onassis was successful, he would have achieved the social coup of a lifetime, but he had also persuaded himself that marriage to Jackie would do his children no end of good, bringing polish and sophistication into a family that, he had to admit, was sorely lacking in both.

Alexander suspected nothing. As he hid from his father, it did not occur to him that his father might have something to hide from him. And his father, judging that the psychological moment was approaching, gradually began to emerge from the cover he had gathered about himself. In April, 1968, with Robert Kennedy absorbed in his campaign for the Democratic presidential nomination, he flew Jackie to Palm Beach in his Lear jet. Christina, by now enlisted as a member of the permanent Greek chorus that accompanied him throughout his life, was also aboard. Neither father nor daughter emerged from the plane at the Florida airport, but their presence was noted. In May, he took Jackie on a cruise in the Caribbean. Later that same spring—rumors had finally begun to surface, to be greeted, in general, with hoots of disbelief—he gave her a small dinner party at Mykinos, a Greek restaurant in New York, with Dame Margot Fonteyn, Rudolph Nureyev, and Christina as the other guests. (Afterward Christina, who alone of the family had gotten a good look at the woman she later called "my father's unhappy compulsion," told friends that she considered any possible marriage a serious mistake. If she shared her misgivings with her father, he refused to listen.) Presents of unusual lavishness were dispatched to 1040 Fifth Avenue; Onassis knew Jackie well enough by now to have detected a possible high road to her heart. (Once, when her father-in-law Joseph P. Kennedy asked her what she would do if he gave her a million dollars, she replied: "I would tell you to give me another million dollars.") Maria Callas, having slipped across a none too subtle borderline in the Onassis mind, was sent packing to Paris, the elephant's graveyard of discarded mistresses, complaining bitterly to the press. "An aging playboy is awful," said Costa Gratsos later, reflecting the prevailing feeling in the Onassis inner circle. "So is an aging gold digger." A somewhat similar thought had occurred to another observer in 1961 during President Kennedy's state visit to France. "She is unique for the wife of an American president, sir," André Malraux had remarked. "Yes," agreed President de Gaulle, "she's unique. I can see her in about ten years on the yacht of a Greek petrol millionaire."

Of all the Greek petrol millionaire's friends, associates, and relatives, only his sister Artemis—"a marieuse," a matchmaker, in the words of Professor Georgakis—gave the proposed union her unmixed blessing; Artemis thought that marrying Jackie was a wonderful idea. As for Robert Kennedy, he had only a single comment: "It's a family illness," he said, and he made Jackie promise to make no move until he secured the nomination. But in June, Robert Kennedy was dead, struck down by an assassin's bullets in a restaurant kitchen in Los Angeles, and Aristotle Onassis was at Hammersmith Farm, the Newport estate of Jackie's mother and stepfather, Hugh D. Auchincloss.

He had chosen his moment with skill if not with taste; the lady had received another blow, and she had summoned him. The Kennedy family was in disarray, temporarily neutralized as a force by the events in Los Angeles. Edward Kennedy spent two hours every evening calling each of his twenty-seven nieces and nephews, assuring them that he would be alive the next morning. Jackie herself had momentarily given way to hysteria. "I hate this country," she told a Kennedy aide. "I despise America and I don't want my children to live here anymore. If they are killing Kennedys, my kids are the number one targets. I have the two main targets. I want to get out of this country and away from it all!" Robert Kennedy had lent her his strength and his sense of proportion, now, with Robert gone, she called on her sympathetic friend, Aristotle Onassis. He flew to her side at once, bringing Christina.

The Auchincloss cordiality was somewhat strained; the aftermath of a murder was hardly the time for Jackie to introduce an exotic stranger, and her mother had not forgotten London. Christina did her best to worsen the situation. She clung to her father and spoke to no one else; when Jackie tried to draw her out, she remarked that Americans were boring and drank too much. "She was a very unpleasant person," says Jamie Auchincloss who, as the only young man at the gathering, was given the task of entertaining her. "Very uptight about a lot of things. I don't know whether she was trying to get to her father or get to Jackie or get to us, but I had a certain sympathy for her. It couldn't have been a trip that she herself had planned, and she was sort of a fifth wheel. I don't like to bring these things up because they're good wounds to bury. I know that we're often placed in situations—everybody is, but Christina and people like myself more than others—where we're relegated to the position of reacting to what the other people in the room are doing, and she'd probably been through quite a lot of it. It just wasn't a good weekend for her. I never got to know her well enough to say 'Christina, are you angry or are you sad or are you a jerk or are you anything?' I think she must have been sad, and she didn't look in the best of shape. I've never quite figured Christina out. In her father's marriage, it was going to be Jackie who triumphed or Christina who triumphed, and in the end it was Christina. I think everybody probably tried to make it work; it was just, so to speak, that there wasn't enough love to go around. It was a Greek tragedy."

As the old Greeks might have said, it was a union ill begun, touched by the element of improbable and now sinister melodrama that Aristotle Onassis seemed to carry with him wherever he went: the great house shadowed by a statesman's murder, the vulnerable heroine, the arrival of the interloper, and the inept young Cassandra who would not have been heeded even if she had been more skilled at her work of prophecy. It was as though Onassis needed to watch his daughter watching him or the event would not take on the added dimension his ego craved, as though his victory would be incomplete without his daughter's presence as he focused his attention on a woman she barely knew, disliked, and would presently come to hate. He was about to get everything he had always thought he wanted, and the omens were extremely poor.

CHAPTER SEVEN

The Emotions of a Simple Person

For once, Alexander was told in time, although just barely so, at the Glynfada villa two days before the ceremony. Unlike Christina, he had never met the woman (he had heard of her, as who had not?) and he had no personal objections, but he resented being informed at the last moment, and he said so with his new assertiveness. Jackie, his father explained, would bring them all refinement and culture.

Intellectually if not emotionally, Alexander could understand his father's problem perfectly well, or so he claimed afterward. His father was not a young man, but he was as vigorous as ever and he was by no means in his dotage. In all probability, his needs included a wife, and Maria Callas, like Ingse Dedichen before her, was obviously no longer in the running. (Christina, if not Alexander, would later come to appreciate Callas's virtues.) No, if his father wanted a wife he should surely have one, even this absurd Kennedy woman of whom Christina so obviously disapproved, if she was his choice. Alexander had nothing against the lady personally, never having made her acquaintance—which was, in Alexander's view, precisely the point. It was as though his father had selected his bride-to-be in a shop, paid for her at the till, and was now placidly awaiting the delivery truck, meanwhile inviting his children to admire the aptness of his choice. There had been none of the consultations commonplace in normal families; the lady in question had not even been introduced to the only son; nor had the only son—who was, after all, an adult on the verge of acquiring a stepmother—been solicited for his opinion. It was the same thing all over again, the story of Alexander's life to date: his father's intolerable self-absorbtion, and his refusal to acknowledge that his children were human beings with feelings of their own. With Christina in tow, Alexander raced from the house, and they drove wildly for hours through the streets of Athens in his Alfa Romeo.

Meanwhile, Professor Georgakis was a busy and distracted man.

The pre-nuptial agreement had already been drawn up with the assistance of Jackie's American lawyers—a document customary in unions where at least one of the prospective partners is a person of substance, making clear his financial responsibilities in the event of his death. Presumably, the Onassis will had been appropriately altered, or would soon be. The guests were invited, and transportation for the bride and her immediate family had been laid on at Olympic Airways. The professor, however, found that there was still much to do; nothing that touched upon the intimate affairs of Aristotle Onassis was ever as simple as it might have been. On his friend's behalf, Georgakis had to deal with the American embassy, where the chargé d'affaires exibited vigorous and not exactly cordial surprise when he learned the identity of the happy couple. In addition, the professor had to obtain—on short notice and without the bride's signature—the papers necessary to secure the blessing of the Bishop of Levkos. Somehow he also had to locate the English-speaking, short-bearded Orthodox priest whose well-groomed and bilingual presence, the professor's friend believed, would do much to calm the presumed fears of the bride's children, John Jr. and Caroline. Last, but by no means least, the professor had to discover a way of persuading Alexander to attend the ceremony on Skorpios, no easy task until Fiona Thyssen intervened. Jackie's family and certain Kennedys would soon arrive on Skorpios in force, and Onassis felt it essential to present a united family front, as though he planned a showdown rather than a wedding. (Christina, equally reluctant, was left to her Aunt Artemis, and somehow the trick was done.) The founder of the feast, as usual, was occupied elsewhere, and the professor was uneasy in his mind. Despite his careful preparations, he was unable to shake the uneasy premonition that he was about to preside over a circus.

On October 18, 1968, the groom met the bride at the remote airport in Andravida, 192 miles west of Athens. As a chaste kiss was exchanged on the tarmac, those reporters who had ferreted out the location of the rendezvous were locked in the waiting room and their film was confiscated by the police, but as the professor and Alexander feared, their presence marked only the beginning of a concerted journalistic assault. While the wedding party shuttled to Skorpios, first by plane and then by helicopter, some 250 other reporters descended on the neighboring island of Levkos and prepared to lay siege from the seaside village of Nidri. Onassis owned Skorpios, but under international law he did not own the five or six meters of its beach, and it was here that the press proposed to make its landing once the bridal couple were in residence and newsworthy activity was detected. An offshore picket line of caïques was established, binoculars were brought into play, and the *Christina* 's Piaggio seaplane and an Alouette helicopter were observed as they went about their business. Finally, after a day, a night, and most of another day of waiting, a quarry was sighted: John F. Kennedy, Jr., riding in a cart along the shore. As John-John watched with delight and the *Christina* signaled furiously from its anchorage, thirty-six photographers, most of them Greek, hit the beach, to be met by a determined party of Onassis seamen. The encounter was not in good fun; it was growing plain that someone was going to be hurt, perhaps seriously, when Jackie arrived on the scene and put a halt to the proceedings. "These men also have to make a living," she explained to the sailors, and with Professor Georgakis's assistance a truce of sort was arranged.

For days, the professor had attempted to make Onassis deal with the press in an orderly and reasonable manner. Now he was finally able to persuade him to establish a pool of respectable newsmen who would witness the wedding and share their findings with their colleagues afloat. If the battle on the beach had proved anything, it conclusively demonstrated that Aristotle Onassis had finally achieved his heart's desire. By marrying Jacqueline Kennedy in what was already being described as the wedding of the century, he had driven the Vietnam war and the American presidential elections off the front pages of the world's newspapers (JACKIE, HOW COULD YOU? headlined Stockholm's *Expressen*, voicing a fairly typical sentiment), and for a brief and shining moment, he had become the most interesting man on the planet.

On the morning of the wedding day, October 20, Jackie made one last attempt to restore a measure of balance and dignity to the undertaking. "We know you understand that even though people may be well known," she wrote to the press, "they still hold in their hearts the emotions of a simple person for the moments that are the most important of those we know on earth—birth, marriage, and death. We wish our wedding to be a private moment among the cypresses of Skorpio [*sic*] with only members of the family present —five of them little children. If you will give us these moments, we will gladly give you all the cooperation possible for you to take the pictures you need." In England, Tina expressed her indifference by hunting partridges.

It was raining on Skorpios, always considered a good sign at any Greek wedding. At 5:15 in the afternoon, loudspeaker-equipped Onassis helicopters circled the island while fast patrol boats from the coast guard base on Levkos tried in vain to keep the press fleet at the agreed on 1000-meter distance. A glum American Secret Service agent with a *PT-109* tieclip (it was the torpedo boat that John Kennedy had shot from under him during World War II, and he had made it his trademark) barred the door of the Chapel of the Little Virgin while the half-hour service was performed by Archmandrate Polykarpos Athanassiou, the golden-robed, English-speaking priest the professor had finally unearthed at the University of Athens. The interior of the chapel was a tiny place, and although the wedding party was small—twenty-one people, including Caroline Kennedy, John Jr., and Princess Lee's two children— some of the guests were compelled to stand against the walls. Jackie, looking drawn and seldom taking her eyes off her daughter, wore a long-sleeved two-piece dress of ivory chiffon lace, designed by Valentino, that ended three inches above her knees. Her hair— thickened, as usual, with a fall; it was naturally sparse—was secured by an ivory ribbon, and she wore matching low-heeled shoes so as not to tower in too obvious and willowy a fashion over the bride-groom, who was two inches shorter. He was garbed for the occasion in a blue suit, white shirt, and red tie—"the sort of thing," Mario Modiano of the London *Sunday Times* dryly cabeled his colleagues, "Onassis loved to wear." The professor noticed that he was perspiring even more freely than usual.

Artemis took her place as *koumbra*, the sponsor. As the priest chanted, it was her task to place the delicate leather wreaths, shaped like branches with lemon buds and joined by a white ribbon, on the heads of the bridal couple and exchange them three times. The rings were also exchanged three times, and a silver-bound Bible was given to each to kiss, after which they drank from a goblet of red wine. Father Athanassiou shifted into English. "The servant of God, Aristotle," he chanted, "is betrothed to the servant of God, Jacqueline, in the name of the Father, the Son, and the Holy Spirit." Then he took Jackie's hand, Jackie took the hand of her new husband, and they began Esiah's dance around the altar to end the ceremony. No kiss was exchanged; the closest Jackie came to a gesture of affection was when she took her husband's arm. The priest, the married couple, and two witnesses signed a document signifying that the marriage had taken place under the laws of the Greek Orthodox Church and the Greek State. "It was like a business transaction," someone remarked.

The Kennedy children, serious and unsmiling, held candles and kept their heads lowered. Alexander and Christina grimly dodged the very photographers whose presence Alexander had personally secured. A determined attempt had been made to confine the members of the pool to a remote corner of the island, but it had been defeated when Alexander arrived in his jeep and drove them to the church. He wanted, he said, to make certain that a waiting world would learn the smallest detail of the riveting event that would soon transpire. "My father needs a wife," he said, "but I don't need a mother." Now, as his new friends went about their work, he and Christina could hear the shouts and occasionally the screams of his friends' colleagues as they waited impatiently in the boats offshore.

At Jackie's insistence, no pictures had been taken inside the chapel itself—correspondent Modiano thought that she seemed terrified of the photographers—but the party was fair game once it emerged under umbrellas and showered the wedded couple with flowers. The sixty-two-year-old bridegroom was expansive and confident. "I feel very well, my boy," he told a reporter. The thirty-nine-year-old bride wore a radiant, reflexive smile that revealed nothing of her thoughts—it was the mask she habitually assumed in the presence of the media, and it photographed well. The Kennedy children seemed subdued. Onassis slid behind the wheel of a yellow golf cart; Jackie climbed in beside him, clutching Caroline. John Jr.

and Princess Lee Radziwill with her daughter, by coincidence named Christina, took up their stations in the back seat, and they led the procession to the yacht. The pool of journalists—their number swollen by colleagues who had swum ashore in their clothes— were given pink champagne as the caïques closed in, the reporters aboard chanting "O-nas-sis, O-nas-sis" until Ari—he was Ari to the world now, and Daddy O as well—appeared at the rail with his wife and posed obligingly. Then they briefly joined the pool of journalists and accepted their good wishes. Jackie looked blank, Modiano thought. She came briefly to life when Jim Pringle of the Associated Press introduced himself. "Are you Irish?" she asked, and giggled— the last echo of another time and another place, the young politician's wife working the crowd, and then the moment was gone. She and her husband turned to rejoin their guests in the drawing room. The doors closed behind them, the reporters raced to the windows, and the crew closed the curtains.

"My God," said Pat Kennedy Lawford, wife of the actor Peter Lawford, looking around at the vessel's fittings. "I can't quite believe it."

"Almost makes you feel poor, doesn't it?" said her sister, Jean Kennedy Smith, attending against her husband's wishes. The Kennedys, like the Onassises, were split. Ethel, Robert's wife, pregnant with her eleventh child and still in mourning for her husband, sent her best wishes, but nothing was heard from Senator Edward Kennedy or the other active sister, Eunice Shriver; and Rose, the family matriarch, was silent.

Jackie reappeared in a black blouse and a long white skirt circled with a jeweled belt that had been given her by the sultan of Morocco; on the third finger of her left hand, in place of John Kennedy's simple gold wedding band, was a gigantic cabochon ruby surrounded with diamonds. Gifts were distributed: zodiac rings from Zolotas, the Athens jeweler, for the ladies; gold bracelets set with diamonds and sapphires for the girls; Accutron watches for the boys. At dinner the bride and groom sat side by side, with Christina on her father's left and Alexander on Jackie's right; the evening was given over to toasts and weeping. "I want to toast my dear sister," said Jean Smith, raising her glass, and Jackie cried. Janet Auchincloss wiped away tears, rose, turned to her new son-in-law, and said, "I know that my daughter is going to find peace and happiness with you." The host replied that the presence of seven sisters was a good portent for the future. Then it was Jackie's turn. She too rose, with the happy inspiration of picking up the thread where her husband had left it. "I wish to make a toast to the only brother at the table," she said, turning toward Alexander. Christina threw her arms around her father and sobbed. Downstairs, in the master suite, Artemis scattered charms around the bed to ward off the wrath of Callas.

True to their word, the journalists in the pool reported on Jean Smith's silver lamé pajamas, Pat Lawford's tunic decorated with platinum accessories the size of small doorknobs, and even Caroline's nightie, but there was also an omission, a significant one, of what Christina Onassis wore. Of what she said or did, there was scarcely a word. It was true that she had avoided the press that day, much as Alexander had done once he had accomplished his purpose of sabotage. But it was Jacqueline Kennedy and her relatives that the press was interested in—Jacqueline Kennedy and, as it happened, the way she spent Aristotle Onassis's money, and there, no detail was either too foolish or too small. Christina's father had said his new wife would bring the family refinement and culture; what she brought instead was a vulgar extravaganza of press coverage.

As the beautiful young widow of a martyred and popular young president, Jackie had been entitled to her budget of news. Indeed, a case could have been made that she was actually obligated to share some measure of herself with the public, but as long as Robert Kennedy had been alive her activities had been chronicled with the respect and even reverence due to a woman whose position was not merely unique but symbolic. In the American pantheon, she had achieved a position much more closely akin to the one formerly occupied by Mary Pickford than to the niche once inhabited by Eleanor Roosevelt. Jackie, in a way peculiar to her time and place (and considerably assisted, it should be added, by a certain amount of romantic myopia in the reams of newspaper and magazine copy that were generated concerning her doings), had become America's Sweetheart. For her to have married *anyone* and still retain her place in the public heart would have been difficult. Any prospective husband would inevitably be measured against the tall ghost of John F. Kennedy, surrounded as it was by an aura of myth and nostalgia. For her to have married Aristotle Onassis, a parvenu tycoon with no visible taste and nothing in the way of a social conscience, was intolerable. He was, moreover, foreign and short.

That the press coverage would be intense, sometimes bordering on the absurd, was only to be expected. That it would be intensely hostile, however, was apparently not anticipated except by Alexander, the professor, and perhaps Christina. The press thought it had made her into what she once had been; now that she had evidently sold herself to the high bidder, it would atone for its sins by subjecting her to a scrutiny that was more intense, perhaps, than any woman in history had ever received. The reputation did not exist that could survive a thing like that. If his friends' reading of the situation was correct, Aristotle Onassis had gotten exactly what he had bargained for, and like the celebrities he had so devoutly courted, it was not what he had wanted at all.

At a press conference called in Athens a few days after the ceremony to announce the giant aluminum mill he proposed to build in cooperation with the junta of colonels who had overthrown parliament and, in 1967, exiled the king, he told the assembled reporters to go to hell, and stalked from the room when they persisted in asking him about his marriage. He was jealous of his privacy on Skorpios; twice, in 1970 and 1972, he hauled an aggressive photographer named Nikos Kouloris into court. Although Kouloris was acquitted the first time, on the second occasion Onassis succeeded in having him sentenced to six months in jail. (According to one witness, Kouloris had thrown stones at John Kennedy, Jr. and snapped the boy's picture as he threw them back. One witness at the second trial testified that "Mr. Onassis is thinking of giving up Skorpios because of Kouloris." The photographer, the same witness said, had made Jackie's life "unlivable.") When Onassis and his new wife visited Turville Grange, the Radziwill country house in England, a burglar made off with $12,000 in jewelry; the police obtained a picture of the thief from an Italian photographer who had stationed himself nearby with a telephoto lens. When Jackie flew to New York with a Pekingese named Daisy, the event—including the hot dog that Jackie devoured in flight—made the front page of *The New York Times* and the pet dog received fifteen lines of precious newsprint. Christina, who met the plane, received five. Yet her father sent clear signals that, under the proper circumstances, he did not consider the publicity entirely unwelcome. In 1969, he called the press together for a drink at the Grande Bretagne Hotel in Athens and expanded on this theme. "Why, I always answer the phone," he said over a glass of scotch, "even if I have to get out of my bathroom. I am always accessible to the press. I am not like some people who sit on top of the Himalayas." (He could seldom resist an opportunity to take a good dig at Niarchos.) While none of the press had his number and most calls were channeled through Amalia Hatziargyri at Olympic Airways, the confidential secretary whom one reporter described as "his private Cerberus," there was no lack of publishable copy. When Aristotle Onassis spent money, he wanted the world to know about it. And Jackie was very, very expensive.

Her extravagance was well known within the Kennedy circle; accommodating it was something that came with the franchise. "That Jackie," President Kennedy once yelled in the presence of his old friend, Senator George Smathers of Florida. "She's unbelievable. She absolutely does not know the value of money. Thinks she can go on spending it forever. God, she's driving me crazy, absolutely crazy. If the taxpayers ever found out what she's spending, they'd drive me out of office." (Another time, in a calmer mood, he asked if there was such a thing as Shoppers Anonymous.) He brought in Carmine Belluno, an expert at cracking the secrets of Mafia bookkeeping, to bring her accounts under control, but not even Belluno was equal to the task. In 1962 alone, Jackie disposed of an estimated $121,461.61, or roughly $350,000 in 1986 money.

Fred Sparks, a Pulitzer Prize-winning reporter (who went on to make headlines of his own at the time of his death, when it was learned that he had willed a substantial portion of his modest estate to the Palestine Liberation Organization), estimated that Jackie and her second husband disposed of $20 million during the first year of their marriage. Sparks's figures were at times conjectural and occasionally fanciful, but he may not have been far wrong if the houses, servants, airplanes, and yacht were added into the total. "God knows Jackie has had her years of sorrow," her husband was quoted as saying. "If she enjoys it, let her buy to her heart's content." In New York, *Women's Wear Daily* called her "the retailer's best friend," a title that was earned and not merely bestowed. The retailers in question estimated that she spent $1.25 million in clothes the first year she was married to Onassis. "Jackie O continues to fill her bottomless closets," the fashion paper continued. "She is making Daddy O's bills bigger than ever with her latest shopping spree. She is buying in carload lots."

Although Daddy O would later have some pointed questions about what, exactly, happened to all those clothes (she was selling them to thrift shops), at the time he professed to find it all perfectly normal. "There is nothing strange in the fact that my wife spends large sums of money," he explained. "Think how people would react if Mrs. Onassis wore the same dresses for two years, or went to second-class beauty salons, or rode around in a family-type automobile. They would immediately say that I am on the verge of bankruptcy and that my wife will soon be forced to work for a living." In his more euphoric moments, it must have seemed like a fairly even trade-off. Business was good, he could afford to indulge her, his name was in the Social Register (at last!), and for once he had all the publicity he wanted. How that publicity made him look was something he did not consider closely until later.

At the wedding, he had given her a million dollars' worth of rubies. At Christmas that year, with two trees, fore and aft, adorning the yacht, the villagers of Nidri greeted Jackie and Caroline with *"chronia polla"*—many happy years—when they stepped ashore to attend Orthodox services. It was tactfully ignored that the Vatican had labeled Jackie a public sinner on the occasion of her remarriage and that Cardinal Cushing of Boston, her principal defender in the church, had announced his retirement from his see and his intention of spending the rest of his life as a missionary in the tropics. To her husband, she gave a portrait of herself by Aaron Schickler. In return, he presented her with a pair of earrings worth $300,000. "Jackie," he said, "is a little bird that needs its freedom as well as its security, and she gets both from me. She can do exactly as she pleases—visit international fashion shows and travel and go out with friends to the theater or any place. And I, of course, will do exactly as I please. I never question her and she never questions me." For her fortieth birthday he have her a forty-carat diamond with a matching ensemble, a diamond necklace and a bracelet worth yet another million dollars, and a pair of earrings, designed by himself and executed by Zolotas, commemorating her first husband's interest in the Apollo space program. One earring, rendered in gold with rubies and diamonds, represented the moon on which

American astronauts had recently landed; the other, gold with diamonds and sapphires, was the earth, and the two were joined with a chain of tiny golden space vehicles. As far as is known, Jackie wore the ensemble once.

Her husband announced that he had ordered a new yacht in Japan. It would be, he announced, even larger and more splendid than the one he had named for his daughter, a vessel of which Jackie did not quite approve. The whale scrotum upholstery in the bar did not amuse her, nor did the decor in general, and she proposed to do something about it. (She seldom seemed happier than when she was moving furniture around. "The syndrome seemed almost pathological," said the late Willi Frischauer, the semiofficial Onassis biographer. "Find a place, rent it, buy it, decorate it, then leave it. Find another place, et cetera.") Her husband gave her one of the villas on Skorpios to furnish as she wished: during the honeymoon, she had seen more of her decorator, Billy Baldwin, than she did of Aristotle Onassis, and that, too, was to her taste. She was always more comfortable in crowds than at individual encounters, and she preferred the company of men who were cultivated but absorbed in their own affairs: actors, artists, and the elderly captains of the more genteel of the demanding professions, such as banking. (By contrast, her new husband was charming rather than cultivated, and as his children would attest, his self-absorption took the form of absorbing everyone he believed he owned.) She was deeply devoted to her own children—even her enemies conceded that she was an excellent mother—but she could not manage to win over Alexander, whom she seldom saw, or Christina, who was rounding out her education, such as it was, with a few months at Queen's College in London following a year of finishing at St. George's College in Lausanne, Switzerland.

"Jackie made the same mistake that Callas did," says Professor Georgakis, perhaps the one man in the Onassis entourage who was closest to her, although they always spoke together with a certain restraint. "She ignored the children. Unlike a Greek, she did not view the family as a horizontal entity but as a vertical one, as an American would view it. She didn't realize that, in becoming a part of the Onassis family, she was expected to develop deep and close relations with Alexander and Christina, and she didn't attempt to. That, and not the money she spent, was her greatest error. The children hadn't liked Callas, they didn't like Jackie, and they saw the marriage as an extension of the same thing—Callas had also been wrapped up in herself. In time, Onassis came to share this view."

When he grew tired of marriage and its diversions, Onassis could always return to the other world he had made for himself, to the hangers-on that his friend, the British diplomat Sir John Russell, called his "yes men and yes-please women," and to his ships and his planes and his endlessly entertaining war with Stavros Niarchos. Alexander, too, had his means of escape. (He also had a habit of giving everything a name. The yacht was "the tub," his father's Piaggio seaplane, which he disliked and mistrusted, was "a heap of junk," Callas was "the singer," and Christina was shortly to become "the queen of the maze." Jackie was "the geisha." To Christina, she was simply *"kyria"*—madame.) Under the patient tutelage of Fiona Thyssen, it had finally occurred to Alexander to ask his father for something and to refuse to take no for an answer: Olympic Aviation, the airline's small-plane subsidiary. His father had always known that his son's interest in speed and internal combustion would eventually lead him to airplanes, but he had tried to postpone the evil day for as long as possible. Nevertheless, it had come at last, and despite his bullying and his misgivings, he was never able to refuse his son when he really wanted something. Alexander learned to fly with ease and, more importantly, with extraordinary care. Yorgos Zakarias, who refused to accompany him in a car (largely because he quite literally had no desire to be caught dead with his friend and employer) experienced no such qualms when Alexander took him aloft. "I trusted him in planes," Zakarias said. Alexander was eager to win the respect of the professionals who flew for his father, and he did not propose to waste his newfound skills on hobbyism and recreation. He bitterly regretted that his inability to wear contact lenses prevented him from qualifying for a commercial pilot's license.

At Olympic Aviation, he found himself in the grip of a novel situation: He discovered the pleasures of popularity. His father regarded the small planes as a minor enterprise and was openly annoyed when Alexander began to do well with them. Professor Georgakis considered the whole undertaking a frivolous diversion—"playing with planes"—that distracted the heir from the vital task of learning the shipping business. But there was no denying that Alexander's labor relations were better than his father's and his business methods were more modern. He extended air service to islands that had never seen a plane, where hitherto the national capital was as remote and exotic a place as Peking. He personally flew mercy missions in weather that kept other pilots grounded; the flights became legendary. He took care of his customers and he took care of his personnel. And as his confidence grew and the distance that separated him from his father narrowed, he began to watch Jackie very carefully.

Christina was not so fortunate. A satisfactory marriage, not a distracting career, was to be her portion. Cosmetic surgery may have corrected her eyes and nose, but apparently nothing could be done about her thick, unmanageable hair, her oily skin, or her tendency to put on weight—she was a heavy girl in a family her father had always populated with slender women. If anyone had ever attempted to teach her how to dress, the lesson had not sunk in. Her expensive garments, chosen under the supervision of Madame Porthault at Yves St. Laurent, seemed to hang from her stocky frame. Her manners lacked polish, another aspect of her education that had been neglected, and while she occasionally exhibited her father's unerring sense for the natural balance of an English sentence, she also tended to prattle like her mother. She seemed unaware of the saliva that gathered in the corners of her mouth and she seemed unable to control the compulsion that led her to consume dozens of Coca Colas every day. Like Alexander, she was largely ignorant of literature, poetry, philosphy, or politics. Her taste in music extended to rock and later to disco, but no farther. The tantrums of her childhood had been succeeded by deepening episodes of depression, and to the pills she took to control her weight, she added pills to elevate her moods—hardly an encouraging development, in view of her mother's growing addiction. Nor were she and her mother particularly close (Tina had in the meanwhile developed an obsessive jealously for Fiona Thyssen) although she was fond enough of her. "Christina liked her mother, but not as a mother," says one of Tina's friends. "She liked her as a sister."

In short, Christina was an ideal potential ally—indeed, with the exception of Artemis, she was the only possible one in the family—

for Jackie, who had much to teach her in return. Jackie's taste in clothing was exquisite, as were her manners. She knew how to hold herself while being photographed and she knew how to conduct a conversation, how to introduce the names of the proper books and authors, the proper painters and paintings, and how to show interest in a boring subject until the talk could be artfully steered into more productive channels. Jackie was well versed in food and wine, and she knew how to write: One of her pieces appeared anonymously in the *New Yorker*, a "Talk of the Town" item about an exhibit at the Jewish Museum. Her room on the yacht resembled a room in a college dormitory, with clothes thrown about and pictures taped to the walls and a good deal of cheap madras spread around, but while her fascination with interior decoration may have been, as Willi Frischauer claimed, a compulsion, it was also informed. Christina's father would be proven wrong about many things concerning his second marriage, but he was right about one of them: Jacqueline Kennedy was the first truly cultivated woman, aside from teachers, that Christina had ever had a chance to know intimately.

And yet Jackie made no useful moves. If Christina was resentful and sullen, she was also immature, starved for attention and affection, shy, and vulnerable; it seemed as if she could be won over by only a little kindness, but care would have to be exercised. "Like her father," says Professor Georgakis, "Christina is an emotional rather than a rational person. If one approaches emotional people with the arguments of reason, they are like someone awakened from a deep sleep. They are confused, they are disoriented, they do not know where they are." At first, to please her husband, Jackie made a few half-hearted attempts to do the right thing by her stepdaughter, holding little dinner parties for her at 1040 Fifth Avenue and—characteristically—taking her shopping, but the effort was not sustained. "Jackie told me that Christina was a spoiled monster with fat legs and chunky ankles who dressed like a Greek peasant," one of Jackie's friends told Kitty Kelly, and there were no attempts to probe beneath the surface. Jackie's feelings were richly returned. "Make no mistake about it," one of Christina's friends told Kelley, "she hated Jackie from the start. At the best of times, they tolerated each other—were just barely civil." In any event, it seemed that Christina would soon be gone.

"When the time comes," her father told Peter Evans, a prospective biographer, in 1968, "she'll marry a Greek." Indeed, there had never been any other possibility in his mind. He was vastly more generous with her than he was with Alexander—for her eighteenth birthday that year, he gave her $50,000 worth of jewelry wrapped in a Greek shawl—but her destiny was just as settled and just as out of her own control, he believed. At first, a possible alliance with one of her Livanos cousins was briefly scouted and other possibilities were explored in the usual fashion, but when the search seemed to end in 1970, it was Peter Goulandris who appeared to meet all the necessary criteria. Though not conventionally good-looking, he was a pleasant and intelligent man of twenty-two—"and so naturally," says one of his friends, not an unbiased witness, "Christina treated him like shit." More to the point, he was Greek, of established family, interested in shipping, and wealthy. Taken together the Goulandris clan owned 130 vessels and commanded assets that were estimated in the vicinity of two billion dollars. Peter's branch alone owned 60-odd vessels and flew the flag of Orion Shipping. Originally, the family was headed by four cousins, all named John after their paternal grandfather. Peter's father, John P., known as "Megaleas," the Great One, had died of a heart attack in 1948, the year of Peter's birth. His mother, Maria, was the sister of Costa Lemos, the richest of all the Greek shipowners and one of the most elusive. Like most of the maritime Greeks, the family lived principally abroad but maintained powerful ties to Adros, its native island, marrying into other Andros families such as the equally wealthy Embiricos and Dembassi clans. It seemed, however, that a possible Onassis connection was not entirely out of the question.

Christina met Peter at his mother's home on Lyford Cay in the Bahamas; he returned the call by accepting her father's invitation to Skorpios. As a young maritime aristocrat with an impeccable pedigree, Peter was clearly and in all ways the perfect catch, and the necessary arrangements were made. The date was set for the formal announcement of the betrothal—and in April, 1970, at almost the last possible moment, Christina fled Skorpios and joined her mother in the south of France. "Nerves," said her father. "There's no hurry. She's still a child." In any event, he had other and far more pressing business to consider.

For it had come to pass as the others had predicted: Despite his bold announcements of husbandly indulgence and his public proclamation of an open marriage, he had begun to realize that Jackie, unlike Maria Callas, was not the woman for him. "Within a year of the marriage," Gratsos reported, "he would come into my office and say, 'My, God, what a fool I have made of myself. This woman is a bore. Why didn't I see that before I married her?' " As is often the case when a man becomes disenchanted with a woman without quite knowing why, his bill of particulars was sparse and the items on it were not things that reasonable people would have found insoluble. It was just that everything was somehow wrong. He had publically encouraged her to spend money to her heart's content and had likewise announced that she could do exactly as she pleased. Now, it seemed, she was to be blamed for doing precisely that.

He complained that she was "always reading." He wondered what became of all the clothes she bought; all he ever saw her wearing was jeans. She professed to love Sirdar, the magnificent horse given her by President Mohammad Ayub Khan of Pakistan, on which she rode to hounds, and she bought a home in the New Jersey hunt country with her new husband's money, but she all but ignored the Arabian stallions he gave her and she almost never visited the little farm—the "Petite Trianon"—he had built expressly for her on Skorpios, where they were kept. He was outraged to discover that on 23 occasions she had taken Olympic Airways planes and helicopters out of service for her personal use. He complained ceaselessly about the $5,000 she spent for messengers to deliver the gifts and letters she preferred not to mail. Maria Callas had discussed his affairs with him and taken an intelligent interest in his doings; Jackie seemed positively to resent his aides, particularly Johnny Meyer, the former Howard Hughes associate, who helped Nigel Neilson with publicity, and she seemed to resent even more the fact that her husband's affairs were frequently conducted in languages she could not understand. Moreover, she seemed to prefer the company of her sister, Lee Radziwill. During the first year of the marriage, a mathematically inclined observer calculated that she and her husband were together 225 days and apart for 140, although that, too, was in part his own doing. "He did not like having her around, but he couldn't be without her for long, either," said one of his aides. "If he didn't see her for more than ten days in three months, life would be hell in the office. If he spent more than a month with her, he got fed up."

He discovered that he was regarded as a mildly comical figure among his wife's sophisticated friends in New York, Mr. Jacqueline Onassis, the rug merchant who had married Jackie. (Moreover, when he gathered these friends together for some social function that would presumably please her, she seemed absolutely incapable of arriving on time.) In Paris, where he was far better known, he was able to reverse the situation, a circumstance that gave him a certain grim satisfaction without doing anything to improve the situation. "Paris was his revenge for New York," says a longtime observer of the continental social scene. "She was nothing here, absolutely nothing." Still, the cure was imperfect. Jackie did not share his taste for nightlife (she had tried, but he evidently gave her no credit for the attempt), and she was absent so often. There was no question of disciplining her with the tip of a hot cigar, as he had done with Tina, and his other options—at least, as far as he saw them—were nonexistent. To divorce her would be to admit a humiliating defeat and perhaps openly expose him to the derision that was now politely if imperfectly concealed. After all, he had been warned. There was no question of trading up to a superior model, as he had done when he left Tina for Callas. There was no superior model. Like many unreflective men, he was unaccustomed to looking deep within himself, and it had been many years since he felt obliged to examine his life. He did so now, and he found the experience agonizing.

In February 1970, certain letters Jackie had written to Roswell Gilpatrick, a prominent lawyer who had served as Jack Kennedy's undersecretary of defense, surfaced in the possession of the well-known New York autograph dealer, Charles Hamilton. Both the members of the press and Jackie's disenchanted husband found them of keen interest, particularly the one dated November 13, 1968 and dispatched from the yacht during the honeymoon cruise.

Dearest Ros—
   I would have told you before I left—but then everything happened so much more quickly than I'd planned.

I saw somewhere what you had said and I was very touched—dear
Ros—I hope you know all you were and are and ever will be to
me—

> With all my love,
> Jackie."

Gilpatrick's third wife, Madeline, filed separation papers the next
day. She repeatedly suggested that there was more to the relationship between the sixty-three year-old lawyer and the wife of Aristotle Onassis than an exchange of letters and an occasional compan-
ionable evening on the town; she told friends flatly that her
husband's fawning on Jackie had broken up her marriage. To the
press, she said "They were certainly very, very close. Just say that
it was a particularly warm, close, long-lasting relationship."

"I'm afraid my wife is a calculating woman, coldhearted and
shallow," Onassis confided to his friends when he heard the news,
but it is possible that he inwardly rejoiced. Here at last was real
ammunition, hard evidence that Jackie had never been the woman
she had seemed to be, an excuse for action, and he loved nothing
more than a good fight on his own terms. It may have been impossible to leave Jackie, but now he could humiliate her in the eyes of
the world. Possibly, too, he hoped to redress an old injustice. Aristotle Onassis was a man who rarely did a thing for a single motive,
or even for reasons that he himself entirely understood.

In May, it was reliably reported that he had begun to visit Maria
Callas in her Paris flat on the avenue Georges Mandel, and presently the paparazzi were invited to witness a more public reunion
at Maxim's restaurant. Jackie flew in the next day, either playing her
husband's game or responding to a summons. That evening, she
dined with him at the same table. The photographers were again
present.

For Maria Callas, it was not a game, whatever the motives of her
old lover. Four days after Onassis dined with his wife, Callas was
admitted to the American Hospital in Neuilly. Her condition was
officially diagnosed as sinus trouble. A nurse leaked word to the
press that it was an overdose of sleeping pills.

And so perhaps, after all, Aristotle Onassis finally learned something about himself. On August 15, the feast day of the Holy Virgin
when every Maria in Greece is kissed and congratulated, Maria
Callas reclined beneath an umbrella on Perry Embiricos's private

island of Tragonisi just south of Euboea. An Olympic helicopter landed on the beach and a familiar figure stepped forward. He leaned over, kissed her full on the mouth, sat down, and kissed her poodle. *"Chronia polla,"* he said.

After that, they met quietly in the homes of friends.

PART TWO

The Daughter

CHAPTER EIGHT

A Very Nice Relationship

Stavros Niarchos later admitted to the authorities that his wife had been "grieved" by his behavior on the evening of May 3, 1970. He told the investigators that at dinner he and Eugenie had discussed the proposed visit of Elena, his four-year-old daughter by Charlotte Ford; it seemed possible that Charlotte would also visit. Around 9:30 in the evening, Elena and her mother called from America. It was settled that the child would come to Spetsopoula for July and August and that Charlotte would come for ten days. During the course of the conversation, Eugenie entered the room and left abruptly, but there was nothing unusual about that. The perfect Victorian wife (as she was often described), who had earned such high marks during her husband's small adventure a few years before, had developed a very Victorian propensity for hysterics, which she treated with increasingly large doses of barbiturates.

Niarchos hung up after about twenty minutes of talk and went to bed, but at 10:15 he decided to visit his wife's room and clarify the situation. He told the authorities that he found Eugenie lying on the bed in her nightgown. He spoke; she failed to respond. Assuming, he testified, that she had taken a larger than necessary number of sleeping pills, he attempted to awaken her by slapping and shaking, but the vigor of his movements caused her to fall to the floor. He reported that he took her first by the neck and then by the shoulders and attempted to lift her back onto the bed, dropping her several times before he succeeded. He said that he then called for strong coffee and summoned his valet, Angelo Marchini. Together, he and Marchini tried to force Eugenie to drink the coffee, but her teeth were clenched, and they failed. Her pulse rate was 65 beats per minute; it soon fell to 19. Around eleven o'clock, Niarchos called his sister in Athens and asked her to summon a physician. She in turn called Panayotis Arnautis, the company doctor, who arrived by helicopter at around 12:25. His patient was dead.

There was a note. "For the *first* time in all our life together I have begged you to help me," Eugenie had written in English with a clear hand, using a red pencil. "I have implored you. The error is mine. But sometimes one must forgive and forget." Then, in a violent scrawl with a ballpoint pen, she had added: "26 is an unlucky number. It is the double of 12. 10 b of whiskey." It was never discovered what, if anything, she had meant.

Amid a low snarl of rumor and speculation (for Stavros Niarchos was not a popular man), the body was brought to Piraeus for a postmortem and then returned to Spetsopoula on the *Creole;* it was the last time Niarchos ever sailed on his splendid vessel. A source familiar with the situation reported that, with his usual instinct for making himself look worse than he was, he ordered an in-ground burial rather than (as was customary) interment in a vault. It was said that he wanted the body to decompose as rapidly as possible.

The postmortem report listed fourteen separate injuries, concentrated on the face, the neck, and the abdomen. One of its authors was Dr. Demetrios Kapsakis, director of the department of forensic medicine at the ministry of justice. He and his colleague ruled that Eugenie's death was the result of an overdose of barbiturates and concluded that the wounds on the body were the result of "old-fashioned attempts at resuscitation." The ever active Athens rumor mill called it a murder and a cover-up. There was a second investigation and then a third. Each time, the regime cleared Stavros Niarchos and convinced almost no one. "Now my antagonists pour accusations and gossip against me," he railed, "and try to detroy what I have made for the good of Greece, I repeat, for the good of Greece." But he explained nothing.

Eugenie had in fact died of an overdose, just as the doctors said, although the bruises on her body would continue to vex her friends and blacken her husband's reputation for years to come. A fatal dosage of Seconal, Eugenie's drug of choice, is .5 milligrams to a hundred cubic centimeters of blood, although hardened addicts can tolerate somewhat more. Eugenie's blood contained 2 milligrams per hundred cubic centimeters, four times the fatal concentration, and she was not a strong woman. It was her husband's misfortune to be a man of whom the worst was often believed, and to have been cleared by a government that was almost universally loathed, whose menacing, brutal, and humiliating inept leaders were known to be deeply in his debt.

The Onassis chief of security, Mirto Yannicopoulos, monitoring the situation for his employer, detected what he believed to be a counterintelligence probe moving in their direction from the Niarchos camp. Evidently Niarchos believed that Onassis would perceive an irresistible opportunity in his present weakness. The war went on, but Yannicopoulos's employer was no longer certain that it should. Perhaps his own experiences with Jackie had taught him something about a rich man's capacity for self-destructive folly, or perhaps he realized that the situation was too serious for pranks and diversions. He did not believe that his old enemy was guilty, and he had prepared no raid. Surveying the wreckage Stavros Niarchos had made of his life and the agony that Eugenie's death had caused Alexander and Christina, he concluded that the game was no longer worth the candle. Alexander maintained contact with his Niarchos cousins; Yannicopoulos had his own means of communicating. Aristotle Onassis began to send messages that it was time to make peace.

His children were appalled. They had never understood the element of play in their father's rivalry with their uncle, and they had always regarded the struggle with the utmost seriousness. Christina, especially, was ready to believe that her uncle had murdered her aunt and she later said so openly. Apparently she never learned of the investigation Alexander conducted, which (according to Fiona Thyssen) resulted in a mysterious piece of paper, written in Greek, that exonerated their uncle and attributed all of their aunt's injuries to a third party whose identity was never revealed.

The actual situation Christina confronted, as with so many of the tangled events in her family's history, was never made very clear. With virtually all of the participants either dead or incommunicado, only the testimony of outsiders exists. It is a definite fact that her mother, Tina, believed herself in love again. It is equally definite that the object of her affections was Stavros Niarchos. Not that many people believed she needed much urging in that area, although the story was current that she was cheered on by her own mother, Arietta Livanos. (The restraining hand of old Stavros Livanos had been absent for seven years. As secretive as ever, he had died in 1963.) Mirto Yannicopoulos, for one, came to believe that there were great schemes afoot, that Mrs. Livanos was maneuvering Eugenie's not inconsiderable dowry and inheritance by keeping Stavros Niarchos in the family by marrying him to Tina (who had recently filed for divorce from Blandford), and that Christina's mother planned an even grander, if murky, alliance that would somehow unite the Livanos, Niarchos, and Onassis fortunes in a single immense concentration of wealth beneath the Livanos banner. But, yes, it was definitely a fact that Tina had fallen in love with Stavros Niarchos.

"I meant to call Christina and invite her to come here," says Lady Russell (wife of the diplomat Sir John Russell, and a former Miss Greece) in London. "But her mother called just before she was supposed to come and said that they were going to St. Moritz instead, to console Mr. Niarchos. That was when the arrangements for the marriage were made." With Eugenie hardly cold in her grave (although no one had the poor taste to point it out), Tina gathered up the two youngest Niarchos children and took them to London while negotiations continued. The Orthodox Church permits three marriages, or four if the care of young children is involved. This would be Niarcho's fourth, the one to Charlotte Ford not having been properly sanctified. Special permission would have to be obtained. Meanwhile, Mrs. Livanos cast herself in the role of her once and future son-in-law's most conspicuous defender against the rumors and accusations that continued to dog his heels, and Christina once again found herself cast in the role that fate and her family perversely reserved for her: the bystander, the unheeded witness to her family's strange, unseemly, and now almost incestuous private drama. She had seen it happen before, with Callas, with Blandford, with Jackie at Hammersmith Farm, and now, incredibly, it was happening again: all the old preoccupation with self and money and position, and the laundering of everyone's dirty linen in public. Her mother was about to marry the man who Christina believed had murdered her aunt, and there was no one to whom she could turn

in the world she had always known. This time, however, she was not
without options of her own.

Alexander, as usual, was kept in the dark, but he sensed the
direction of the wind. "If you lie to me again," he told his mother
when she returned to the south of France with Christina in tow, "I'll
never speak to you. If you marry Stavros Niarchos, you'll never see
me alive again." Tina denied that she planned to do any such thing.
Christina announced that she was going to Germany for a weight-
reduction cure.

The next time anyone heard from her, she was in California.

In a Las Vegas lawyer's office on July 26, 1971, Judge Carl Chris-
tensen presided over the marriage of Christina Onassis, heiress, and
Joseph Robert Bolker, a divorced real estate developer who, at
forty-seven, was twenty-seven years her senior. "Is this the famous
Onassis family?" asked the judge.

"I am the daughter," Christina replied.

She was over the wall and running free.

Her father was celebrating Jackie's forty-second birthday on
Skorpios when the phone rang and he received the news—apparently from an informant who had read about the marriage in the
newspaper. His intelligence apparatus had detected Bolker earlier
but had dismissed him as no great threat. Christina herself once
described him as "a dinky millionaire in real estate" and therefore
not to be taken seriously. And yet somehow, against all the odds and
in the teeth of probability, the "dinky millionaire" had actually
married the girl. Her father's reaction was almost literally inde-
scribable, in the sense that witnesses found it hard to find words to
convey what it was like. He was wild, they said. He was every
betrayed Greek father since the dawn of time. Jackie had never
seen anything like it, not even in the days when Jack Kennedy
reviewed her household accounts, and she drew back from her
husband just when, under the ancient rules of Greek matrimony,
she should have rushed forward to his support. It was a golden
opportunity, never to be duplicated, to grow close to him, to show
that she was actually his wife and not merely the unsatisfactory
woman who occupied his premises and spent his money. But the
moment slipped away.

Without the benefit of her moderating influence, her husband was able to lose himself in his rage, rather savoring the experience; things had been slow lately. He threatened Christina with disinheritance, forgetting that explicit provisions of Greek and American law prevented him from doing any such thing. He raved about the inconscionable disparity in the ages of the bride and groom, ignoring the fact that Christina was only carrying on an established family tradition and that he himself had once done much the same thing as Bolker. (But he did not, as Bolker came to believe, mention the fact that his new and, he hoped, very temporary son-in-law was Jewish, despite the fact that his Moslem clients might not be pleased by the circumstance. He was angry but he was not cheap, and he had even found it impossible to hate the Turks.) He contacted the members of his trusted inner circle—his sisters, and Gratsos, and Johnny Meyer, and Yannicopoulos (but not Professor Georgakis, perhaps because he anticipated his erudite friend's disapproval)— and parceled out tasks. Gratsos, Christina's honorary uncle, would travel to Los Angeles bearing the arguments of reason and check to pay the detective agency that would tap Bolker's telephone. Johnny Meyer would likewise travel to California, befriend the treacherous couple, look into Bolker's background, and if possible besmirch his reputation. Yannicopoulos would search for a possible Niarchos connection. No doubt there was one in there somewhere.

Gradually, the reports came in. They were muddled and illogical, but they spoke to his favorite obsessions and they were what he had expected to find. To further an ingenious plot concocted by Christina's grandmother, Arietta Livanos—her object appeared to be the amalgamation of the Livanos and Niarchos fortunes—Tina (Onassis was told) had decided to neutralize Christina by placing her in a position from which she would be unable to disrupt the impending union between her mother and Stavros Niarchos. ("We will marry," Niarchos was supposed to have said, "but first we must get the little girl out of the way.") To this end, Onassis believed, Tina had positively thrown her daughter at Joseph Bolker, and Niarchos had given him $300,000 for his trouble. If Onassis had stopped to think, he would have realized that none of the supposed conspirators could possibly have known that Christina would suddenly bolt for California, that it was unlikely that they would have known of Bolker's existence, and that Tina's ultimatum—marry the girl or send her home—had all the earmarks of a more-than-slightly peculiar snap judgment, not the triggering phrase of a long-maturing and well-laid plan. There was no reason for Christina to have fled for any motives other than her own. But Aristotle Onassis did not stop to think.

There was only one thing to do. Joseph Bolker, whoever he was, must be destroyed.

The reality of the situation, as Alexander discovered, was rather different. He obtained copies of the transcripts yielded by Gratsos's telephone tap; evidently his father had never read them. Alexander looked them over carefully and passed them to Fiona Thyssen. "What shall we do?" he asked when she finished reading. Fiona went to the telephone and placed one of the few calls she ever made to Aristotle Onassis. "Leave your daughter in peace," she said.

Joseph Bolker had never heard of Arietta Livanos until Christina drew up a chart of her genealogy. ("This is my grandfather," she said. "This is my grandmother. This is my father, this is my mother, and this is the man who murdered my aunt.") He had shaken hands with Stavros Niarchos at a couple of parties, but he had never engaged him in conversation and he had never been offered nor had he received $300,000. When he first met Christina at the Lido Pool in Monte Carlo in 1971, he had no idea who she was.

Bolker was a slender, handsome man with silver hair and spectacles. He bore a faint but undeniable resemblence to the father of his bride-to-be. Like her father, too, he was fond of celebrities, especially film stars, but he was also unmistakably American, almost an American type, an innocent abroad who had come to Europe with his heart on his sleeve, the tan of the sunbelt on his face, and his total ignorance of Christina's world in his eyes.

"Joseph is not in the least in awe of me," Christina told a friend at the time. "Do you know how refreshing that is?"

Ten years, two wives, and much water under the bridge later, he would be living in a huge, neo-Palladian house in the Hancock Park section of Los Angeles, pickled pine paneling on his walls, condensed novels and mystery anthologies on his shelves. He was the honorary consul general of the Republic of Senegal and the owner of the Forty Carrots chain of health-food restaurants. He was fond of serving his guests herbal tea and wholegrain cookies, and at the age of fifty-eight, he pronounced himself as fit as he had ever been.

His first marriage to Janice Taper, the daughter of Mark Taper, the builder and philanthropist, had cost him money, he said. His marriage to number three, Dene Hoffheinz—the daughter of Judge Roy Hoffheinz, mayor of Houston and driving force behind the Astrodome—had cost him more money yet. His fourth wife, Victoria, had recently presented him with a son they named Alexander. Framed on the mantel in his living room were photographs that appeared to a visitor to be four studies of Christina Onassis. They were pictures of his daughters.

The man toward whom the Onassis juggernaut prepared to launch itself in the summer of 1971 possessed a degree in subtropical horticulture from UCLA. Through the good offices of his first father-in-law, he had entered the building trades and branched out successfully into real estate development. Unable to bear the thought that his housing tracts might look barren, he sponsored landscaping competitions among the purchasers of his homes. He was innovative; he was personaly congratulated by President Kennedy on the cleverness of his design for Rose Park, a low-income development he built near Oxnard. He was a member of the Young Presidents Organization, an international association of conspicuously successful executives between the ages of 32 and 49, and he interested himself in the affairs of its affiliate, the World Business Council. He had been head of civilian protocol for the City of Los Angeles, and he had been local chairman of the International Sister Cities Program. He supported the Greek Theater and the county art museum, attended the ballet, scuba dived and river rafted and skiied —but in he fall of 1970, he was not an entirely happy man. His wife of eighteen years had filed for divorce in 1967, and although she was a wealthy woman in her own right, she was awarded a seven-figure settlement just at the time, as one of his friends put it, when "Joe was beginning to make some money."

It had not been a pleasant divorce, and its aftermath was slightly bleak. He dated women, but he was also a man who enjoyed going into society, but thanks to the influence of his former father-in-law, Mark Taper, certain sectors of that life were closed to him now. He was well-meaning and ambitious, a good businessman who thought highly of himself, but things had not gone quite right for him, and it was in a receptive and slightly unsettled state of mind that he set out for Europe that year with his widowed friend, Hank Hendler.

They visited Crete and Sicily and Corsica, and Bolker decided to look in at Monte Carlo, where the Young Presidents Organization was meeting.

"I enjoy swimming and getting massages," he says, "and every time I go to Monte Carlo, I stop at either the Summer Club or the Winter Club. The Hotel de Paris has a tremendous swimming pool, glass-enclosed, overlooking the harbor, and they have massage facilities there. So I went for a swim. There was another couple there—an attractive girl in a black one-piece bathing suit and her companion, and we started talking. She said, 'Where are you going next?' and I said 'Germany and London.' She said 'Why, I live in London,' and she offered me her phone number. I remember that there were only the three of us in this huge place. I said, 'I'll call you from Munich.' So she wrote out her name and telephone number. She was Christina Onassis."

He was intrigued, but no more than that. He enjoyed the company of the famous, and on occasion might go out of his way to place himself in their path, but unlike Christina's father, he was not obsessed with fame. Aristotle Onassis had long since ceased to be merely a practical man of affairs, but Joseph Bolker still had to work for a living. He was not well versed in the dynastic and cultural intricacies of Greek wealth; few Americans were. "She was a pretty girl," he says. "Good swimmer."

And he was as good as his word. "I called her from Germany, and we went out in London and had a very nice time together," he says. She spent their first evening together complaining about her father. Christina was eager, almost desperately so, to experience ordinary life—she later confided that she wanted to work on the docks at Piraeus—and her new friend was unique in her experience. Not only did he give the impression of being totally uninterested in her father's wealth and equally unimpressed by it, but he actually seemed content with his own modest millions, confident of his ability to make more, and secure in his identity. Like most of the men in her life, he was fond of the things money could buy, but he preferred the money to be his own. He knew no one in her circle, knew nothing of the unpleasantness she inflicted on her servants, and had never heard that she was supposed to be selfish and spoiled. Unlike many people, he thought her pretty. He was a kindly man with a daughter, Jill, almost exactly Christina's age, and with the exception of Fiona Thyssen, she had known very few kindly people. Indeed, the near total lack of that comforting quality was the dominant characteristic of the world in which she lived—that, and the lack of trust. She believed that Joseph Bolker could be trusted.

He returned to America, to a life of work she could only imagine. "She would write me and . . . well, she was having a lot of problems with her father," he says. "He was a very difficult man. I remember one time she called and said she had the flu, and her father protested the fact that she wanted a television set for her bedroom and he refused to pay for it. Yet she said the week before he gave her a matched set of emerald earrings that were worth two hundred thousand dollars. And she said, 'Why, Joe? Why would my father treat me this way?' I said, 'Well, you understand, Christina, very few people see your bedroom, but everybody sees you when you're wearing his jewelry.' "

Compared to her family, Joe Bolker was a good and honest man, and as she fled north from the Mediterranean that summer, away from her irrational father and addicted mother and Stavros Niarchos, a plan began to take form in her mind.

Bolker and his daughter Jill were in Caracas, attending the wedding of the Venezuelan president's grandson to the daughter of Mario Lanza, the operatic movie star, when a call came in to his Los Angeles office. It was Christina. She said it was a matter of life and death; she had to talk with Mr. Bolker at once. When she was finally put through to him in Caracas, Bolker did not hesitate; he sent Jill home and flew to London. "She needed me," he says. "She was having a terrible, terrible time with her father, and she was extremely depressed. Her father wanted her to marry Mick Flick, the Daimler-Benz heir, and she didn't want to. It would have formed a fantastic family merger, but she didn't love him. Her father was insisting, yelling, threatening—I think he needed a loan, too, and that was part of it. She wanted me to be with her and help her." In fact, her father was perfectly creditworthy, he wanted her to marry a Greek, and she was actually quite drawn to Mick Flick. Other sources in New York and Los Angeles insisted—at times with vehemence—that she told Bolker that she was pregnant, that the baby was his, and that she needed his help in getting an abortion; an allegation that Bolker emphatically denies.

"She needed a confidant, somebody to advise her and guide her, somebody with experience in life," says Bolker, a point upon which he and Christina were entirely in agreement, although their interpretations of how this role was to be performed proved to be somewhat at variance. Bolker returned from London to Los Angeles. Then: "She called from London. She said her father was giving her a terrible time. Could she come and visit me? I said yes. I met her at the airplane. It was a strange moment." ("Everybody was a little crazy then," says a friend of the family.) "Back in the apartment, I said, 'Have you talked with your mother? Does she know where you're at?' She said no. I said 'We must phone Tina in Paris.' So she did. Tina asked to speak to me, said did I intend to marry her daughter? I said I didn't intend to marry anybody. Her mother said, 'Well then, I want Christina to come home on the next plane; I don't want her staying with a man she's not married to.' I said, 'If I was going to marry her, I would have asked for her parents' permission.' She said, 'Ari won't give his permission to anybody. You have my permission.' I said 'Christina will be on the next plane.' Christina didn't like that at all."

In fact, she became hysterical and went into the bedroom to compose herself. When Bolker joined her, he found her on the bed, muttering to herself in a stupor, surrounded by empty plastic pill bottles. Bolker summoned the doctor who lived across the hall.

Tina had said to marry the girl or send her home. Although there were other possible options (her father, for example, was not consulted), there seemed to be only one thing to do. At the ceremony in Las Vegas, Jill stood as witness. Later the workers at the office of Brighton International, Bolker's company, chipped in and bought a cake from a Greek pastry chef at an English bakery in Beverly Hills; the shop displayed a replica in its window. At a subsequent wedding reception given by some of Bolker's friends—"high up in Beverly Hills," says a guest, "in a house literally poised on the head of a pin; I got clammy hands driving up to it"—Christina, her hair done Jackie-fashion, did an excellent imitation of her stepmother's breathy, ethereal, little-girl voice. "It was a pretty good job," says one of the guests, "especially coming from someone whose own voice sounds like a trumpet. She and Joe seemed devoted to one another. The Bolker girls stayed off to one side, not hostile but questioning and bemused, as though to say, 'What's daddy gone and done *that* for?' "

It was an altogether odd episode, and it became no less peculiar with the passage of time. "Joe was ambivalent about the marriage at the beginning, and he was ambivalent about it at the end," says one of his friends. In the Onassis circle, those who did not share (or tactfully imitate) her father's outrage regarded the whole adventure as patently absurd, but there were at least a few, like Professor Georgakis, who were inclined toward sympathy. "It was a desperate thing Christina did," says a friend of the family. "She tried to create something on her own, but she tried it with the wrong man. All those things her parents had done had pulled the rug from under her feet and she felt she belonged nowhere. I think at the time she was acting like a lost person. I'm sounding very complimentary to her, but I'm speaking with my head and not my heart; I think of those times and how a young girl might have felt, putting for example my own daughter in her position. Christina felt rejected, you know. Don't forget that this was—see, here in America, you had the 1960s. The sixties came late to Europe; there; you had the sixties in the seventies, and until then the children behaved very properly. Consider the ambience that was growing around her and among her contemporaries, when every young person was behaving the same way, breaking up the establishment and reading Norman Mailer. The times were right for what she did; before, she could not have done it. Even so, I think if she had married Alexander Andriadis instead, as she later did—a Greek of good family, with the proper nautical connections—it might have lasted."

She entered a life unlike any she had ever known. The entrance to his condominium on the twenty-fourth floor of the west tower of Century City, the luxury apartment development erected on a former movie studio backlot, was dominated by a flashing marquee. The living room was done in gray, with leather director's chairs around a glass table, a chinchilla couch, a lavish display of house plants, and a balcony. The bedroom walls were covered with mirrors. Christina's father maintained a corps of servants; Bolker made do with a houseman who doubled as a chauffeur. "Joe Bolker is a loner," says a friend of the family. "He can exasperate you to death, but there's also something basically good and innocent about him. He's the sort of man who talks about things like the American character." He mailed innumerable letters of advice and criticism to his elected representatives, and he believed the American dream was alive and well. "I used to sell magazines door-to-door in Omaha, where I grew up," he says. "I sold more magazines than any other kid in the city. I had a pop stand in the summertime. I sold more pop than any other kid. I think I originated the idea of carrying food and cold drinks to construction workers. I used to hire two or three boys my age, and they would put buckets of ice filled with soda pop bottles on the backs of their bicycles and go around to the various construction jobs and sell them. I'm just a country boy. When I was back in Omaha many years ago, just after the Second World War —I was in the war—I was introduced at a party to the man who owned the Ideal Bottling Company. He said, 'I know Joe. He got us through the Depression with his pop stand.' "

In college at UCLA he formed his own student landscaping company. Later, he was named Builder of the Year by the American Association of Home Builders. At the age of forty-seven, much to the amusement of his friends, he still collected trading stamps and carefully clipped grocery coupons from the daily newspaper.

His bride, like an immigrant setting up housekeeping in a new country, tried to learn the customs and adjust her life accordingly. Shortly after the wedding she appeared at the offices of Brighton International, requested paper and pencils, and asked one of her husband's employees to teach her the basics of household accounting. (Sometime later, Bolker's office manager came upon the neat columns of figures and realized with a mild shock that she had learned her lessons well, and she knew exactly what she was doing.) "We had a very nice relationship," says Bolker. "We stayed home a lot. She made breakfast for me. She had friends who came through town, and they'd visit her. She'd go out to lunch. She took care of the apartment—we had a cleaning woman, but Christina would tidy up—and she made some changes, bought some furniture, a vanity for herself. Occasionally on Sunday we'd go to St. Sofia, the Orthodox Church built by the Skouras brothers. Not every Sunday. Sometimes. She'd meet people there who knew her father, who knew her family, and they'd talk." He encouraged her to shop at Gelson's, the expensive supermarket near the condominium, and afterward he went over the cash register tapes with her and analyzed her buying habits. Her bookkeeping was excellent, but she had somewhat exotic notions of how much things were supposed to cost. "She enjoyed shopping and going to the market." he says.

"She'd never done it on her own. Before we married, she'd just go into stores and sign the sales slips. I found that she was giving enormous tips over at the Century Hotel beauty shop, like about fifty dollars on a twenty-five dollar hairdo and manicure! A normal tip was fifteen percent, maybe twenty percent if somebody had knocked themselves out. I told her she was going to spoil it for other people, being so generous."

She could be funny. At times, she almost seemed to become the person she had once dreamed of being, a normal young woman leading a normal life. "Dear Joe," she wrote. "I hate you. You ate all the chocolate mousse. But I got even. I found the cake in the freezer and ate it all."

"She had a good heart," says a person who knew her then. "Her instincts seemed right, and she tried to be a good stepmother to Joe's girls, who were almost her own age—in fact, Jill *was* her own age. She bought board games to play with them when they came to visit. I think it's very touching that Christina ever wanted to be a mother to four precocious Beverly Hills teenagers and play Parcheesi with them. They patronized her unmercifully—except Jill, who's one of the nicest people I've ever known. I think the real problem was that Christina was bored, or maybe bored and innocent would be a better way of putting it. She was innocent of real life and had no real tools to make one. She was too European, too cosmopolitan, too Greek, not at all inclined to pursue the hobbies of the California rich, such as growing organic vegetables or building her own furniture. She couldn't understand why Joe had to go to work all day and earn his living, why he couldn't be with her all the time. She didn't know what to do with herself."

She knew Paris and London and New York—or the parts of them that mattered to the members of her set—but Los Angeles, while not without its diversions, often gave the impression of being a town full of people who were falling all over themselves to get to London or Paris or New York. "She was very restless, I think," says an older woman who tried to help. "This is not an easy town to live in, you know. If you work in show business as I do, it's different, and then you have a social life. But it's not as exciting as New York at all. She had nothing to do here except socialize with people she didn't know too well. Joe's friends weren't the kind she was accustomed to."

Once the novelty of her situation wore off, she found that while it had no depth, it was rich in irony. Her stepmother, Jackie, unable to comprehend the complexity of the Onassis life-style, was bored on Skorpios, while Christina, who had rebelled against that complexity with headlong flight, was bored in Los Angeles. "In the morning, you go shopping," says one of her California friends. "In the afternoon, you go shopping. In the evening, you might go to a party or a movie, or you might drive thirty miles to the Music Center. Or you might go down to the beach and throw yourself off one of the piers, clutching an anvil."

Christina took driving lessons and bought a red Ford. At least one observer credited her with introducing backgammon to Beverly Hills. Actually, the game was already popular at a sports club, Pips, to which she and Bolker belonged, and she played it enthusiastically. ("If anyone introduced backgammon to Beverly Hills," says Bolker, "it was Lucille Ball.") Sometimes, on her visits to her husband's office, she wore one of the maid's housedresses and hid in the closet whenever Bolker appeared; he liked her to dress nicely. She never carried a purse or identification; in Saks one day, trying to buy designer jeans with a handful of hundred dollar bills, she was politely escorted to the manager's office by the floorwalker. "Now, young lady," said the manager, "where did you get all that money?" "I am Christina Onassis," she replied. They refused to believe her.

Old habits, in remission during the early days of the marriage, began to reassert themselves. "When she was happy," says one observer, "there was no one funnier or more joyful, but her depressions were awful." She became as obsessively secretive as her father and grandfather, in small things as well as large. "She didn't like to be seen when she didn't know she was being watched. She was very upset when someone saw her coming out of a medical center in the valley. It was silly, but it was also bewildering. You never knew how she'd react to something."

When she asked what she had most enjoyed about her life in California, Bolker mentions the surf at La Jolla and falls silent.

"Joe wasn't really prepared to handle a situation like that," says Stanley Slotkin, one of the founders of Abbey Rents, the rental and leasing firm. "He lived in a condominium just a few floors above mine. It was beautiful but too small for the kind of entertaining and the kind of life that she was used to. One of the things I think Joe did that was wrong was he kept his own style of life. He would go to work very early and come home very late because he did a lot of exercise and jogging in the evening. One day she came down to see me, and she said 'Stanley, is this the way American businessmen live? I didn't want to get married just to sit home all the time. I could do that in Europe.' It was the first inkling I had that something was wrong. I told Joe what was happening—I think she meant for me to tell him. She just didn't fit in. Their life became very social and it could have been a happy one, but there were too many differences. I didn't find her a happy person at all. I think she was . . . seeking. And I don't think that Joe could have made her happy unless he devoted his whole time to her and became a playboy."

He did his best. On their first night out after the wedding and reception, he took her to meet the singer Englebert Humperdinck. He thought she might like Greek restaurants, and he took her to them, too. "When I was single I used to date actresses and movie stars and so on," he says, "so I was used to people coming around and talking and photographing, but with her it was incredible. I don't know whether it was because she was married to an older man or because there'd been so much publicity or what it was, but going out with her never felt peaceful. We had one nice evening out, I remember, with Ronald Reagan at Al and Betsy Bloomingdale's home. We were at their house for New Year's Eve; that was a very pleasant evening. But if we went to a restaurant or a charity event . . . it was just uncomfortable all the time."

In a city with an ambitious but not highly developed social life, Christina was seized upon as a catch, an arresting novelty, the sensation of the season. "There hasn't been so much gushing here since Ed Pauley, Henry Salvatori, and Howard Keck [all local oil millionaires] brought in their last wells," one local hostess told *The New York Times* shortly after the wedding. It was a circumstance that did not exactly displease Bolker. To his delight, he and Christina were taken up by the people Joyce Haber, the gossip columnist, had labeled the A Group, the circle of top-quality hosts and hostesses whose most prominent members were the Bloomingdales, Kirk Douglas, Gene Kelly, and the producer Ray Stark. But even here, pleased though he was to be moving in the city's social stratosphere, Bolker remained ambivalent and sometimes allowed his discomfort to show. "Christina was very unhappy here, I know that," says one hostess. "I don't think that Joe treated her like he should have. I gave a dinner party for them once, and Christina called at the last moment to say that Joe was not at home and how should she get there? I sent a friend of mine, a Hungarian writer, to pick her up, and Joe never came at all. And I had some very chic lovely people. I think she was giving Joe a very hard time."

Bolker took the opportunity of a supper party at the home of James Doolittle, the impresario, to announce that Christina planned to take courses in American history at his alma mater, UCLA. A serious course of study was consistent with her plan to forge a new life for herself. It was not, unfortunately, consistent with her undistinguished history as a student or her growing inability—it would later become one of her most prominent characteristics—to sustain an effort. "I graduated from UCLA in 1950, and I'm active in the Chancellor's Associates," says Bolker, "and so I was able to get Christina registered after the semester had begun and into the courses she wanted to take. She did go a few times. Then she decided it was too much bother, and she didn't go anymore. It was disturbing because I'd pulled a lot of strings to get her into the classes." Like an ex-convict with an intellectual understanding of the consequences of his actions but with larceny firmly rooted in his heart, Christina was finding herself unable to make it on the outside. She had been too rich for too long. As the more perceptive of her father's associates had foreseen, the marriage was doomed from the start, a ninety-day wonder and no end of a lesson, swiftly collapsing under its own unlikelihood and Christina's inability to create a life independent of her father's fortune. Her father, however, was not content to wait.

"The pressure began the day we were married," says Bolker. Christina's aunts called repeatedly, demanding to know, they said, why she always made trouble for the family. Alexander begged her to call it off. A friend phoned with word that Bolker was a member of the Mafia. Gratsos, no longer the avuncular friend of her childhood, bullied and threatened. Johnny Meyer dropped hints that Bolker's background did not bear scrutiny. Jackie, like any well-bred woman of good family, had dispatched a congratulatory letter —something that could hardly have overjoyed her husband if he ever learned of it. Meanwhile, Aristotle Onassis remained incommunicado. He was not at home to his daughter and his son-in-law. "Sometimes he would be right there in the room when the calls came in," says Professor Georgakis. "I would ask him, 'What would it cost you to pick up the phone and speak to the man?' But he never would."

"I remember," says Bolker, "when the LA county sheriff, Pete Pitchess, called one day. He said, 'Joe, I just want you to know that I got a call from Costa Gratsos, trying to tell me that you had a bad reputation, that you were a criminal.' I've known Pete Pitchess for years. He said, 'Joe, I asked him why he didn't leave the two of you alone.' When Johnny Meyer came out, we thought he was our friend, we thought he was going to help. We took him to lunch at the Beverly Hills Hotel. But he tried to sabotage the marriage too, even while he was still in Los Angeles. He went around asking people about my reputation, trying to get them to say bad things. I don't know what else he did. All of a sudden it became difficult to do business with the banks, where I'd never had any trouble before; I've been in business here since 1955. I'd come home at night and Christina would tell me who'd called and what they'd said. Sometimes she was crying. It was kind of, well, unpleasant."

After a while, it seemed as though the unpleasantness and their reaction to it was the only thing holding the marriage together. Bolker, who continued to give some people the impression that he had been little short of railroaded into the judge's chambers in Las Vegas, was both touched in his pride and touched by Christina's suffering. Christina, lacking an excuse to break off and unwilling to yield to her father's pressure, held on grimly.

People called to say that her father had canceled her trust fund. "That was all right," says Bolker. "We had enough to live on. I happen to be a very good builder. I earn a living. This guy Onassis was impossible, a tyrant. It was amazing. Christina disliked her father and she loved her father. She hated what he was doing, but she loved him at the same time. All she really wanted was a family life, and her father wouldn't allow that. He really destroyed any happiness she might have had in her life. It's a pity."

On October 22, 1971, Christina's mother disappeared.

They had last seen each other the month before, when Tina appeared at the St. Regis in New York on what was widely believed to be a mission to save her daughter from Bolker but which in fact was no such thing—Tina was ill again, and she checked herself into a hospital. (Unable to fly, she had come by boat.) Christina stayed the night and returned to California the next day; Tina encouraged her to stand firmly against her father. Whatever the truth of the matter, it was definitely in the Niarchos and Livanos interests for Christina to remain in America. (Tina, as it turned out, had paid the plane fare to California.) Christina's presence there distracted her father and absorbed his associates as the time approached for another wedding that, at all costs, must not be prevented. Alexander posed no real threat, and the Orthodox Church was not an obstacle. As long as the impulsive Christina remained in Los Angeles, she was effectively neutralized, and her father was unlikely to interest himself in anything else. If Niarchos and Mrs. Livanos wished to avoid mischief-making interference, they could not have planned Christina's movements better.

On the day her mother disappeared, Christina, as she often did, made Bolker's office her headquarters. It was more difficult for her aunts to reach her there, and she occasionally saw her husband. Her grandmother Livanos claimed to have no idea where Tina was. That not only seemed odd, it seemed impossible. Tina was the sort of person who needed a great deal of supervision. (Alexander had already been informed of the marriage—by registered mail.) Christina picked up the phone again. "She's the sort of person whose face changes from moment to moment," says a person who was in the room at the time. "As she placed call after call, to friends in Europe, to South America, her features began to darken, and when she finally learned the truth, her eyes were wild. She couldn't understand how it had happened. Her mother had married the man who some people thought had murdered her aunt."

When she and Bolker returned from Bolker's house in Palm Springs, there was a message confirming her mother's remarriage. "It was awful," says Bolker. "There was screaming. There was no talking or reasoning with her. Her mother had married the man who murdered her aunt, and he was going to murder her mother." She went into the bedroom and locked the door. Bolker forced the lock and found a scene much like the one that had met his eyes on Christina's first night in California. The doctor was no longer in residence across the hall; this time, Bolker drove her to the hospital. As soon as she recovered, Christina flew to Europe alone.

"Since our marriage," Bolker told the press, "Christina and I have been subjected to extraordinary parental pressures, which are now seriously affecting her health. She is a young woman and should not be alienated from her father. At my suggestion, she has gone to London to see her doctor . . . and hopefully to resolve family problems."

She promised Bolker that she would return for her twenty-first birthday party at the Bistro, the fashionable Beverly Hills restaurant, but they both knew that their story had only one possible ending. In her London hideaway, a somber smoke-filled room of Greeks gathered in council to resolve the problems of her marriage, her trust fund, and her inheritance. But their conclusions were foregone: her marriage was absurd, it served no useful purpose, and it must be abandoned. It was too late to save Tina—in truth, it had been too late to save Tina for quite some time—but it might be possible for Christina to achieve a more tolerable relationship with her father. It would not be the old, close alliance of father and daughter—he would never trust her again—but it should be possible to persuade him to allow her to lead the life she chose, within limits that he would prescribe. In a few weeks she would come into the $75 million in the Victory Carriers trust, and no matter what her father said, it was the Grace National Bank, and not he, who administered the money. She would no longer be tied to her mother's checkbook and her father's selective generosity. She had lost nothing but her hope of leading a normal life, her father's regard, and (she was convinced) her mother's life.

As she had promised, she did return for the party. Bolker was determined to give her a final moment of the California glamour that he loved, and which had somehow eluded her. He engaged the second floor of the restaurant, floodlighted the entrance, rolled out a red carpet, laid on food and drink, and hired a band to play her favorite rock and show tunes. (She liked the music of Frank Sinatra. By coincidence, Sinatra himself was giving a party downstairs.) As often happens when the filtering effect of the Onassis mystique makes itself felt, it is a little difficult to discover just what happened next; different people witnessed the same event, and they say different things. Bolker and his lawyer and friend, Gil Dreyfuss, who attended, remember an entirely happy occasion, a glittering company, and a radiant Christina. Others saw a party whose existence was in doubt almost until the last moment. They saw a Christina with her hopes in ruins, a young woman by no means inclined to cooperate in her California swan song, who was of two minds about attending, and who finally made her entrance with hardly an excess of enthusiasm.

"There was an ambience of people being very ill-at-ease," says one of the guests, although Bolker and Dreyfuss recall no such ambience. On the contrary, says Dreyfuss, everybody had a very good time.

"There'd been a lot of speculation about whether she really would come back—Onassis was putting the killer pressure on," the guest continues. "Christina was really mental that night." Not so, says Bolker, in fact, Christina was very happy. And perhaps, for Bolker's sake and in his sight, she was.

"She looked distraught," says the guest. "There was no way she could win out over her father, but she didn't exactly hate Joe, either. I remember that Zsa Zsa Gabor was there, and her daughter, Francesca Hilton, and Francis Lederer and Robert Stack and Betsy Bloomingdale and the usual motley crowd of Hollywood has-beens. There was a reception first and then—was there a sitdown meal? I seem to remember eating something really good with Cornish game hen and some sort of elaborate French dessert. I remember thinking, God, Christina looks awful." To Bolker, who has never publicly uttered a negative word about his former wife, she was beautiful. The guest's perception was rather different. "She was exceedingly pale and drawn, and the strain was just radiating out of every side of her. She just floated through the evening wearing a black and white dress. A lot of the A group was there, to see what she was like. And the B crowd. And the D-minus people. Her face was a vicious mask. Almost nobody could bring themselves to wish her a happy birthday." Bolker and Dreyfuss remember that everybody wished her a happy birthday. It was, they say, an entirely successful evening.

The marriage wound down in a kind of twilight sleep. They were marking time, going through the motions, saving face. Gold and silver keys were ordered from Van Cleef and Arpels, one to the apartment in Century City, one to Christina's London hideaway, to be exchanged at parting. There was the New Year's Eve party with Ronald Reagan at the Bloomingdale's, and then it was over. Christina returned to Europe.

Divorce proceedings began on February 4, 1972. "I am divorcing Joseph Bolker," said Christina, inaccurately; he was divorcing her. "His work forces him to live in California and I would have been forced to stay too far away from my family. I couldn't bear that. . . . He may soon be my ex-husband, but he will always be my best friend. I am too Greek and he is too Beverly Hills."

It was rumored that her father had given Bolker five million dollars. In fact, the divorce cost Bolker $50,000 in legal fees. "I wish I had been given five million," he says almost inaudibly. He looks away and is silent for a moment. "I could have put it in the bank. Collected some interest."

He and his associates endured a siege by the press that left him with an enduring suspicion of reporters, and with good reason. Stories about him, most of them untrue and some of them ridiculous, continued to appear in the gossip papers for years. In May, he was granted an uncontested divorce. The court asked him six routine questions, to five of which he answered yes. The sixth was: "Will your wife need financial support?"

"No," said Joseph Bolker.

CHAPTER NINE

Death in Athens

Once the Englishman had examined the wreckage and made his report, they knew what had happened, but they never found out why.

The weather had been good in Athens on Monday, January 22, 1973. The skies were clear, the temperature was in the upper fifties, and the *nefos*—the atmospheric inversion that makes Athens one of the most heavily polluted cities in the world—was nowhere in evidence. Alexander Onassis was in excellent spirits, and with reason. Three weeks before, on January 4, his father had finally accepted Alexander's arguments and had told his son that he would divorce Jackie, promising soon to end an intolerable and humiliating situation and—perhaps as important—clearly acknowledging that his relations with his son were now a partnership of near equals. Elsewhere the news was ambiguous, but at least fresh disasters had been avoided. Neither Alexander nor his sister expected their mother to make old bones, but for different reasons. According to Joseph Bolker, Christina still believed Tina would be killed by Stavros Niarchos, and Alexander believed she would probably kill herself. Tina still took five sleeping pills a day, she was ill with phlebitis, and her disposition had not improved with age. At St. Moritz, during the Christmas season just past, Fiona had kicked Alexander out of the chalet they shared—and Fiona owned—when he refused to wish his mother the compliments of the season. Deciding that Fiona was probably right as usual, he had knocked on the door of the Niarchos chalet, only to be greeted by his mother with words that were hardly ones of yuletide cheer. "I knew you would come crawling back," she had told him, "because you need me." Even Fiona was now compelled to admit that there was little hope in that direction.

Yes, Tina was a sad case, but at least she kept her condition to herself. To the puzzlement of her friends—and Alexander's relief —she was no longer seen in her old haunts since her third marriage, and she did not socialize. Her new husband, Stavros Niarchos, had grown increasingly reclusive over the years—he was known as "the governor" now—and Tina had apparently joined him in his solitude. As far as Alexander was concerned, it was a circumstance hardly to be deplored. He was preparing to make a major change in his life, and the less meddling he received from his impossible mother, the happier he would be.

In great secrecy, he was preparing to resume his education. He knew that there was no real future for him in aviation beyond the narrow confines of Olympic's light plane subsidiary, and his father would never give him the airline itself; for years, it had been the private fiefdom of his father's cousins and old companions in the Argentine, Nikos and Costa Konialidis. Of course, Alexander would one day inherit half of it, along with a similar portion of his father's merchant fleet, and he would be expected to manage both entities, but while he could probably handle the airline, he would be hopelessly lost when it came to the fleet. He and his father had reached a new understanding in their personal relations, but elsewhere his father was directing the same course of study that had taught his son nothing about the business that was significant. Alexander was still expected to keep himself on call and answer promptly when summoned to meetings he barely understood, or to dance attendance on deals he found incomprehensible. He had no idea of how Olympic Maritime was put together and only a hazy notion of what it did—well, yes, it hauled oil and dry cargo, but just how did it go about doing that?—and the maze of Panamanian companies that controlled it was as much a mystery to him as it was to the tax collectors whom it quite effectively foiled. His father betrayed no inclination to enlighten him.

In the absence of a proper education, Alexander had come to understand, his life would go on much as before, with his days spent in his father's long but now more amiable shadow. He would amuse himself with his airplanes and with Fiona, and he would come when he was called. He had come to realize something that Christina had known for years: thanks to the family fortune and his parent's self-absorption, he was almost totally ignorant of the workings of the real world and he could not function there, much less hold down a job. Therefore, he would return to school. It was late, but perhaps he could make something of himself. Like Christina, he wanted to do something on his own. Fiona was willing to subsidize the venture, and she had set aside an entire floor of her London house as his study.

This alone was cause for rejoicing, but he had another and slightly more macabre reason for high spirits on that splendid January day. He was a young man who had just seen one of his favorite theories vindicated. He had always contended that most aviation catastrophes were the result of a number of small errors compounding themselves rather than a major equipment failure or a single large and tragic error, and now he believed he had his proof. In his call to Fiona the previous evening, a Sunday, he had spoken at length about the offical investigation into the recent crash of a British European Airways Trident jet in the London suburb of Staines, and how it was a perfect demonstration of everything he had always said. Perhaps the matter was still in the back of his mind as he crossed the tarmac and climbed into his father's Piaggio seaplane. But he had many things to think about.

He had decided to come to Athens on the spur of the moment. Fiona was attending a London wedding she was sure would bore him, and a friend there had asked for a lift to Greece. With nothing better to do, Alexander had ordered the Lear jet rolled out, and they were on their way. He stayed, as usual, at the Hilton, and he would make use of the opportunity to check out the newly over-hauled seaplane. If all went well—and there was no reason it shouldn't—he would be back in London sometime Monday night.

He distrusted the Piaggio and considered it dangerous, and he was delighted that his father had recently decided to follow his advice and replace it with a helicopter. Alexander had located a suitable one in Germany and his father had agreed to purchase it, but complications arose. His father proposed to take the yacht across the Atlantic to Miami, and it was impossible to take delivery of the new helicopter before the cruise. The Piaggio was really unnecessary—his father rarely used it after he purchased the Lear—but he found travel without some form of aircraft aboard the *Christina* all but unthinkable. A seaplane was one of the first things he had bought once he began to make some money—his first, all but forgotten, and much smaller yacht had been equipped with a crane and storage pad of such disproportionate size that it resembled a miniature aircraft carrier. In the absence of the helicopter, the Piaggio would accompany him to America even if (as was likely) it never flew; it was an essential part of his image. Against his better judgment, Alexander had ordered the plane completely over-hauled. The work was now complete and the Piaggio had not been in the air since. Today's flight would be a test for its certificate of airworthiness, and it would also serve another purpose. Donald McGregor, the regular Onassis pilot, had recently undergone eye surgery. An American, Donald McCusker, had been imported as his replacement. McCusker had extensive experience in seaplanes but not in Piaggios, and the flight would be an excellent opportunity for Alexander and McGregor to familiarize him with the craft.

Alexander filed a flight plan listing his destination as "Athens local;" evidently he planned to handle the takeoff himself, turn the controls over to McCusker, try a few water landings, and return. The Piaggio was not a complex mechanism, he objected to it mainly because it was amphibious. Once before, making a water landing, he nearly hit a floating log. Attempting a landing ashore, the experienced McGregor had forgotten to lower the wheels. Air safety was much in Alexander's thoughts, and not merely because of the crash at Staines. A couple of years earlier, the Kouris brothers, men he worshiped, had disappeared without a trace while guiding the Lear's predecessor on a routine but always tricky night approach to Nice—they had been coming to pick up Alexander. For weeks thereafter, he and Fiona had searched the beaches for some piece of wreckage, some clue to what had happened, but nothing was ever found. The accident had shaken him badly and seemed to have contributed to a new and growing sense of prudence—for example, he allowed Fiona to persuade him to trade his Ferrari for a more sedate Mercedes. And one of the most inflexible rules he laid down for his pilots was his insistence that they conduct their own pre-flight checks of the wings and flaps rather than letting the ground crew do it. Former airline pilots sometimes kept their big-plane habits.

The three men climbed into the seaplane. McCusker was feeling the effects of his transatlantic flight, too many cups of coffee, and the boredom that characterized the life of an Onassis family retainer. (It had been necessary to recruit the new pilot in America because the Olympic pilots declined, to a man, to volunteer.) As Alexander settled into the copilot's seat, he discovered that somebody had neglected to supply the cockpit with the usual preflight checklist. No matter. Athens tower was trying to hurry him as usual, but he was perfectly capable of doing the checks from memory. He had done them dozens of times before.

From the back seat, McGregor noticed that young Mr. Onassis had forgotten to fasten his seat belt.

Christina was in Brazil when her friend, Maria Tzombetsoglou, reached her with the news. "No!" she cried. "It can't be true!" But it was. Alexander, the careful aviator, had crashed in Athens during a normal takeoff, in excellent weather with superb visibility. The other two men were injured but would recover. Alexander was alive, but he was in a very bad way, his head seriously injured. Rescuers reaching the wreckage had been able to recognize him only by the monogram on his handkerchief. An operation was underway to remove the bloodclots from his brain.

They all converged on Athens, all the actors in the drama, excepting only Maria Callas: Christina from Brazil; her father and Jackie from America, bringing a specialist; Stavros Niarchos and Tina; Fiona Thyssen. No one seemed to be in charge. Hospital staff and sympathetic visitors remembered nothing clearly, only chaos. But on one unrelatated point, one mind remained clear. At some point, Jackie took Fiona aside and asked her what she knew "about January fourth"—the day Aristotle Onassis had promised his son that he would divorce his second wife.

At midnight a British neurosurgeon, Alan Richardson, arrived from London, the only passenger aboard a 103-seat Olympic plane. There was nothing he could do. Alexander's brain was dead, his vital signs sustained by life-support machinery. At two in the afternoon of January 23, his father finally accepted the inevitable. "Let the boy die," he told the doctors. "Don't torture him anymore." He instructed them to wait until Christina arrived and said her last farewell. Then he went home to his villa in the suburb of Glyfada to be alone with his thoughts.

Tina (even then, an Olympic employee couldn't help noticing how "cute" she was) remained secluded in the hospital office. Upstairs, Fiona sat at Alexander's side, waiting for the end.

Christina's plane landed at 4:45. She was met by relatives already dressed in mourning. At the hospital, she could think of only one thing. "Where's my mother?" she cried. "I want my mother!" Alexander died at 6:55 in the evening.

Christina drove to Glyfada where, she thought, her father was waiting for her. "Oh poppa," she said. "I'm here."

He looked at her with reproach.

He believed now that he had never wanted a daughter, that he had hoped in vain for a second son, and Christina had lost his trust in California. Like Alexander, she had recently found it wisest to avoid him, although she had been careful to send a clear signal that she was ready for reconciliation. "It is not true what the papers write," she said for the benefit of *Life* magazine while her divorce made its way through the courts, "that Jackie bosses him and he is her slave. It is just the opposite. She always tries to please him in everything. Whenever they are together, she seems to fall more in love with him. . . . Jackie is my stepmother, but she is also my great friend." Her father remained unforgiving.

Since her divorce, Christina had tried to lead the life he wished for her, and indeed it was no great task. No more was heard from her about the little house by the sea or the job on the docks at Piraeus. An ordinary existence as represented by Century Towers, Wilshire Boulevard, and Joseph Bolker was not for her. Her rebellion, which her father never understood, was over. Yet by a paradox, she was more liberated than she had ever been before. She now had all the money she needed from the trust fund. Her mother was a spent force and her father kept his distance. As a divorced woman, under the stringent but unwritten rules of Greek maritime society, Christina was free to be seen in public, to go about on her own, to enjoy the company of suitable young men, and to express her opinions on a variety of subjects. She had returned to Paris; she was seen in the company of the Baron de Rosnay, a friend since childhood; Patrick Gillis, the skier and former constant companion of Brigitte

Bardot; and especially Mick Flick, the Daimler-Benz heir. Alexander, seldom original but always apt, had called her "the prodigal daughter."

"What happens next?" he had asked.

"I have no idea," his sister replied. "Isn't it exciting?"

For the last time in her life, during those months between her divorce and Alexander's death, she claimed to be happy in the way that other people are sometimes happy, taking simple pleasure in her pursuits, living in the only world where, she had found, she was comfortable. "It was the best time, the best time there ever was," she told a friend. And yet there were those who had detected a flaw in the design. "I always felt a terrible sadness for her," Jean-Jacques Cornet-Epinat, who wanted to marry her and who died young, told the writer Peter Evans. "She never seemed to be traveling to see new things, to find new people and adventures—it was always as if she was trying to get away from people and places that bored her. She was so determined to be happier than any woman ever could be, but I always suspected that she was less happy than most."

All that was over now. Alexander was dead. Her mother had given way to hysteria, her father was mad with grief. "In moments of tragedy, a volatile character swings into unforeseen dimensions of illogic," remarked Professor Georgakis, who found himself with his hands rather full. For one thing, Onassis flatly refused to have his son buried. On some occasions, he seemed to want Alexander's body embalmed so that he could carry it around with him forever. On others, he seemed to have cryogenics in mind, keeping the cadaver frozen until science could repair the damage, although it was far to late for even that faint hope. On his own authority, the professor went ahead with the funeral arrangements. He also wrote his friend a letter. Seeking and finding his precedents in ancient Greece, Georgakis pointed out that Onassis had no right to dispose of the soul of his son, and he bluntly stated that Onassis was unqualified to discuss the theological aspects of the question. Very well, his friend replied, he would bury Alexander's remains as the professor wished, but only on Skorpios and only beneath the floor of the chapel. Impossible, the professor said. The Orthodox church permitted only saints to be buried in a sanctuary. A compromise was reached. Alexander would not be buried in the chapel but beside it, and the structure would later be extended to cover the grave. It was an outlandish and therefore typical Onassis solution, but it was the best the professor could get.

While the preparations went forward, Alexander's body was laid out in the chapel at Athens' First Cemetery. Tina threw herself into the coffin. Stavros Niarchos wept. Of all the family, only Christina seemed in command of herself. "Things never happen the way you expect," she said. "It would be comforting to say, with Medea, 'I, myself, am enough.' That would be an exquisite kind of exile, the best asylum. Isn't that what we really want?"

Lines of citizens formed to view the bier, many shops closed for three days, and mothers who had lost sons wrote letters of condolence. "It was as though a child of Greece had died," says an official at the airline. In the newspapers and the tavernas, Alexander was remembered fondly—"perhaps it was just as well that he died young," observed the professor—but the prolific Athens rumor mill was also busy, and each rumor as it emerged was progressively more bizarre than the last. It was murder, of course. The CIA had done it; Alexander's skull had been crushed with a hammer to prevent him from consolidating his father's operations in Greece. No, the plane had been sabotaged in revenge for the death of the Kouris brothers. Stavros Niarchos had done it for reasons that were obvious, Jackie had done it for reasons of her own—the theories were various. Yannicopoulos gathered up the stories one by one and reported them to his employer. Meanwhile, the official investigation moved slowly forward. If its preliminary findings were correct, something was very wrong indeed.

With McCusker at the controls (though Fiona remained convinced that Alexander would have handled the takeoff himself) the Piaggio had taxied onto the runway at 3:15 P.M., directly into the jet wash of a departing Air France 727, a thing that Alexander, who never let the tower hurry him, would never have done. The Piaggio began its takeoff roll, accelerated to 100 mph, and lifted off. At less than 100 feet in the air, it had banked sharply to the right, hit the ground with its starboard float, veered yet further to the right, and cartwheeled along a curved path for 460 feet. McGregor, in the rear seat, claimed that things happened too fast for him to see what was going on. McCusker claimed amnesia.

Onassis hired Alan Hunter, a British expert, and instructed him to get to the bottom of the matter. Meanwhile, he posted a million dollar reward—half to the person who brought him conclusive information, half to that person's favorite charity—which generated a blizzard of crank mail and triggered another flaming row with the professor. Georgakis tried to point out that all this talk of sabotage and murder could only harm Olympic Airways. Onassis responded by forbidding the members of his inner circle, including the professor, to have anything to do with the airline until the crisis was resolved. He had no time for his daughter, who was in need of emotional support, and he had no time for his ships, which were experiencing the most fabulous year in their history. When Alan Hunter's report came in, he was convinced he was on the trail of something big. Unfortunately, however, the Englishman's report made no sense at all.

At some point between the beginning of the overhaul on November 15 and the takeoff on January 22, Hunter found, someone had reversed the Piaggio's aileron controls. When McCusker tried to obey the air controller's order for a left turn when airborne, presumably to escape the wake of the French 727, the seaplane had banked to the right. When McCusker, reacting, had tried to correct the situation by applying more left wheel, he had driven the amphibian into the ground. That much was clear, but how had it happened?

The steering column, Hunter discovered, had been removed by an Olympic mechanic on November 15 as a routine part of the overhaul Alexander had ordered. A new column had been installed by a different mechanic on November 25. The plane had been examined (and passed) by the Greek Civil Aviation Authority and by officials from Olympic Airways on January 18, following a two-hour inspection. It was true that Alexander had come to Athens on short notice, indeed on impulse, and it would have been difficult to reverse the controls at the last minute, but how was it possible that the meticulous Alexander, even without benefit of the preflight checklist, could have missed something as obvious as malfunctioning ailerons? And yet there the trail ended, firmly impaled upon a series of improbable happenings. The answers had died with Alexander. McGregor and McCusker were useless as witnesses. No leads —none—were generated by the offer of a reward, an unusual occurrence in a country where money is an exceptionally powerful lubricant—unless, of course, there were no leads, which in turn could mean only one of two things. Either there were no leads because there had been no crime and Alexander had received dramatic and final proof of his theory of aviation disasters, or there were no leads because the murder had been done by someone powerful enough to enforce silence. Arguing powerfully against the latter supposition was the fact that Alexander was not the seaplane's regular pilot (and, in fact, disliked it) and had come to Athens on an impulse that could not possibly have been predicted. Furthermore, the Piaggio was a murder weapon of almost surreal clumsiness, and the risk that any tampering would be prematurely discovered was astronomical. Nothing was proved by the fact that it had passed its ground inspection except, perhaps, that the inspection was inept, nor was it possible to predict that the methodical Alexander would, for once in his life, neglect to make the one test—of the flaps—by which he set such store. But given a choice between a simple if baffling explanation and an ornate, unprovable one, there was only one path for the Onassis mind to follow.

"He built himself a whole edifice of suspicions and paranoia," remarked the professor with resignation. "The number of suspects and possible motives was almost limitless." Like the gossips sipping their ouzo in the tavernas, Onassis considered the CIA an obvious choice. He had never trusted the Americans since the oil boycott of the 1950s. Stavros Niarchos was also prominent in his list of suspects, notwithstanding a complete lack of evidence suggesting his involvement. But in the end, after much deliberation and obsessively circular thinking, he settled on Tina as the most likely culprit. Her ex-husband believed that a clear pattern of intrigue had emerged at the time of Christina's preposterous marriage. Perhaps, too, he knew about Tina's outburst at St. Moritz during Alexander's last Christmas. Tina's objective, as before, would be the consolidation of the Livanos, Niarchos, and Onassis fortunes. Eugenie's death had opened the way, the next step had been Tina's marriage to Niarchos, and now the Onassis male line had been irrevocably severed, making the untrustworthy Christina the sole heir. The last phase of the plan would doubtless consist of luring Christina into a second, strategic marriage. Stavros Niarchos had eligible sons. It was all so very clear; He had been checkmated at last. "He was crazy," sighs the professor.

Turning away from his daughter, Onassis sought the only comfort he knew: a cruise on the yacht with Jackie, for whom he felt a brief rekindling of feeling, and Pierre Salinger, her first husband's former press secretary, a man Onassis barely knew. For once his wealth failed to console him. It had all come down to this: his fabulous, topheavy vessel wallowing across the sea; his son cold in the ground on Skorpios; his untrustworthy daughter the target of a monstrous conspiracy; and the strange, incompatible woman he had married in his pride sleeping in her cabin below amid her madras throws and her taped-up prints, "the sort of things," a guest once remarked, "that you'd do up your Manhattan apartment on the cheap with." His insomnia intensified.

It was summer when Christina brought the packing cases full of Alexander's belongings to Skorpios from Monaco. Outwardly, her father seemed much the same, as though living his life from habit, going through the practiced motions. There was the usual assembly of guests. He still charmed the women, entertained the men, and gave personal tours of his kingdom in expectation of praise for his handiwork. Jackie, as usual, was missing. On an island hill, her pavilion and farm were finished at last. He told his guests that she was no longer interested in them.

The sight of Alexander's effects clearly depressed him, but he refused to be diverted from his guests. Instead of spending more time with his daughter, he turned his attention to his sister Artemis and a visiting archeologist. Christina had brought a Greek friend with her, a woman her father seemed to dislike on sight. A pair of American girls were on the island, attractive young women about his daughter's own age. "Why can't you have friends like that?" her father demanded querulously. Nothing about her pleased him, and he was at no pains to hide his feelings. "Though Christina was quite pretty," said one of the visitors, "he didn't like the way she dressed and thought she hadn't enough class. These things are hard to explain. I think he thought Christina wasn't the sort of person he would have been attracted to. He undoubtedly loved her, but by the standards of the women he had known, she did not rate." More to the point, she was not Alexander.

Christina struggled unhappily on, waiting in vain for a sign that her father was himself again, and that she had recovered his love. Overweight and looking desperately sad, she took care to appear in the sorts of places he approved of, in the company of the sort of people he liked. Friends reported that she was at least half-convinced that Jackie had brought a curse to the family, either some acquired Kennedy taint or one that was uniquely Jackie's own. Christina also believed that she knew how to exorcise it. She had only to persuade Mick Flick to marry her, something that the young Daimler-Benz heir had no intention of doing.

She knew the match would please her father. Something of the sort had been scouted in 1970, before the family settled on Peter Goulandris and Christina ran to California, and from the highly specialized Onassis viewpoint, the Flick bloodline was impeccable despite its being German rather than Greek. The Flicks were citizens in extremely good standing of the country of the rich and they had gotten there on their own, not once but twice, triumphing over the available competition, the rigid German social structure, and the determined assaults of the victorious wartime Allies. They were self-made, their track record was stunning, and the parallels with the Onassis experience were compelling. Mick, christened Gerd-Rudolf, his brother Friedrich Christian (known as "Muck"), and their sister, Countess Dagmar Vitzethum, were the grandchildren of the legendary Friedrich Flick, the Rhineland farmboy who began his business career as a clerk, rose to company director in eight years, and expanded his empire until he manufactured 10 percent of Nazi Germany's steel, mined 8 percent of its coal, and stood second only to Alfred Krupp in the country's industrial pantheon. During the war, the munitions ministry proclaimed the Flick group a "model armaments enterprise," and in 1947 the United States Military Tribunal agreed; Friedrich Flick was sentenced to seven years in Landsberg Prison (later reduced to five and then to three) for using Russian slave labor, looting German-occupied countries, and various other crimes. East Germany confiscated three-quarters of his assets; the Americans and the British ordered him to divest himself of either his remaining coal or his remaining steel.

Released from Landsberg in 1950, he set out to rebuild. By the time of his death at eighty-nine in 1972, he owned Dinamit Nobel, Alfred Nobel's old explosives company, the Feldmuhle pulp and paper enterprise, the Buderus foundries, 39 percent of Daimler–Benz, the automobile and truck manufacturer, and much, much more. The Old Gentleman (as he was called) was easily, very easily, a dollar billionaire. Mick's father, Otto-Ernst, quarreled with the

Old Gentleman in 1962 and died in 1974, a family outcast but not a disinherited one. At thirty-two, Mick Flick was a well-off young man even by the demanding standards of an Onassis, and he was on the verge of becoming better off still. Shortly before Mick's grandfather died, he had executed a document awarding Mick and his siblings important voting rights in the Flick group of companies, where Mick and Muck briefly worked under the tutelage of their shy but extremely shrewd uncle, Friedrich Karl. The brothers discovered that they were not cut to the corporate cloth, but their parting had been an amiable one. Now Friedrich Karl, preparing to reposition the empire for the hard times he correctly saw coming in the latter half of the decade, exhibited an eagerness to regain control of his relatives' voting rights. Once this was accomplished, Mick and the others would split at least $150 million and probably hundreds of millions more. He was, in short, a catch. Not incidentally, he was also a means of reestablishing the Onassis male line.

Christina flung herself into her project of entrapment with innocence and zeal. "I think she wanted to get a catch by herself," says one of her friends. "Mick speaks quite funnily about it. He says, 'Gee, my family was poor at that time.' I don't think his family's ever been poor at any time. In any case, he was young and she was young and they got thrown together. I remember a lot of stories he would tell me about her, one being that she tried so hard to impress him by being, you know, domestic. Once she was staying at his house and he went out to work, and Christina decided to clean the house. She started to work on the walls with a brush. What she ended up doing was taking off all the wallpaper. She had no idea of how to clean a house."

"She went for Mick, but he didn't go for her," says another friend. "He said to her, verbatim, 'I can't go with you. Your legs are too thick. Anyway, I like blonds.' She dyed her hair blond, but she couldn't do anything about her legs." Nevertheless, by the end of the year she believed that matters had advanced to the point that she could approach her father with news of the impending match.

It was January 1974, the first anniversary of Alexander's death. The new wing of the chapel was completed and ready for dedication. The archbishop flew from Athens to officiate, the island's population—120 servants and retainers—was summoned to the spot, and Christina stood at her father's side, bubbling over with her news.

(Jackie, once again out of favor, had chosen not to attend.) Wrapped in his private grief, his thoughts elsewhere, Christina's father was too preoccupied to remember to invite the archbishop and his entourage to join him in the customary light meal and cup of tea. It was difficult to tell how much, if anything, he absorbed of what his daughter had to say.

Confident that her plan was working, Christina returned to New York and broke the news to her intended husband, who proved to be rather less than overjoyed. Young Flick immediately requested an audience with her father and proceeded to set matters straight. He said that he had no intention of marrying anyone until he reached the age of forty, and he certainly had no intention of marrying Christina then or at any other time. It cannot have been an easy interview. Onassis, however, quite saw the point. Indeed, he heartily approved. Johnny Meyer, for one, believed that Onassis considered the young German a prince of a fellow. Christina, understandably, saw matters in quite a different light. Of all the men in her life says a close friend, Mick Flick was the only one she never forgave.

At the same time, her father was gradually recovering, or so it seemed. Gratsos was convinced that he no longer wanted to live, but Gratsos and Onassis's New York banker, George Moore, saw more of the private man than his other friends and even his daughter were permitted to see. In New York, he seemed almost unable to bring himself to return home to Jackie's flat at 1040 Fifth Avenue, spending long evenings with Gratsos or the Moores, complaining about his wife, wishing aloud that he had spent more time with his children when they were younger, raiding the refrigerator when he grew hungry. When Moore, not a night person, gave up the struggle and went to bed, Onassis would turn his attention to Mrs. Moore, spinning out his long, gloomy monologues as he had once written the endless letters that Professor Georgakis had called "the Onassiads," the writing of which had been one of the greatest pleasures of his life. At the end of the evening, alone or in the company of Johnny Meyer, he would look in at El Morocco, one of the four restaurants that stood like the milestones of his life. (The others were Maxim's in Paris, Neraida in Piraeus, and "21.") Seated at his usual table, he seemed his old self again, telling his stories and sipping his drinks, talking to anyone who approached him unless they were obviously drunk or obviously crazy, but his public man-

nerisms, long and carefully cultivated to conceal his crippling shyness, were by now as instinctive as the migration of birds, as habitual as the Dunhill cigarettes he always lit with matches, the Dom
Perignon he always drank after lunch and dinner, and the cream
silk shirts and black ties, loosely knotted, that he wore with the
invariably rumpled suits that were almost always blue or gray. He
had never carried large sums of money but he had always had
enough for tips; now, he tipped rarely or not at all.

His day still began with his boiled egg, his toast, coffee, and juice.
If he was in Athens, he would lunch either at home, in the noisy villa
he shared with a cook and a boy valet (there were three bedrooms,
his own, the one Alexander had rarely used, and a spare; guests
were sent next door to his sister's house), or at the Grande Bretagne
hotel where, for some reason, he always paid cash. He would nap
from five to seven and would then return to his office and work until
midnight, trying to make some sense of his life. In the old days, he
would top off the evening with a visit to Neraida, but his visits were
infrequent now. It was in Neraida, on an evening of newfound
intimacy, that he and Alexander had broken every plate in the
house.

It was some time before he realized that he was slipping. He had
deliberately structured his life and his business to be as mobile and
elusive as possible, with bases ashore but no real homes. If labor
difficulties threatened his operations afloat, his ships could put into
the nearest port and engage a new crew, and in practice his
Liberian flags and Panamanian companies meant that he belonged
to no country whatever. Ashore, at the first sign that fate was at last
closing in, he could slip the anchor of his yacht and leave nothing
of value behind. Skorpios, where he had entrenched himself in
luxury, was the exception, but Skorpios was an island where he
controlled the population, the foliage, and the architecture. If the
nameless enemy he seemed to fear ever found him there, he would
see it coming in time, and he would escape. And yet there was no
escape from the fact of Alexander's death.

He seemed to feel a need to create something permanent. Here,
at least (or so he believed), circumstances had conspired to provide
him with an opportunity that seemed irresistible. Since April, 1967,
Greece had been ruled by a junta of army officers that governed the
country with a rare mixture of comical ineptitude and mindless

brutality yet seemed to provide an element of stability that had been conspicuously lacking in the country's public life for the better part of its modern existence. A royal countercoup later that year by young King Constantine and elements of the air force had been a complete failure that resulted only in the monarch's exile and eventually in the loss of his throne. In July, 1973, the country voted to become a republic, but a republic that was still firmly in the grip of the political colonels and their secret police. Although Onassis professed to a vague and never very clearly defined liberalism (and tartly defended Professor Georgakis, a genuine liberal, when his friend's beliefs were called into question), the altered state of affairs in his nominal homeland was not necessarily a bad thing. His dual citizenship—he carried both Greek and Argentine passports—and his failure to establish a strong business presence in Athens were only partly a function of shipowning tradition and the paranoia of wealth; he kept his distance for compelling practical reasons as well. Despite the rightist victory (with considerable British and American help) over the Communists in the bloody and divisive civil war of 1944–48, the chances of a Communist takeover in the postwar years had always seemed fair to good. The sad truth was that democracy was not firmly established in the land that had been its cradle. The country was corrupt; the royal family was meddlesome and was, moreover, an imported German dynasty; the tradition of public service was not well established; and the ruling classes were widely perceived as regarding politics as a business venture much like any other. Greece, in short, was a country rather too much in the Onassis mold for comfort, and although Onassis had allowed himself to take over the national airline in 1956 during a persuasive government campaign to lure the wandering shipowners home (Niarchos had taken over the shipyards at Skarmonga at the same time), he was not otherwise an active participant in the development of the country whose language he had first spoken.

Given these circumstances, the military junta seemed to be a thing of great promise. At home, it needed to justify its continued existence as well as the stringency of its measures—such as arbitrary arrest, torture, and the austere puritanism it wished to impose upon its unruly citizens if not, in fact, on its own members—and this justification could only come through forms of vigorous economic development that had hitherto proven elusive. Abroad, the junta craved respectability, a thing that (the junta felt) could be achieved in precisely the same manner: If Aristotle Onassis and men like him could be persuaded to make major investments, it would be a powerful signal to a hostile Western Europe that the junta was a bluff, hearty group of legitimate rulers worthy of a cautious tycoon's confidence.

Onassis himself needed little persuading. He had always wanted to own an oil refinery. Greece, for its part, had plenty of bauxite, one of the few raw materials it possessed in abundance, and when the two combined in the Onassis mind, the Omega Project was born. He would build his refinery in Greece—on preferential terms, of course. The by-products of the refining process would, in turn, be used to power a complex that would convert the raw bauxite into marketable aluminum. It seemed like a foolproof scheme, especially in view of the fact that the colonels needed him badly, while he needed the colonels not at all. But as always, Onassis had his own personal agenda, and it was not an entirely rational one.

Immediately after his marriage to Jackie, he had flown back to Athens and called a news conference to announce the details of his new scheme, only to stalk out in a rage when the reporters insisted on querying him about the recent and far more fascinating events on Skorpios. He was under no illusions that his marriage to a president's widow had brought him close to the center of American political power, but Omega by its very nature brought him to the new reality in Greece. In the 1950s he had nearly been crushed by the oil companies and the United States government. Now he dealt with a somewhat smaller but definitely sovereign government, an experience that, as with his celebrity-hunting, was both heady and humiliating. On the one hand, he developed a fascination for the junta's leader, Colonel George Papadopoulous (a man whose fine qualities and breadth of intellect were elusive to less partial observers), and even went so far as to provide him with a villa at a modest rent. On the other hand, Onassis's mania for dickering (perhaps, in all due charity, it was partially fueled by his doubts about the quality of the men with whom he was dealing) got the better of him, and in the end, a very long and drawn out end, he simply bargained Omega to death.

"One of the most tragic things was to see this most enchanting and fascinating of men become a bore," said Professor Georgakis.

"He became obsessed with the subject, constantly repeating himself, constantly returning to it and distorting it. In the end he bored even Papadopoulous. He ground on and on about Omega, wrote him letters, twenty-four page letters, pleading, accusing. Papadopoulous said: "I *can't* help you. Why don't you withdraw?" In the end, the refinery project was awarded to Stratis Andriadis, a businessman more to the junta's liking (and one with whom Christina would shortly have some very odd dealings indeed).

The $400 million Omega Project had been abandoned in 1971, two years before Alexander's death, but in October, 1973, nine months after the Athens crash, the idea was revived in modified form on somewhat more stable political ground, in the American state of New Hampshire. In Meldrum Thompson, New Hampshire had one of the most conservative governors in the country and a strong supporter of a refinery there, but it also had an institution that Onassis, who never read books and who knew next to nothing about politics, had apparently never heard of. This was the annual town meeting, an exercise in an unusually pure form of participatory democracy. The politician who ignores its recommendations does so at his extreme peril. In 1973, the United States was riding a cresting wave of environmentalism, but Onassis gave no sign that he was aware of this movement's existence. He and his wife were not personally popular. His land acquisition policy was underhanded. Worse, it was discovered to be so. Gratsos wrote an unfortunate letter deploring the fact that all of nature would eventually disappear but waxing lyrical on the beauty of an oil refinery at night, and the letter found its way into print. A personal appearance was a disaster; Onassis was a spent force without either charm or wit, and even his command of English seemed on the verge of deserting him. The American refinery went down to resounding defeat.

Even at sea, the old touch was missing. Rich with cash from the unprecedented profits of 1973, he ordered four new Very Large Crude Carriers (VLCCs) and his first two Ultra Large Crude Carriers (ULCCs), unaware of (or unable to face) the consequences of the dramatic upward movement in the global price of oil; the Arabs had begun to extract the revenge he had foreseen so clearly twenty years before. He was old and sick, and he knew it. Once before, he had met and defeated a serious disease, diabetes, but in the spring of 1974 it became impossible to ignore the symptoms of myasthenia gravis, an incurable degenerative muscular disease whose symptoms are aggravated by alcohol, which he consumed in quantity, and fatigue, which now seldom left him. Meanwhile, in New York, another of his land-based projects, an office and condominium complex he called Olympic Tower, was about to open in the midst of one of the worst real estate markets since the Great Depression.

He had always enjoyed his last walk of the day at three o'clock in the morning, strolling hatless and coatless in all weathers through the deserted streets of whatever city he happened to be in. Now, if he was in New York, he left El Morocco at dawn. In London, friends who dropped him off in front of Claridge's, where he habitually stayed and where Jackie was presumably waiting for him, saw him turn away from the door in the glow of their headlamps and walk away down the street. The second flowering of the marriage following Alexander's death had been feeble and brief. Jackie's habits had reasserted themselves, and he did not regard her ways as winning ones. "There was a looming matrimonial problem between the Onassises," said Roy Cohn, the lawyer Onassis retained to begin divorce proceedings, as he relaxed in his diminutive office amid his extensive collection of stuffed toy animals. Outside in the hall, a crew of workmen busily uncrated a life-size statue of the late Louis Armstrong. "It was predicated on her, quote, overspending, number one, and number two, on the fact that she was always where he wasn't and she was never where he wanted her to be. According to him, she considered him nothing but a money machine. Whether there were other things behind it which he didn't tell me, I don't know. He was contemplating that there would be a breakup of the marriage."

The problem, Cohn found, went far deeper than the spending spree that had so delighted the newspapers in the early years of the marriage. Under the terms of the premarriage agreement negotiated by Jackie's lawyers, Eliot Bailan and Ben O'Sullavan, she had received from Onassis a lump-sum payment of $3 million at the time of her marriage. "In his mind, that was not a gift," Cohn continued. (Outside in the hall, it was discovered that Louis Armstrong was chipped.) "That money was to cover certain items, and one of his complaints was that it was used twice. In other words, it was treated as a gift and socked away in Jackie's bank account, and then he was billed a second time for the clothing and jewelry she was supposed to have purchased with it." Her husband was not best pleased, but the episode, or so he felt, was only the beginning of a long raid on his wallet.

He had brought her expenditures under a degree of control by insisting that she follow his own practice of charging everything to the Onassis offices in New York, where she could be audited. But she also sued Ron Galella, a free-lance photographer who made an estimated $50,000 a year by peddling pictures that were taken without her permission. Her lawyers, Paul, Weiss, Rifkind, Wharton, and Garrison, won the case, Galella was suitably enjoined, and Onassis was presented with the bill, which he flatly refused to pay. "It's not that I couldn't afford it," he plaintively told Cohn. "It's just that, well . . . " But it was a legitimate bill, and Jackie was his wife; in the end, he produced $235,000. "Everyone is happy now," he said.

His wife also presented him with her aunt, Edith "Big Edie" Bouvier, and Big Edie's daughter, Little Edie, when the Suffolk County (New York) Health Department threatened to condemn their twenty-eight-room mansion, Gray Gardens, on the grounds that it was infested with cobwebs, feces, raccoons, and eighteen diseased cats. Little Edie was occasionally glimpsed by the neighbors wearing a miniskirt, tattered stockings, and a headcloth that imperfectly concealed the fact that either her hair had fallen out or she had cut it off. Not one member of the Bouvier family would lift a finger to help them, not Bouvier Beale, Big Edie's lawyer son who publicly rejoiced at the news that his mother and sister were finally to be forced out of the decaying old vine-covered house, and not Jackie, who professed to believe that the two Edies were living as they preferred to live. The Bouviers remained unmoved when the newspapers, including the distinguished *New York Times,* flashed word of the Edies' plight around the world, but Onassis did not. He knew a public relations disaster—and opportunity—when he saw one, although it was unlikely that he was aware of how much his benign intervention was about to cost him. Not only did he have to pay $50,000 to fix up the house—a trifle—but he was compelled to listen for forty-five minutes while Big Edie sang love songs to him over the telephone. He also assumed responsibility for the Edies' utility bills.

In all, it was a relatively harmless episode, the sort of thing that showed him in a favorable light as a generous member of an old, established family with the inevitable eccentric branch, but the gratitude of the rest of the family was not conspicuous. Nor was gratitude in particularly abundant supply much closer to home. Quite the contrary. At a dark moment in her life, Jackie had regarded him as her savior and her children's protector. Now she complained openly to her friends about his lack of taste.

He cut her allowance from $30,000 a month to $20,000 and moved her account to Monte Carlo, where his people could keep an even closer eye on it. She complained that she was short of cash. He acidly suggested that she sell her jewelry. They were rarely seen together in public and then only as members of a group. When he was in New York, he resumed the use of his suite in the Hotel Pierre, which he had always patronized because it was owned by his hero, J. Paul Getty. He was distressed by the fact that she let her children, whom he genuinely liked (Alexander, too, had developed a soft spot for John Jr.) wear dirty blue jeans. She accused him of being vulgar. As had been obvious to everyone from the start, they had little in common, and they had come to dislike each other. (One Christmas Onassis called Alexander from Turville Grange, the Radziwill home near London, and begged to be rescued.) For her part, Jackie was outraged that he exhibited no more than mild interest when nude photographs of the pair of them appeared, separately, in the gossip press. She was appalled by his yacht and bored by his taste for nightlife, although she had once attempted to redecorate the former and to enjoy the latter. After a brief flurry of possessiveness, she seemed uninterested in his renewed affair with Maria Callas, whose return to the operatic stage he was wrongly accused of having spoiled. Indeed, Jackie seemed interested only in spending his money and keeping as much distance between them as possible. Her husband concluded that she was sleeping with someone else. (She was not.) And he remembered that he had promised a divorce to his son.

In fact, his plans had been maturing in this direction for some months. Back in January of 1974, in a last, ill-advised attempt to save the marriage, Jackie had suggested a vacation in Acapulco, the Mexican resort where she and Jack Kennedy had spent their honeymoon. They had visited the ruins at Oaxaca and dined with former president Miguel Aleman. Within the hearing of reporters, Onassis let it slip that he was thinking of buying a house in the vicinity. It was an agreeable remark, nothing more, the sort of thing he sometimes said. He still liked to see his name in the papers. (Once, in Los Angeles, he actually went so far as to examine a mansion that had once belonged to comedian Buster Keaton. The local press covered the historic occasion and captioned the resulting photograph "Aristotle Contemplating the Home of Buster.") But Jackie took him seriously.

She brought up the matter of the house as they flew home on the Lear. Her timing proved exquisitely poor. In New Hampshire, his refinery deal was foundering. After the unprecedented year of 1973, the world tanker market was on the verge of collapse, with no sign that it would improve for at least a decade. Onassis scrambled to cancel the huge new ships he had recently ordered, but he would have to take delivery of three new VLCCs that had been too far along to kill, and there were no cargoes anywhere for them to carry. His new illness was making itself felt, and the first anniversary of Alexander's death, which Christina would make so memorable with her own bad timing, was fast approaching. Now Jackie wanted him to buy her a house in Mexico. He saw it as more of the same old thing, more needless extravagance, another attack on his wallet, and he told her as much. As it happened, he was not the only one who had reached the end of a personal tether. Jackie screamed that she had given up her reputation to marry him (which was true enough), that she'd signed away her rights (also true), and that she didn't want any of his goddamn money (which was—and would prove to be—debatable).

He assured her that she would have her wish. Moving to a different part of the plane, he produced pen and paper and set to work. Someone asked him what he was doing. "Writing letters," he replied.

He was revising his will.

CHAPTER TEN

The House of Atreus

"Although he cheered up during dinner, it was all very sad," said Prince Rainier. "To have come so far just to end up heartbroken and ill on board this vast yacht with only your daughter for company seemed unfair." It was the spring of 1974. Aristotle Onassis had returned to Monte Carlo for the last time.

Perhaps, like Jay Gatsby, he had learned what a terrible thing a rose can be. Like many very rich men, he had always believed himself immortal, a law unto himself, almost a force of nature, and possibly a minor god. Now, with his life in ashes and his health deteriorating, he was preparing to die. With Christina as his only companion, he took his yacht out for one last cruise. His mind was clear again, clearer than it had been in many years. He was without illusions, and he no longer entertained fantasies about Alexander's death. His myasthenia gravis was making it necessary for him to tape his eyelids open much of the time now. The disease, though not necessarily fatal, was making itself felt in even the tiniest of his muscles, but he could still crack lame jokes about it. "I am only wearing these tapes on my eyes to keep myself awake in this boring company," he explained. Who, he asked, had ever died of drooping eyelids?

The prince and princess seemed to understand. Monte Carlo was the place where his vessel had once ridden at anchor in unrivaled splendor while its master ruled the legendary games of chance ashore. It was the place where he had awakened the world to his existence and the place where he had experienced his first great defeat, and it was the refuge Alexander had sought during the long days of their estrangement. It was fitting that he should return; there was a bittersweet symmetry to it, and also something of the personal nobility he admired but which, in his days of power, he had honored as much in the breach as in the commission.

The yacht continued on to Egypt and the eastern Mediterranean. His conversations with his daughter, held in the privacy of the vessel, were not recorded, but it was clear from his subsequent actions that he had settled upon a new course. With the new realism that had come to him since the death of his son, he was giving thought to his succession.

There could be no question about Christina's inheritance. Not only were her rights protected by Greek law, but it was important for the ships and the money, his only tangible achievements, to survive intact. Even in death, his name would remain a power in the world. Naturally, he had devised certain safeguards, but when all was said and done, it would be best for Christina to learn something of the business. Alexander's instruction had been woefully deficient in this regard, but the sad truth was that Alexander had never seemed very interested. As Onassis saw it, Christina's marriage to Bolker had demonstrated that she had no sense of loyalty or proportion, but she had a good mind; he had always granted her that. Greek women had owned ships in the past—Tina, for example, owned quite a lot of them—but no Greek woman had ever participated in the management of a fleet, and just such a novel event was doubtless not without its appeal. He had lost much, but he had not lost his fascination with the astonishing.

In any event, it was important for Christina to learn something about fleet management, if only for her own protection—he knew his executives, some of them, all too well. She had always been interested in the ships in her trust. When she was married to Bolker, she had received and studied detailed reports on their operations. By the time the *Christina's* Mediterranean cruise was over, it was clear that her father's mind was made up. It was time to teach a woman the shipping business. Perhaps, after all, she could somehow redeem herself in his eyes.

As he had done with Alexander, he required her to be present when he conducted his negotiations and closed his deals. He introduced her to Y. K. Pao, the Chinese master of the long-term charter, and he asked Sir Eric Drake, the head of British Petroleum, if she could attend a chairman's luncheon. Sir Eric consented, although the presence of a woman at such a function was all but unheard of, "except for the odd minister," said Drake, who added, "I think we once had Margaret Thatcher." During the meal, Christina remained almost totally silent despite Sir Eric's best attempts to draw her into the conversation, but he noticed that she was a different person at his birthday party that evening, where she "chattered away like a little cricket." He asked her why she had been so withdrawn at noon. "Daddy told me," she explained, "to listen to everything you said and not open my mouth."

It was not an easy course of study. The business was an intricate one at the beginning of a full-blown chartering crisis, and her personality complicated matters. In New York, Gratsos called up a business acquaintence and asked if Christina could come over and talk to one of his vice presidents. "Why doesn't she want to talk to *me?*" asked the executive. "Because you're older and a friend of her father's," said Gratsos. "She's afraid of you." At the offices of Victory Carriers, she was placed in the care of an officer named Harry Gatzionis. "It was very hard at first because she was thinking so much of her brother, who she loved very much," Gatzionis told Erich Morgenthaler of the *Wall Street Journal.* "She would interrupt me and say, 'Where is my brother?' and I would say, 'He is in heaven, he is gone. Now you must learn.'" Everyone seemed to sense that there was little time. The lessons began at nine in the morning and lasted until seven in the evening. "Christina knew about shipping when she came to me," said Gatzionis, "but she had a lot of empty spots. She knew things on ship financing—tricks and secrets I never knew. What she didn't know was the mechanics. You really had to pump things into her, going over and over things, push and push and push. Sometimes she resented me pushing her." Nevertheless, she learned fast. "Her father was amazed at what she was learning."

When different people looked at Christina, they often saw a series of very different young women. Like her father, she seemed to change as her surroundings did, and the kindness of others did wonders for her shaky powers of concentration. "Her father called here," says the man who supervised her training at Frank B. Hall, the great maritime insurance brokers, "and said, 'I want to send Christina around to see you.' Naturally, I wanted to know what she was going to do. 'Well,' he said, 'I want her to learn some insurance.' We said fine and asked when she was coming. He said, 'I'm sending her around in the morning.' That was the way Ari did things. The next morning she came down with a colleague of hers, a young woman, and another young fellow, a member of the staff. They came to my office; I've known her since she was that high. I think the two areas he told her to pursue were insurance and chartering. Now, insurance is one of the big high costs in the shipping business. You got something floating out there worth twenty or twenty-five or thirty million dollars, and you've got to pay others to take the risk on your behalf unless you want to take the risk yourself. Costs quite a bit of money to insure a vessel, because you not only want to insure the hull, you want to insure the people in it—against sickness, accident, third-party liability, collisions, or a Texas City situation like you had many years ago when a ship blew up and practically wiped Texas City off the map.

"Christina arrived punctually at nine o'clock. My secretary greeted her and brought her in—I was on the telephone at the time. I stood up, shook hands with her, told her I'd be right with her, finished my call, and we had a good, old reminiscence. We asked her what she wanted to do. While her father hadn't been vague, he'd spoken in general terms, and we wanted to be more specific. She said, well, she wanted to study all phases of marine insurance. She didn't expect, of course, to become a technician. She wanted to get some overview of what marine insurance was, what it entailed, and the risks a shipowner runs so that she would know how to cover herself for any eventuality. We said, well, we'd be happy to assist her in every possible way because her father had not only been a valuable client of ours for many years, but he was also a very dear friend of ours, a lovely man. Naturally, we wanted to know how much time she had at her disposal. She said, 'Several months. I'd like to come at nine in the morning and leave at three, when a car and driver will pick me up and take me to our uptown office where I can follow other aspects of my business.' She wanted to start the next morning. I said, 'Fine. We'll have someone here. I'll work out a program this afternoon and we'll put it in place so you'll know what you're going to do each day.' Next morning, sure enough, there she was, very nicely and simply dressed with a little notebook and pencils—nine o'clock, on the button.

"She had a penchant for drinking Tab, she loved Tab, so we ordered her one and I had my usual coffee, and I told her about her abbreviated curriculum, starting with the actual ship itself and the engine room and all the things that could happen. So I called in one of our senior technicians and we gave her two hours of this, and then the next technician came in and gave her two hours of something else, and then we broke for lunch, [a meal which] she rarely ate. Then sometimes we'd take a little walk around downtown Manhattan and show her some of the sights she'd never seen before. I think it was the first time she'd ever been downtown in her life. We'd come back after an hour or so and she'd resume in the little anteroom outside my office. There were so many phases to cover; it would be difficult for me to describe in a short time how ramified the subject is. We have a thousand people here, on seven floors, doing nothing but insurance.

"She kept at it for about a month, every day, punctual, which I was very pleased about because I think she got, well, a raw deal from some of the press people, and she was actually a very serious person. If she has a short attention span, we didn't see it here. The questions she would ask our technical people astounded them, simply astounded them. It was extraordinary how she grasped a subject she knew nothing about when she walked in here. The technical people commented on it. I didn't ask them; they came to me. One of them said, 'What did you bring in here?' I wanted to know what he meant. He said, 'This girl's grasp of the subject is phenomenal.'

"Then, about a month and a half after she started, she didn't appear. Of course, I didn't think anything. She's a girl, she might want to go shopping or something like that, but at eleven-thirty, I got a phone call from her. She said—she always used my first name —she said, 'I want to apologize to you that I didn't show up this morning. I hope it didn't disrupt your people.' I told her not to worry about it. There was no ironclad rule that she had to be here at nine o'clock; she wasn't paying tuition. She said, 'I have to explain to you why I wasn't there. The president of Mobil Oil asked me to have lunch with him and Mr. Gratsos. I'm sure my father would have taken a very dim view if I'd turned him down. I don't want you to feel that I came to Frank B. Hall just to pass away the time. I promise I won't do it again.' I said, 'I'm not going to ask you to promise that at all.' She said, 'I feel a little guilty. I feel that I tie up your staff all day long, and then not to show up one day is disruptive.' I said, 'No, not at all.'

"Another month, two months passed, and one morning she failed to show up again. This time, I got a call from LaGuardia airport. 'Now, Christina, don't start that all over again,' I told her when she tried to apologize—said she'd broken her promise. 'I was in a very difficult position,' she said. 'Jackie asked me to go to Washington with her to meet Teddy Kennedy, and I felt it was a nice opportunity to get to know him.' She told me all about it when she came in, as usual, punctually and religiously at nine the next day. She never spoke ill about the Kennedys all the time she was here. If she had, I think I'd know; we had some very confiding sessions.

"One day she came in and asked if I minded if she went down and worked on the third floor. The third floor is where our marine department is, about a hundred and fifty some odd people who write the policies, place the insurance with the underwriters, and advise the owners of the sort of coverage they need; it's a very specialized profession. Christina just wanted to mix in with the people without any special privileges. I told her of course I had no objection. Everybody just adored her down there. All the girls wanted to take her out to lunch. She had her desk and she had her files. It wasn't exactly a crash course we were giving her; we were trying to show her things that would stand her in good stead in the future, certain key things we thought all owners ought to know for their own protection. I remember one time—it was very cute—she learned something downstairs and she couldn't wait to get uptown where she had her daily communication with Ari. She told him, I'm just paraphrasing now, she told him, 'You know, there's something you didn't cover on the fleet.' Her father said, 'Of course we covered it.' She said, 'No, you didn't. I've been looking at our files here, and there's not enough coverage.' He said he'd check with his insurance manager and get back to her in the morning, and when he did, he said, 'Christina, you were right, you were absolutely right. We aren't covered.' Of course, she just glowed when he told her that.

"After she'd been here about five months, I had to go to Norway. She stayed for about three more weeks, and then we met at Monte Carlo, where we had a session with the fleet's insurance manager. Ari sat in during the last stages. Afterward, he and I had a chat. He

said, 'How's Christina doing?' I said, 'You're not going to believe
this, but she's not the best, she's extraordinary. I've never seen a
person so young encounter a subject so foreign and grasp it so
quickly.' He didn't show much reaction, but I could tell he was
pleased.

"When I got back to New York I wrote him a letter and told him
how proud of his daughter he should be. Of course, to someone in
your position, sitting where you're sitting, it's probably running
through your mind that she could do no wrong as far as I was
concerned. I don't want to leave that impression; I'm just telling
you the positive things I observed. She's a generous person, a very,
very generous person. The things she did that nobody ever heard
of, paying people's hospital bills and things like that, have never
found their way into print. All you ever hear about is Studio 54.
There are things about that girl that are very touching."

Others, though, were less complimentary. An oil company executive who knew her during the same period described her as "inquis-
itive about what the business was all about, but rather like a fifteen-
year-old trying to catch up on things she's missed." She also studied
at the Charles R. Weber Company, her father's tanker brokers, who
maintain a polite but complete silence on the subject. In Monte
Carlo, she was tutored by her father's chartering expert, Constantine Vlassopoulis, "a saintly man, extremely patient, the only one
who could relay his wisdom to Christina," but at the fleet's Springfield Shipping Company in Piraeus her dedication once more
flagged. "When her father was in Greece every day, she would go
to the office," a former Onassis manager told Erich Morgenthaler
of the *Wall Street Journal*. "But when her father would go away,
she would disappear." In the hands of the patient, understanding,
mostly older men who were able to substitute themselves for the
better angels of her nature that her parents had neglected to supply, she was able to work with diligence and even with skill, but in
the end the burden was too much. As she herself had seemed to
understand when, to the amusement of her California friends, she
had spoken of working on the docks, her upbringing was no preparation for life, much less the enormous responsibilities she was
being trained to assume. She had never been required to accomplish something, to work for the same reason other people worked
—not as a hobby or an interest, but to keep groceries on the table.

One day, possibly soon, her powerful father would no longer be able to guide the destiny of the fleet, and she would be alone in the world with her meager skills. She was supposed to enjoy her fortune, not administer it in the middle of the worst tanker crisis in forty years. "One minute she'd be fine, smiling, relaxed—then *wham*," an Onassis executive told Peter Evans. "Her fuses were getting shorter all the time."

At the same time, Johnny Meyer began to circulate a story that she was in love with Philip Niarchos and that the couple intended to marry. It was as though Meyer had reached back into the swamp of his employer's temporary madness to produce a tale perfectly tailored to the Onassis paranoia and Christina's persistent fears— her father may have become reconciled with his old enemy, but Christina most emphatically was not—and the story was rich in specifics. During the last two weeks of July, 1974, Meyer said, amid the festivities that marked the opening of Prince Rainier's new Winter Sporting Club, Onassis had met with Tina and Stavros Niarchos in Monte Carlo to decide what to do about the smitten youngsters. Away from the prying eyes of friends and servants (Meyer continued), the family council had met several times in a restaurant called Chateau Madrid, with Philip and Christina sitting in as their fate was decided. (Christina was reported to be glowing with new slenderness and cosmetics.) Because of the confidential nature of the talks, Meyer said, no one would ever know exactly what had transpired, but Onassis had definitely returned to Paris muttering "I don't give a damn what she does."

Certain elements of the gossip press found the story plausible and printed it—after all, Niarchos and Tina had actually visited Skorpios the previous summer, an event that was without precedent and one that was rich with possible portents. In Athens, Professor Georgakis heard the story and believed it, or some of it. So did Yannicopoulos, who later provided a postscript in the form of a fight between the sweethearts in St. Moritz, Philip Niarchos trudging away through the snow, and a final interview with Onassis where the young man was supposed to have declared, "Your daughter is mad. I want nothing more to do with her."

Perhaps he was thinking of Alexander and Tina. The truth, it seemed, was rather different.

"Philip Niarchos has gone to bed with Christina precisely as often as you've gone to bed with me," says a source close to the situation. "The whole thing was totally, totally a figment of the gossip columnists' imaginations. There's no connection between the two of them except that they're cousins. I don't want to hear about it; it's complete bullshit. Johnny Meyer, don't forget, had to have items for the columnists to keep them coming to him; if he didn't have something, they'd stop. I don't like Christina, but I'm telling you that there's never been anything between Philip and her. They're civil to each other and they see each other at Christmas. Print anything you like, but if anything had happened I would know, and nothing did."

"Nothing ever happened, no," says a friend of the Niarchos family. "There was never, never any serious talk of marriage, no, never. You and I might think, gee, that would be a great merger, but it was never seriously considered and she never went out with him. I mean, she's his cousin. There was no meeting at Monte Carlo; that's ridiculous. Stavros would never discuss his son with anyone else. There was never any fight at St. Moritz. Philip is a gentleman; he wouldn't do a thing like that. It's true that a lot of people thought they'd been out together—I know that Mick Flick thought it was okay for him to go out with Christina because he thought Philip had —but they never did. I think Philip was her escort once at some family thing, but that was it. No big deal."

In August 1974, Christina disappeared. On the sixteenth of the month she was admitted to a London hospital under an assumed name, suffering from an overdose of sleeping pills. Her mother immediately came over from France to be at her side. It was a reunion of the lame and the halt.

As Alexander had feared, Tina was in a very bad way. At first she kept herself somewhat visible, at least in the glossier of the fashion magazines, with her involvement in the decoration of Niarchos's enormous new sailing yacht, the *Atlantis,* a project that had begun before Eugenie's death. Eugenie had been permitted to supervise such "feminine" aspects of the decor as the color of the towels, and Tina took up where her sister had left off, assisting the interior decorator, Larraine Dubonnet. The *Atlantis* was a top-heavy but elegant craft with twin docking propellers in the bow, twelve staterooms named after such painters as Degas, Cézanne, Picasso, and Matisse (all featuring examples of their namesakes' handiwork),

winding staircases, onyx "his and her" bathtubs, and murals by the
artist Poucette—"Little Thumb." Tina's bedroom was done in pink,
her favorite color. The photographers were invited in, the obliga-
tory articles were written, the sea trials were completed, it was
revealed that Niarchos intended to sail around the world, and cocktails were served aboard during the summer of 1974. But subsequent guests were rare. Niarchos, preoccupied by his affairs—his
fleet and operations had at last overtaken those of his former brother-in-law—rarely made himself available anymore, and as time
went on, Tina was hardly fit to be seen.

More than one observer had noticed the dangerous predilection
of various of Niarchos's wives (specifically Melpomene, Eugenie,
and Tina) to seek refuge in drugs, but Tina's dependence had long
predated the wedding day. Now with Alexander's death weighing
on her mind—and, or so Stavros Niarchos believed, Christina's latest suicide attempt—she sought chemical solace with suicidal determination. "She was so doped up in the morning that she couldn't
speak," says one of her friends. "She just went to pieces. The last
time I saw her was just maybe two weeks before she died. I was in
my car on Avenue Montaigne in Paris, and Tina was coming along
with her mother. I saw the mother and then I looked again and
there was Tina, looking old and haggard. She looked so awful that
I didn't get out of my car because I thought that if I said hello to
her, she would see the look on my face. She was completely another
person. And before, she had been so young looking and so gay,
always laughing."

On October 10, 1974, Tina Livanos Onassis Blandford Niarchos
was found dead in her sleeping quarters at the Hotel de Channal-
lille, the Niarchos mansion on the Left Bank near the Swedish
Embassy. The Niarchos family lawyer, Count Rene de Chambrun,
left Paris for Switzerland the same day. By the following morning,
the German but not the French press had the story, and a family
friend confirmed the news. At noon, Niarchos went to the telex
machine he increasingly used to convey his thoughts to the world
and typed out the formal announcement. With his usual genius for
placing himself in the worst possible light, he had allowed more
than twenty-four hours to elapse since the time the body was discovered by the servant who brought in the breakfast tray, and his
numerous detractors were not slow in drawing their own conclu-

sions. The rumors that had surrounded Eugenie's death were certain to be revived, and one of the servants helped matters along by revealing that de Chambrun had been the first person the grieving husband called. (Nobody thought to point out that Tina was to be buried in Lausanne, and that arrangements quite naturally had to be made.) It was clearly time for cooler heads to prevail. Aristotle Onassis soon made contact with the suggestion that an autopsy, however belated, might do much to clear the air. If everyone would only be sensible, the crisis would soon pass. But Onassis had reckoned without his daughter.

On hearing the news, Christina immediately rushed to Paris and made a public demand for the autopsy that—although she was unaware of it—had already been planned. *People* magazine later claimed that when she arrived at the Niarchos residence, she found her latest stepfather preparing to sit down at a formal dinner for eighteen guests, with candles on the table. Whatever the truth of the matter (and she apparently never told anybody any such thing), it was clear that her old suspicions had never been laid to rest, and they were now in full cry.

It was one thing for Stavros Niarchos to take sensible advice from Aristotle Onassis. It was quite another to be confronted with what, in effect, was an accusation of possible murder on the part of the Onassis daughter, and Niarchos was no diplomat. He immediately returned to his telex machine and typed out a new message. "In fact," he wrote, "Mrs. Tina Niarchos was in London August 17–24. She rushed there because her daughter Christina Onassis has [sic] tried to commit suicide with a massive dose of sleeping pills and was at Middlesex Hospital under the name of Miss C. Danai from August 16–24 at a time when her mother still mourned the death of her son. Tina never recovered from the depression into which these blows plunged her." He may very well have been right, but for such an anglophilic man, he was far from being (as one would say in England) correct. ("That son of a bitch," said Christina's father.)

The official autopsy, when it was completed, showed no signs of violence on the body. Death had been caused by a pulmonary edema, a swelling in the lung resulting from an excess of fluid, almost certainly complicated by her dependence on barbiturates.

"My aunt, my brother, now my mother—what is happening to

us?" Christina wept at her mother's graveside. "Surely fate can't be that cruel." In Greece, people began to refer to the Onassis family as the House of Atreus. And there was worse to come.

It was clear to everybody who had seen her father that summer that he was desperately ill, but he seemed far from finished. He still swam his mile a day, and he got through a full budget of work. "He tried to get back from Athens for the evening meal every night," said Sir John Russell, the bluff diplomat who visited Skorpios in September. "We'd dine with them late, past ten most nights, then drink a bit and chat. Jackie would disappear, she didn't like late nights much, and we'd potter off to sleep on the yacht. Half an hour later, around one A.M., there'd be a great shout, Ari with a few bottles in his arms coming aboard, crew on deck, my daughter with her guitar, and we'd go singing and dancing for hours more. We often saw the dawn up that way, and Ari never packed it in first, even if he was off to Athens in a couple of hours. He always loved singing, you know. He had a very pleasant voice, small but with excellent pitch, and he would sing the rudest versions of the dockside songs with great glee; the sailors would be falling about."

The symptoms of myasthenia gravis are worsened by lack of sleep.

For once Jackie was exactly where he believed he wanted her to be, at his side, but like hostage royalty in a rival court, she was both there and not there. "It didn't seem to suit her," said Sir John. "She would often turn up, smiling and pleasant, and one sensed she was making an effort for Ari's sake. But she much preferred swimming on her own or doing a bit of sailing. There was nobody there who had much in common with her, you appreciate, nobody she could relax with." On occasion she joined in the dancing but appeared to take little pleasure in it. She impressed her husband's visitors as stiff and inhibited, going through the motions, her mind elsewhere.

Christina was present as well. She was no longer the dutiful daughter; she wanted out of the whole thing. In the presence of Sir John and the others, she and her father had "endless, very noisy, and violent" arguments that they could neither conceal nor stop, endlessly skirting the central issue between them—the fact that Christina, untrustworthy, inconstant Christina, was alive and Alexander was dead, taking a Greek father's hope of immortality with him. ("It is impossible for a non-Greek to understand the shattering impact," said Sir John Russell.) Onassis accused Christina of being wild and complained about her supposedly execrable taste in men. He claimed that she had no real interest in the business, that she never listened to him or did a thing he wanted, that she laughed when he tried to enforce obedience, all of which may have had some truth but none of which addressed the point: He had conspired with fate, and together they had ruined his daughter's life. He was consistent to the end. With others (except Jackie), he was the soul of kindly understanding, but his own daughter's latest suicide attempt had taught him nothing. A ghost stood between them, and there were days when he could almost see it.

He took the Russells out on a long sail that ended with a picnic on a small, distant island. Two elderly shepherds wandered by; he offered them food and drink. They were impressed but not overawed when they discovered his identity, and they told him how saddened they had been by the death of his son. Onassis broke down and wept.

Back in New York in the fall, he still soldiered on. A private detective was engaged to shadow Jackie (he found nothing of value) and an attempt was made to plant a story with Jack Anderson, the syndicated columnist. Once, this had been the element—litigation, covert operations, manipulation of the press—in which he had thrived, but his heart was no longer in it. At lunch with Anderson, Onassis began to talk about his wife, stopped, began again, and finally returned to the office with the puzzled journalist and turned the distasteful task over to Gratsos and the others. In October, using the name Parker, he checked into a hospital and underwent an extensive course of treatment. In December of 1974, against the advice of his doctors, he returned to Athens and began the last battle of his life.

Olympic Airways occupied a position in his empire that was at once typical and peculiar—typical in that he ran it much like his other enterprises, peculiar in that his continued tenure as its owner was legally dependent on the pleasure of others. Like his fleet, Olympic Airways was mobile in the sense that it was a form of transportation and its planes moved about, but it was also tied to its bases—airports, with their boarding gates, maintenance sheds, landing rights, and fixed supplies of fuel. He called it a hobby enterprise and he was clearly pleased to be the only human being in the world to own a national airline, but he also intended for it to make money. More than one observer had noticed that while the line itself posted fairly consistent losses, its parent company, Victoria Financeria Panama S.A., was in splendid financial condition. Moreover, Olympic was strangely run. For a time, its chairman was Professor Theodore Garofalidis, a dentist and the husband of Onassis's sister, Artemis. Until 1970, the president of its executive committee was Professor Georgakis, who was an expert in criminal law and justice, and whose enemies claimed he lost his post because of excessive tipping at the Grande Bretagne. The company had no computerized reservation system, no catering organization, and no serious pension plan for any of its employees except the pilots, who were paid below international scale but who, like sea captains, were exempt from all but 3 percent of Greek taxes. Labor relations were terrible and the company's organization was chaotic. Olympic's installations were owned by other companies in the Onassis group, and the planes were either leased or purchased from yet another Onassis entity, Leyborn Ltd., of Panama. It was true that the line was a government concession, but because it received no government loans it was without government oversight, and because of the usual Onassis system of ownership, he could slip loose from it at the first sign of serious trouble. However—although he did not believe it—he could also be replaced. "Onassis was not a modern businessman," said Professor Georgakis. "He was a hero of our times without accepting the truth or principles of modern business. It was why he lost Olympic, and with it his courage."

He preferred to keep the management of the airline in the family. His cousin, Nikos Konialidis, ran it until 1970, when he was replaced by his brother, Costa, another old companion from the Argentine days. Onassis and Costa agreed that the latter would be considered a success as long as he never had to ask the boss for money, a fairly simple criterion that Costa was able to meet until the Middle Eastern crisis of 1973–74 drove the price of aviation fuel up to forty-four cents a gallon, adding $17 million a year to the airline's bills. At first, Costa Konialidis deemed it prudent not to acquaint his relative and employer with the new situation, but when the mounting losses could no longer be concealed, he was ready with a plan. They would sell the airline back to the government. For purely tactical reasons, Onassis agreed. In the days of his prime, one of his principal forms of recreation had consisted of war-gaming his countermoves if the government ever threatened to revoke his concession, but the threat of a voluntary pullout had always been implicit in all his negotiations with whoever happened to be in power, and experience had taught that it usually achieved the desired result. Until now, an Onassis withdrawal had been unthinkable. The military junta responded, as anticipated, by offering to sell the airline its fuel at thirty cents a gallon. Costa Konialidis suggested that they hold out for twenty-eight cents and anything else they could get, but before any deal could be closed he was again overtaken by events. The Turkish invasion of Cypress in the summer of 1974 brought down the junta, and the crisis kept the tourists away from Greece in droves—and tourists were the airline's principal source of revenue.

It was easy to misread the new situation. The newly elected democratic government was preoccupied with developing events on Cyprus, where the Turks had occupied half the island, including the main areas of Greek settlement, displacing the inhabitants to the undeveloped south. At home, the displaced colonels remained to be dealt with and their works dismantled. In Europe and among the international banking community, it was essential to redeem the nation's reputation and maintain its credit rating. All these circumstances seemed to militate against the assumption of costly new burdens, such as a (on paper) money-losing major fleet of airplanes. In any event, bankers were not conspicuously fond of nationalizations. Moreover, the head of the new government was Constantine Karamanlis, the man who had granted Onassis the concession to begin with, in 1956, and a politician to whom he had once been close. Distracted by the fiasco of his marriage and the tragedy of his son's death, preoccupied by illness, innocent of politics, and shielded from reality by his staff, Onassis neither understood how profoundly the experience of military dictatorship had changed Grecian reality nor did he comprehend the implications of his own close relations with the departed oligarchs. Instead, the moment seemed to cry out for the continued application of his usual methods.

He renewed his demand for subsidized fuel and added to it a request for low-interest government loans. To underline the seri-

ousness of the situation, he also implemented a program of man-
power cuts, always an effective tool in a country where wages and
employment were chronically low. The airline's personnel retaliated with a strike. Never one for half measures, Onassis proceeded
to fire all 7500 employees and threatened to break up the company.
Instead of caving in as he expected, the government swiftly passed
a law forbidding him to dismiss more than 2 percent of his workers,
an action without precedent in his experience. Onassis grounded
his planes, froze wages, and invoked clause 25A of his agreement
with the government, surrendering his concession. At the same
time, his hand-picked board of directors resigned. To his astonish-
ment, the government immediately appointed a new one and ap-
propriated the money to get the company going again, without
benefit of his assistance. When he tried to retract his withdrawal,
the government refused to recognize him, and when he proposed
a partnership, the government refused again. A negotiating team
was assembled. Professor Georgakis, well known as a political liberal, made the rounds of various government offices, doing what he
could. Nothing worked. The Onassis bluff had been called.

In shirtsleeves, perspiring, complaining about the heat, he labored on through the last days of December of 1974, trying to save
the situation. He would reach an agreement in the evening and
forget about it the following morning, make excuses, float new
proposals, refuse to sign documents. As always, he expected everyone concerned to accommodate themselves to his personal sched-
ule. On New Year's Eve, he ruined the holiday by keeping his staff
at work until ten at night in the hope of passing a miracle, but no
miracle was forthcoming. The airline's 1956 charter contained a
complex booby trap that seemed to offer great possibilities for creative mischief, as no doubt it had been designed to do. The government was entitled to take over Olympic's aircraft, its installations,
personnel, and goodwill, but the legal shell of the company would
remain an Onassis property, which meant that the government
would have to renegotiate Olympic's debt, contracts, and labor
agreements, but only with Olympic's permission. On the other
hand, the government controlled Olympic's landing rights, and
with the takeover of the board, it was also in possession of the
company's books, which provided abundant ammunition for a time-

consuming and disruptive investigation. It was a classic case of a Mexican standoff.

By January 15, 1975, the general outlines of an agreement finally emerged. The government would scrap the provisions of the original concession and make an outright purchase of the 15,000 Olympic shares for $68,788,310, less the company debt, for a net payment to the former owner of $50,622,110 plus $32 million a year for the leases and installment payments on the aircraft. Onassis continued to stall. Ten million dollars was still in dispute; Onassis had yet to surrender the stock certificates. "If I had to continue dealing with Ari, I believe we would still be haggling to this day," said George Theofanos, the airline's new president, a year later.

In America, at the beginning of February, Jackie, making a public display of her financial straits by putting her country furniture up for auction, received a call saying that her husband had collapsed. Telling her friends she hoped to be back in a few days, she flew to Athens with Dr. Isidore Rosenfeld, a heart specialist. Her husband, she found, was suffering from pneumonia and gallstones, both maladies at least partly traceable to his cortisone therapy. His sisters were in favor of keeping him at home in the Glyfada villa. Dr. Caroli, a French liver specialist, was in favor of an immediate operation to remove the infected gallbladder, a position that was flatly contradicted by Dr. Rosenfeld, who stated that the patient was so weak that any operation would surely kill him and who called for a long, recuperative stay in a New York hospital before any decision was reached. Jackie, however, was firm on having him moved to Paris. "He's my husband and I believe this switch is necessary," she said. "Let's not argue about it."

There was at least one person who believed he knew what the certain outcome would be. On February 6, the airline's lawyer, Tryfon Koutalidis, dialed the wrong number at the villa and unexpectedly found himself talking to his employer. "I have to go to Paris," Onassis told him. "I want you to know that I shall die there. Everyone wants me to go but I don't like the idea." He made Koutalidis promise to carry on the fight against Niarchos on Christina's behalf.

They made the trip in the Lear—Jackie, Artemis, Christina (who apparently had not been consulted), Dr. Caroli, and the patient.

Onassis told the doctor that he felt very close to Alexander now. "You understand, doctor, the meaning of the Greek word *thanatos*—death," he said. "You know I will never come out of the hospital alive. Well, please practice *thanatos* on me."

At the airport he refused a stretcher and insisted on going home to the flat on avenue Foch where the press, waiting on the sidewalk, photographed him for one last time—a shrunken old man in an overcoat, broken by misfortune and disease, his fate written in his eyes. The next morning, accompanied by a composed Jackie and an agitated Christina, he entered the American Hospital in Neuilly through the door of the morgue. The gall bladder operation was performed and a hopeful bulletin issued, but Dr. Rosenfeld had been right. The patient would linger but not survive. Attached to a life-support system, massively injected with antibiotics and suffering from jaundice, he began to waste away.

Christina and Artemis established a death watch. Whenever Onassis awoke, he found one of them at his bedside. At first Jackie joined them, riding to the hospital with Christina in the family car, serenely facing the usual mob of photographers while Christina sat beside her in a state bordering on panic, but Jackie's situation was different from that of her stepdaughter—she was an experienced hand at tragedy, she had her own ideas of dignity, and her husband's end was not unexpected. Soon she began to come to the hospital only once a day. She was observed dining at Deux Magots with a friend; later they visited the Peggy Guggenheim art collection. She went to the movies, shopped, had her hair done, and was photographed, smiling, with the president of Air France. Sharing the apartment on avenue Foch with Christina, she began to move the furniture around into new and more pleasing configurations, experimenting. Christina stood it for as long as she could. Then, without bothering to pack her clothes, she abruptly moved across town to the Plaza Athenée.

There was one last thing that could be done, a gift that could be given. Christina summoned Peter Goulandris. Standing with him hand in hand at her father's bedside, she announced that they intended to marry, as he had wished, and she asked for his blessing. Later it would be said that this was a harmless deception and a needless one (Johnny Meyer reported that the old man was semicomatose), designed to ease his last hours by allowing him to drift off in a final dream of dynasty, with his fleet and his daughter secure and his wishes granted. Christina, however, was in deadly earnest.

Her father's condition seemed to stabilize toward the end of February. More dead than alive but lingering tenaciously, he was placed on a kidney dialysis machine and given oxygen. The doctors could offer no firm prognosis. His condition, they said, might remain unchanged for months. Jackie flew back to New York to view a documentary on Appalachia that her daughter had made for NBC; she would be gone, Christina believed, for the weekend. In her absence, Maria Callas was admitted to the sickroom for a last farewell. Jackie called on Monday, learned that there had been no change, and remained in New York. She was still there at the end of the week, when her husband's condition suddenly and dramatically worsened.

Aristotle Socrates Onassis, born in a Smyrna that no longer existed, late of Buenos Aires, Montevideo, London, Paris, New York, Monte Carlo, Athens, and Skorpios, died on March 15, 1975 with his daughter at his side and his wife, as usual, no place in the world where he wanted her to be. When Christina emerged from the hospital, her left arm was heavily bandaged. It was reported that she had suffered an accident.

Jackie remained secluded in her Fifth Avenue apartment until the evening when, dressed in mourning, she flew with her mother to Paris. They were met at Orly by the Onassis chauffeur and driven to the empty flat on avenue Foch, where Jackie remained for the next ten hours. Christina was under heavy sedation elsewhere and made no attempt to see her, the outraged Artemis did not appear, and the Onassis men avoided her. She was informed that her assistance would not be required in making the funeral arrangements.

Accompanied by her bodyguard, she visited the chapel at the hospital, viewed her husband's corpse, prayed briefly, and departed. When she saw the photographers waiting outside the building, she broke into a smile.

In Athens, after the funeral, she gave a short and, as always, carefully composed statement to the press. "Aristotle Onassis rescued me at a time when my life was engulfed in shadows," she said. "He meant a lot to me. He brought me into a world where one could find both happiness and love. We lived through many beautiful experiences together which cannot be forgotten, and for which I will be eternally grateful. . . . Nothing has changed both with Aristotle's sisters and his daughter. The same love binds us as when he lived." She declared her intention of bringing up her children "in Greece, amid Greek culture." Asked if she and Christina had begun to fight over the will, she replied, "I'll answer with something my husband often told me. 'Throughout the world people love fairy tales and especially those related to the lives of the rich. You must learn to understand this and accept it.' "

Then she flew to Paris and had her hair done. Later she attended the bullfights at Gageron.

CHAPTER ELEVEN

Necessary Arrangements

Yannicopoulos took the airline shares from the safe in Artemis's house and brought them to Christina. With her brother and her father both dead, only he and the lawyer, Stelios Pappadimitriou, knew the combination. They had been gathering the certificates ever since 1972, when it had been decided that Costa Konialidis had too much power—his status as sole signatory for the line was also withdrawn—and with the process almost complete, these shares represented almost the whole value of the company. They were Christina's now, or would be until she surrendered them to the government, and although some people might question the wisdom and propriety of placing them in her possession—the will of Aristotle Onassis had placed the shares in the ownership of his assets in a corporation beyond her direct control—Yannicopoulos was not among them. He was a great lover of gossip and the secrets of the rich (and the uses to which these could be put), and he talked about them frequently. He was seeing Niarchos, or so he claimed. He also claimed that he occasionally took tea with the British ambassador.

The tasks facing Christina were immense, and her nerves were not in the best of shape. Even Professor Georgakis, initially one of her supporters, began to lose faith. She believed, rightly, that her phone was tapped; Yannicopoulos was listening in—to prevent his new employer from doing herself a mischief, or so he claimed. The situation at Olympic Maritime was poor and deteriorating. Civil war had broken out among her father's old associates, with Gratsos and the Konialidis brothers on one side and Pappadimitriou and Nicos Cokkinis, the fleet's managing director, on the other. It would have to be stopped. Methods would have to be devised to adapt the fleet to the lean years of the late 1970s and possibly beyond. Most immediately, something would have to be done with the useless new supertankers just emerging from the French yards. There was the old problem of Stavros Niarchos, the ongoing problem of Jackie, and an entirely new problem with Nikos Konialidis. And there was the especially pressing problem of the will. Everything (except Stavros Niarchos) went back to the will. Everything depended on it. It would have to be circumvented. Trustingly, she had given a copy to Nikos Konialidis, her father's cousin, companion in Argentina, business associate, and (to complicate matters further) brother-in-law by virtue of his marriage to Onassis's half-sister, Merope. Furious, in the view of Professor Georgakis, because of his failure to obtain a major legacy, Konialidis made a photocopy and threatened to publish it in a year's time. No doubt there would be a certain amount of attendant publicity, something that should be avoided at all costs, for Christina, too, had read the will, and the news it contained was not good. Mistrustful of her to the last, her father had tried to reach out from beyond the grave and, while he had not disinherited her, he had established a mechanism that prevented her from gaining direct control of the ships and properties in her portion of his legacy. Her personal feelings in the matter aside—and they were great—it was absolutely essential for her to assert her rights if she was to bring the situation in the fleet under control. This she could do only by challenging the will directly—later, they would call it a "reinterpretation"—not by rewriting its provisions, but by applying certain provisions of Greek law that had been devised for just such situations. But if the law was on her side, the situation was nevertheless one of great delicacy. Jackie was also likely to launch a legal challenge. If Nikos Konialidis chose his moment well, he could at the very least embarrass Christina with the revelation of her father's sad lack of confidence, something that might undermine her with the fleet's major suppliers, the oil companies. At worst—and the future, as always was hard to read—publication of the will could upset the intricate negotiations that would necessarily be in progress between Christina and Jackie on the one hand, and Christina and her father's old associates on the other, for the will had given many of these associates positions of great power. Christina called the professor, a man well-versed in the law, at two in the morning and told him what had happened. Georgakis saw the dangers quite clearly.

Some of her father's intentions were open to interpretation, while others were all too abundantly clear. He proposed to accomplish three things: to effectively disinherit Jackie, render Christina powerless, and honor his son. To these ends, he had ordered the establishment of an interlocking trio of new entities: the Alpha Company, the Beta company, and "a cultural institution in Vaduz, Liechtenstein, or elsewhere under the name of 'Alexander Onassis Foundation,' its purpose among others to operate, maintain, and promote the Nursing, Educational, Literary Works, Religious, Scientific Research, Journalistic and Artistic endeavors, proclaiming International and National Contests, prize awards in money, similar to the plan of the Nobel Institution in Sweden." Alexander had been after him to establish just such a fund, but like most of the things his father conceived, it had more than one use.

The linchpins of the plan were Alpha and Beta. Each was to issue a thousand shares. Into the Beta company, the executors were to pour the assets of the Onassis empire, the ships, the properties, the bank accounts, the lot. Nine hundred and fifty Beta shares were then to be issued to Alpha. Christina was to receive the remaining 50 Beta shares, 450 shares of Alpha, the American-flag ships and landholdings not previously assigned to her under the 1955 trust, a three-quarters interest in Skorpios and in the yacht, an annual allowance of $250,000 adjusted for inflation, and the residue of the estate after the other bequests were distributed. Jackie, as stipulated in her marriage contract, was to receive $250,000 a year and nothing else, except for the remaining quarter of the island and the yacht.

With its 550 shares of Alpha, the foundation was to control Beta, and Beta controlled the fleet. At the very moment that Christina needed a free hand to bring matters under control, she therefore found that, legally speaking, she had no power at all. She was on the foundation board, of course, a life member enjoined (as were the others) to continue her father's policies and preserve his legacy, but so were Gratsos, Vlassopoulis, Pappadimitriou, Nicos Cokkinis, and possibly (here the will was vague) the Konialidis brothers—the very

men Christina somehow had to neutralize or bring into line. For
reasons that her father had taken with him to the grave, Jackie was
on the board, too, like Christina a life member, embedded in the
heart of the inheritance. Appointed chief executor and chairman of
the board was "my first wife and mother of my son, Athena (maiden
name Livanos) Onassis-Blandford-Niarchos," which would have
meant, had Tina lived, that her brother George or, most probably,
Stavros Niarchos, would have run the show. At least Christina
would not have to cope with that.

First, she had to head off Nikos Konialidis. Pappadimitriou was
summoned, a taciturn and pious man who operated out of a small,
cluttered office on the Piraeus waterfront. Nikos Konialidis was
more a nuisance than a threat, but it was important for Christina
to demonstrate her mastery of the situation. The press was largely
interested in Jackie, whose inheritance had been somewhat fever-
ishly pegged at anywhere from $3 million to $200 million, and it was
unlikely that many of the reporters were versed in the complexities
of Greek civil law. In any event, someone who was determined to
read the will would shortly be able to do so simply by applying at
the First Court in Athens, by which time Christina hoped to be well
on the way to asserting her rights. There was nothing to be lost if
Christina published the will herself, and she proceeded to do just
that. Nevertheless, Nikos Konialidis was given a million dollars for
services rendered; in fairness, the will had treated him rather shab-
bily. The press predictably concentrated on the amazing news of
Jackie's pittance.

At the same time, Christina made peace with Stavros Niarchos.
Back on March 9, less than a week before her father's death, she had
filed suit to recover the three-quarters of her mother's fortune—
estimated by the press at somewhere between $300 million and
$350 million and at $180 million by insiders—that she claimed was
legally hers under Greek law. Moreover, she had claimed that her
mother's marriage was void, on the ground that Niarchos had already been married three times by the Greek church. Now she
abruptly withdrew her suit. Both sides issued statements of mutual
regard, and Niarchos returned six of her mother's ships, $50 million
in cash, and Tina's jewelry and paintings, retaining $30 million in
property to which he was entitled. Whatever Christina's private
thoughts might have been, the epochal rivalry between the two

houses was over and would never be revived. That flank, too, was secure.

Despite the persistent rumors of her growing emotional instability, she made a tour of the London nightspots and seemed none the worse for wear. She also visited Sir Eric Drake at British Petroleum and Sir Frank MacFadzean at Shell. It was let out to the press that she told them: "Although I'm a woman, I'm also an Onassis. If there's anything to discuss, you will deal with me." Then she flew to New York, presumably to relay the same terse message to the petroleum companies there.

She visited the U.S. embassy in Paris and took the necessary steps to divest herself of American citizenship. Like a flag of convenience, it had served its purpose and was now a liability. American citizenship meant American taxes and the prying eyes of an efficient and troublesome bureaucracy. Because an American-flag vessel could only be owned by an American citizen, giving up her citizenship meant giving up the four obsolete American-flag vessels that were all that remained of Victory Carriers, but with creative use of the law this could be accomplished with a minimum amount of pain. In fact, publishing the will enabled her to cloak a tactical maneuver as a charitable endeavor. Simultaneously, she announced that she had transferred the American vessels to a trust administered by George Moore for the benefit of the American Hospital in Paris. The executives of Olympic Maritime continued to manage the ships as before, Christina retained her New York headquarters, Gratsos kept his comfortable corner office overlooking St. Patrick's Cathedral in Olympic Tower, and only one thing had really changed—the operation was now tax-exempt. The American Hospital eventually received a check for $100,000 from the foundation, but no one in Neuilly ever laid eyes on the four aging vessels. "The hospital was never notified," says David McGovern, one of the hospital trustees. "We don't know what happened to the trust. We don't even know if it was ever created. We saw all the stuff about it in the press and we received a check either the next year or the year after, but that was it. Of course, it doesn't necessarily have to be an income trust, and if a nonincome trust exists, the hospital wouldn't necessarily know about it." Christina's father could hardly have improved on it. And it was all perfectly legal.

Even the problem with Jackie had its uses. In June, a Greek movie producer named Nick Mastorakis announced plans to make an unauthorized film of the Onassis life, and the story began to circulate that Jackie had been offered a million dollars to play herself opposite Anthony Quinn. Jackie's lawyers denied everything. Christina threatened action in the courts and, more importantly, seized on the story as a heaven-sent opportunity to give her executives a much-needed kiss of the lash. "Disturbing events in Athens," cabled Philip Jacobson of the London *Sunday Times* to his colleagues. "Two days of reverses and sources drying up. The promise to deliver you Kokkinis [*sic*] reneged on. [Nicos Cokkinis had long served as the managing director of the Onassis fleet.] I may be overreacting, but Christina's ability to discipline her brass already demonstrated by her successful ban on all contact with Nick Mastorakis, who making Ari film. This ban was reason everybody told me Costas Konialidis would not talk. Because his job vulnerable." Slowly, without making a single misstep, Christina was finding her way.

Jackie herself was not quite so tractable, although on the advice of the opposing lawyers—Christina's and her stepmother's—appearances were just barely preserved. On April 12, John Corry of *The New York Times* published the story of Onassis's planned divorce and his approach to Roy Cohn, although the source of Corry's highly specific information remained a mystery. The paper refused to print a retraction even when approached by such a redoubtable figure as Andre Meyer, the legendary investment banker and Jackie's sometime escort, nor was Christina inclined to issue the rebuttal her stepmother demanded. "Why should I do that?" she asked. "The story is true." Still, the lawyers insisted; negotiations were in a delicate phase. On April 17, after a more than decent interval, Christina finally issued a statement whose lack of candor was written in every line.

"Miss Christina Onassis is very much distressed at the distorted stories and speculations which appeared in the international press about her late father and Mrs. Jacqueline Onassis," it said.

"These stories are totally untrue and she repudiates them. In fact, the marriage of the late Mr. Onassis and Mrs. Jacqueline Onassis was a happy marriage and all rumors of intended divorce are untrue.

"Her relationship with Mrs. Jacqueline Onassis was always and

Above: Christina and her father in 1972, leaving the Crazy Horse Saloon in Paris with Mick Flick, the young Daimler-Benz heir Christina came to deeply resent.
(AGIP/Robert Cohen/Black Star)

Left: Aristotle and Christina leaving Maxim's in Paris, 1972.
(AGIP/Robert Cohen/Black Star)

*The dying Onassis as he arrives at the morgue entrance of the
American Hospital in Paris, 1975.* (UPI/Bettman Newsphotos)

Christina in 1975, outside the American Hospital in Paris as her father dies. Jackie, as was often the case, was not present.
(UPI/Bettman Newsphotos)

Above: Christina with her third husband-to-be, Sergei Kauzov, on the beach in Brazil. At the time, 1976, Kauzov was still married to his first wife. He was also a Soviet official. (UPI/Bettman Newsphotos)

Right: Christina, the heiress, at New York's Studio 54 in 1977. (UPI/Bettman Newsphotos)

With husband Sergei Kauzov, 1978. (Stern)

Christina with her fourth husband, pharmaceutical heir Thierry Roussel, following their 1984 marriage in Paris. Roussel chose the dress. (UPI/Bettman Newsphotos)

still is based on mutual friendship and respect and there are no financial or other disputes separating them."

She and Jackie met on Skorpios three days later for the traditional Greek memorial service that occurs forty days after a death. A certain coolness was observed between them, but it was neither the time nor the place for the confrontation that was now inevitable. They met again for two hours in the presence of lawyers on May 7, during Christina's fence-mending trip to London.

Jackie had decided that she would abandon her claims against the estate for a basic settlement of $20 million. (She would require more money to yield her shares of Skorpios and the yacht.) "I'm strapped," she told one of her relatives. "I haven't been able to get a single cent out of Greece, not even my allowance. I've had to borrow money and sell stock just to pay my bills." She was also in a surprisingly strong position. Under Greek civil law, it is theoretically impossible for a man to disinherit his wife. Thanks to the specific and rigidly enforced provision known as the *nomimos mira* —literally, legal destiny—a surviving spouse is entitled to at least 12.5 percent of her husband's estate, and a full 25 percent if he dies without making a will. In the premarriage contract that awarded Jackie the $3 million bride-price (plus a million dollars for each of her children), she had renounced her right to the *nomimos mira*'s protection, and following the fight in the Lear jet her husband had taken steps to make certain that the renunciation stuck. In May, 1974, Onassis had sent Pappadimitriou to pay a visit to the minister of justice in Athens. A month later, parliament passed a law entitled "For the Settlement of Hereditary Questions of Greek Citizens Living Abroad," which voided the claims of foreign spouses—a reform that was, in fact, long overdue. Jackie, then, would seem to have had no strings in her bow, but in fact she had a great many. Christina detested her, but there was no disputing the validity of her seat on the board or her claims to the yacht and the island. Only God knew why Christina's father had done that; perhaps it had pleased him to imagine the difficulty Stavros Niarchos would have in dislodging her. If so, the joke was on Christina now—that last mistake of a man who had begun his career by making none, and who had ended by making so many.

To overthrow Alpha and Beta and secure physical possession of her half of the estate, Christina herself planned to invoke the *nomi-mos mira*, which likewise made it impossible to disinherit a child. It was delicate work—not so much a challenge to the will, her lawyers said, but a reinterpretation—and it was possible that every-thing would come undone or at least suffer serious damage if Judge Simon Rifkind, Jackie's attorney, succeeded in overthrowing the entire document in the process of asserting his client's rights. Greek civil law stipulated that a will be composed in a single uninter-rupted sitting in a single location, but Onassis had written his will on a moving airplane as it flew over several Mexican and American states. Was an airplane, legally, a "place" under Greek law, or was the will invalid because it had been composed in (actually, over) a remarkable number of jurisdictions? Moreover, the plane had made a fueling stop in Florida in the middle of the composition process, where Onassis had paid the bill with his credit card and signed the receipt, clearly interrupting himself. In a spectacularly good year like 1973, the fleet and the other assets were worth a sum in the vicinity of a billion dollars; in a bad year like 1975, the value was down to around $400 million. If Rifkind overturned the will, they would all be back where they began, with the *nomimos mira* and the 1974 law and a possible claim of $100 million—25 percent of the estate—from Jackie, a catastrophic sum.

"I don't know what happened," Nigel Neilson, the longtime Onassis public relations man, told the press with calculated indis-cretion after the London meeting between Jackie and Christina. "But it is fairly safe to assume that the question of finances was one of the things discussed. There is not a lot of love lost between them." For years, until the deliberate leak to Jack Anderson, Neil-son and Johnny Meyer had been at pains to portray a happy family at peace with itself and its money. This protection was now with-drawn. Appearances would be preserved, but there was no point in pretending that Christina was overjoyed with the situation.

For the last time, Jackie returned to Skorpios and gathered up her possessions. The rumors began almost immediately. It was said that Christina slipped her two fake El Grecos, claiming that they were her stepmother's share of the four that adorned the bulkheads of the yacht. No, wrote Helen Bistikia, an Athens columnist, there were never four El Grecos, only two, and their provenance was doubtful (there was one, and it was genuine). Jackie, she said, had removed nothing from the yacht except "a work of art by a known Frenchman" and a jade Buddha, which only made matters worse —Christina's father was said to have owned a jade Buddha that was literally priceless. Jackie did not look good.

Neither, unfortunately, did Christina. So far, she had done well, moving decisively and with intelligence to consolidate her position, and she had used the press skillfully. Now, half a world away from her stepmother, she began to blunder—not in business, where her movements remained as skillful as ever, but in her personal life, where she had never learned how to behave herself. She would get no credit from the members of her circle for her business ability in any event. Although most of her friends had money, remarkably few of them had made it themselves, and their knowledge of business maneuvers, to say nothing of their appreciation of them, was extremely sparse. When told that Christina was an accomplished businesswoman, one of her acquaintences credited tarot cards and moved on to other subjects. But they all knew, or thought they knew, what had happened on Lyford Cay.

Her reasoning was sound. No Greek woman had ever ruled a fleet, at least not openly. Christina herself was little more than a girl, and not a particularly popular or respected one. The shipping business where she had no allies except, ironically, the even more unpopular Stavros Niarchos, was exclusively a masculine preserve, and her father would have been a difficult act for even a son to follow; her rivals were certain to test her strength. She was alone and, truth to tell, her nerves really were not in the best of shape. The answer to the problem was obvious. She needed a husband, and she believed that she knew where to find one.

Peter Goulandris and his mother had attended her father's funeral. Peter had taken her to Monte Carlo afterward, and he was waiting for her, or so she believed, at his mother's home at Lyford Cay in the Bahamas. "I'm tired of everyone trying to marry me off," she told the London *Daily Mirror*. "I'm not going to marry Peter, not because it's too soon after my father's death, but because I don't have any plans to marry him or anyone else." The next day, spokesman Nigel Neilson said she had been misunderstood. She had neither made up her mind about the marriage nor had she ruled out the possibility. In fact, it seemed that marry was exactly what she intended to do.

By the end of May she was back in Athens, still single, still unbetrothed, and the local gossipmongers, so recently and so gratifyingly busy with Jackie, had an explanation for this fascinating circumstance. It was certain that Christina had visited Peter and his mother at Lyford Cay, the enclave of exclusive homes west of Nassau in the Bahamas. It was also repeated as a certainty that Christina had insulted both Peter and his mother, although the nature of the supposed insult was never very clear. Christina—all parties agreed on this—had been ordered from the house, Christina had been instructed to leave Peter alone, Christina had fled the island. Yannicopoulos, as usual, gathered up the stories as they appeared. And he repeated them.

Christina remained determined, but her field of choice was not a spacious one. Her father had wanted her to marry a Greek, a powerful factor in her thinking. The dutiful daughter once more, she was anxious to bring peace to his restless shade. There was a compelling tactical reason as well, and a problem. Her father's associates and the other maritime oligarchs would be inclined to look favorably on a Greek, but the number of possible candidates was small. The groom should be a man of proven commercial ability or connected with a family of talent and wealth, preferably one with a nautical background. Peter Goulandris had been the perfect catch, but Peter was no longer a possibility, and her father had rarely approved of any of her other young men.

It was her aunt Artemis who finally proposed the solution. Professor Georgakis considered Artemis something of a *marieuse*—a compulsive matchmaker—but with Christina determined on marriage (a course of action her conservative aunt could only have regarded with approval), the talents of a marriage broker were clearly called for. Moreover, Artemis believed that she knew of the very young man who would meet all the requirements. Once, when she and Christina's mother were indulging in their favorite pastime of building dynasties in the air, Tina had suggested "one of the Andriadis boys." Nothing had come of the idea, but it had made sense. The clan's seventy-year-old patriarch, Stratis Andriadis, was a doctor of laws, a corresponding member of the French Academy, and the son-in-law of one of Greece's many former prime ministers. With his seventeen company directorships, his fleet of merchant vessels, his fertilizer factory, his insurance companies, his banks, his owner-

ship of the Athens Hilton, and his shipyard at Elefsis, Stratis Andriadis was comfortably off. His wife, Rena, was a former lady-in-waiting
at the defunct royal court. (That Andriadis and his spouse had been
forceably reunited by the military junta after a long, open separation was ancient history now.) Most important of all, especially to
a person of Artemis's way of thinking, he originally came from
Vrondades on the island of Chios, the traditional homeland of the
Livanos clan.

Stratis Andriadis's older son, George, possessed a reputation as a
good businessman and a connoisseur of fast cars, big yachts, and
pretty girls, but his imminent marriage removed him from the
running. Alexander Andriadis, the thirty-year-old younger son, was
the more likely prospect, although Christina had never met him.
(This was not necessarily a drawback. It meant that her father had
never been given an opportunity to disapprove of him.) Alexander
Andriadis had a long-standing relationship with a Greek-American
girl, Denise Sioris, but that was no great obstacle. Her father was
an insignificant officer in the American foreign service, with no
fortune and no fleet. Alexander himself was widely regarded as a
good fellow but no ball of fire—again, not necessarily a drawback
considering Christina's determination to manage her own affairs.
Officially, he was the general manager of his father's shipyards, but
his true interest ran to his collection of antique Rolls Royces, his
sailboats, and the eight or ten plates of macaroni he consumed each
day, at least when he was not in the army, as he was now. Because
of a trick shoulder, he had been ineligible for military service as
long as his father was on good terms with the cabinet, but when the
short-lived and otherwise confused government of Brigadier Demetrios Ioannis came to power in 1973, it had not been inclined to
be as lenient as its predecessors on the subject of Alexander's obliga-
tions to his country. After six years of increasingly inept military
dictatorship, the country had been in turmoil, the rich were universally hated, the end of the regime was in sight, and the black flags
of anarchy flew in Megara, a town and region on the coast just west
of Athens and north of Salamis, where Stratis Andriadis was expro-
priating land and uprooting olive groves to build the very oil refinery that Aristotle Onassis had vainly coveted for so long. In an
attempt to curry popular favor, the Ioannis government dispatched
the dreaded EAT/ESA interrogation unit to procure Alexander. He

was sent to a military hospital, pronounced fit for duty, and packed off to a unit on the Turkish frontier. The gesture had failed to save the brigadier and his government, but the hapless Alexander was in uniform still, "the richest private," it was said, "in the Greek army." At the moment he happened to be in Athens.

The press would later, and somewhat charitably, describe him as "hefty," but his features were regular and perhaps he possessed latent talents of some sort. He was, after all, an educated man, having done graduate work in economics in both Switzerland and Britain. The fact that he kept late hours, rose at eleven, exhibited no ambition, and failed to cut a great swath as either a playboy or a businessman could all be dismissed as the harmless vagaries of a pampered youth. His father and his brother were competent enough, and blood always told.

The necessary arrangements for the courtship were soon made, with all the initiative coming from the Onassis side of the proposed match. Christina disliked the yacht she had inherited from her father, but young Andriadis was fond of the water and a cruise had been her father's preferred form of dalliance. A cruise was therefore arranged, with Artemis embarked as chaperone. Afterward there were several evenings of dancing at the Hilton. It was decided that Alexander Andriadia would do. If he was unlikely to be of much help, he was equally unlikely to get in Christina's way. It only remained to persuade his father of the wisdom of the choice.

Stratis Andriadis needed little persuading. He was an experienced and skillful trimmer who had always managed to give at least the appearance of backing each of the factions that, turn and turn about, came to power in Athens, but for once he had seriously miscalculated.

In the unruly cockpit of Greek politics, the secret of the game lay in knowing your man and discovering his price. Often the cost was trifling. When the Liberals were in power under General Plastiras during the early 1950s, Stratis Andriadis seldom failed to remind the distinguished warrior of how, as a young captain stationed on Chios during the First World War, the general had been most generously entertained by the Andriadis family. Forty years had passed, but the old general was still grateful. Andriadis carefully kept his distance during the unpredictable election of 1964 until it became clear that the Center Union had won, whereupon he drove immediately to the home of George Papandreou, threw his arms around the victor, and cried in a great voice, "Congratulations, Mr. President! We won!" (At the same time, through an anonymous entity called Martha's fund, he secretly contributed to the Marxist E.D.A., headed by his old friend Elias Elion.) And if the necessity arose, he could be blunt. Bringing an action for libel against an Athens publisher, he arrived in court with a large briefcase, proclaiming, "I have you all in here. If this case is opened, Greece will stifle with the stink." The publisher won the suit, but Stratis Andriadis had made his point.

The military junta had placed him under house arrest when it came to power in 1967, but he soon wriggled free. "The queen of England collaborated with pirates," explained one of the colonels. "Why should we not do business with Andriadis?" The resulting bargain seemed to satisfy both parties. Andriadis named the first bulk carrier launched from his new Elefsis shipyards after the wife of the junta's chief. In return, he received permission to build his oil refinery at Megara on terms that would cost the Greek state $178 million a year.

But astonishingly, Constantine Karamanlis was no longer inclined to play the familiar game. He seemed to have forgotten that he had once been the expansive friend of business who gave the national airline to Aristotle Onassis and the great shipyard at Skaramanga to Stavros Niarchos. The nation's democrats were eager for revenge, and Karamanlis's investigators had begun to move in on the Andriadis banks at the worst possible time, before their owner could cover the $20 million in losses resulting from the transfer of certain sums abroad—to Panamanian companies that might well prove, if the investigators persisted, to belong to Stratis Andriadis. With the banks under close scrutiny, there was no plausible way to call the funds back without calling attention to them and creating yet another, easily followed trail. Faced with what promised, at the very least, to become a scandal of major proportions, Stratis Andriadis was a man who desperately needed $20 million, and there was no way in the world for him to lay hands on it. Until now. It may very well have occurred to him that separating an immature and unstable young woman like Christina Onassis from the necessary funds should be child's play.

Artemis leaked the news of the impending marriage on Monday, July 21, but *France Soir* had somehow sniffed it out the day before.

By Tuesday the word was all over Athens. The wedding would be held that evening in "the Standing Hymn," the beautiful little Byzantine chapel that Father Marius Bapergolas had built with his own hands on the slopes of Mount Hymettis in the suburb of Glyfada, directly across the street from the villa of the elusive Costa Lemos. The church was a tiny place, barely able to accommodate six people, and surrounded by cypress and olive trees, geraniums and jasmine, and the unfinished apartment buildings that stood everywhere in mute testimony to the severe recession that had ruined the tanker business. Denise Sioris (Alexander Andriadis's girlfriend for "two years and two months, to be exact," she told the press) had been informed the week before. George Andriadis, married only twelve days, broke off his Canadian honeymoon and hurried home for the service. "Yes," Stratis Andriadis admitted, "it did catch me by surprise. But then that's life. It's filled with surprises."

As the time for the ceremony approached, a small crowd of a few hundred people gathered. To Steven V. Roberts, who again covered the story for *The New York Times,* the scene resembled Sunday at the beach. There were babies in carriages, men in bathing suits, the inevitable old women in black who stood witness to the principal events in Christina's life like a mute chorus, and the equally inevitable paparazzi. (A number of Greek photographers among them whiled away the time before the arrival of the wedding party by systematically destroying the cameras of their foreign competitors.) The police, the newspapers later reported, "attempted to maintain order."

Alexander Andriadis arrived first, wearing a blue suit with red pinstripes and carrying a cigarette in a holder; he seemed surprised when the crowd applauded him. Christina and her stepmother were forty-five minutes late. Ignoring both the bride and John Kennedy, Jr., the crowd surged forward as Jackie stepped from the limousine. Only two weeks before, she had accompanied a frigid Artemis to the dedication of a summer camp for Greek-American children in the town of Vartholomio. Concerning her stepdaughter, she had words of hope.

"I so love that child, and I'm so happy she had found him," she told the assembled press. "At last I can see happy days ahead for her. They are a wonderful couple."

Dressed more for a confirmation than a wedding, Christina

emerged from the car in an off-white layered gown with a purple sash. There was a gold cross at her throat, and she carried a small bouquet of pink roses. The bridal party filed through the geranium-filled courtyard and entered the tiny sanctuary.

"No zisete!" cried the crowd when the small group reemerged. Long life. The women reached out to touch Father Marius's robes.

"Gosh, it was hot in there," said John Kennedy, Jr.

"It is like being made a king for life," said Alexander Andriadis.

"Big deal," said Denise Sioris when she was contacted at her father's home.

There was no honeymoon. Alexander returned to his barracks; his enlistment expired in January. And suddenly, more or less out of the blue, he seemed to want Christina to place a $20 million deposit in his father's banks.

In the meanwhile, there was still the will to be dealt with, and dealing with the will meant dealing with Jackie. In order to base her challenge on the *nomimos mira,* Christina had the document registered and probated in Athens rather than Argentina, where her father had retained his citizenship, or in Paris, where he maintained his principal residence. Then, in her father's best manner, she sat down to dicker. "She seems to remember everything he told her years previously," said George Moore, "almost as if she has a computer in her brain that was programmed by Ari." She offered her stepmother eight million dollars.

Jackie wanted at least $20 million and she was not inclined to bargain. In conspiratorial Greece (and elsewhere) there were plenty of people ready to imagine that she had something on her deceased husband, that she knew something—no one could say what—that she was not supposed to know. It was $20 million or nothing, the basic $20 million that, amazingly, everybody seemed to want those days, *plus* the proceeds from her share of the property and additional monies to settle the tax bill. Christina countered with an offer of $22 million, payable from her own half of the estate and transferred in such a way as to avoid as much American taxation as possible. For awhile it seemed as though Jackie might be happy with $23 million, but in the end her final demand proved to be somewhat higher: $26 million, a lifetime allowance of $150,000 per year, and the return of her personal correspondence. In exchange, she would renounce all further claims on the estate (for the second

time; she had already renounced them in the marriage contract of
1968, but that was a dead letter now), and she would surrender her
rights to Skorpios and the yacht, resign from the foundation, and
agree (if Christina would do likewise) never to discuss the matter
for the rest of her life. "Jackie did the best deal of the century,"
observed Professor Georgakis, but the lawyer Stelios Pappadimitriou, negotiating for Christina, had not done badly either. Once the
Onassis foundation turned over the money, Jackie would be out of
Christina's life forever, a highly satisfactory result but not the most
important one. More to the point, the will itself remained intact.
The settlement was between Jackie and Christina, not Jackie and
the estate. With Jackie out of the way, Christina was free to seize
control of her legacy—if she could.

Though married again, she was utterly alone, a circumstance that
her detractors (and they were many) could never seem to grasp.
Alexander Andriadis was no help whatever. The first fights began
when the marriage was less than a month old, and he seemed to
have developed a particular interest in the money he wanted
deposited in his father's banks. Perhaps he handled the matter
badly, or perhaps Christina was not the easy mark Stratis Andriadis
apparently believed her to be. On Pappadimitriou's advice, she
refused to transfer the funds and her husband was instructed not to
meddle in her affairs, a prohibition that effectively destroyed his
usefulness to his father, whose banks were shortly seized by the
state. The marriage was clearly doomed.

Nor did it seem that Pappadimitriou could be relied upon for the
long run, although he was an effective ally. Yannicopoulos described him as "a man of God, quiet and not interested in trickery."
Pappadimitriou, who was one of the youngest of her father's former
associates, was fed up with the endless bickering within the company, he was fed up with the marriage, and he was threatening to
leave just when his counsel was most urgently needed. Costa
Konialidis had been brought under discipline, and Christina had
actually considered firing him; she was persuaded otherwise. Gratsos, who had been her father's right-hand man, was a Konialidis ally.
Vlassopoulis, the chartering expert, was preoccupied with his attempts to mediate between the warring factions in the company.
The professor's confidence in his old friend's daughter had eroded
(and the professor had his own enemies), and Artemis was out of her

depth. With the threat from Jackie dissipated by the settlement, it was now possible to seize control of the fleet, but badly needed guidance on just how that could be accomplished was not exactly in abundant supply, nor was it entirely trustworthy.

The answer—it was unclear who found it, although in all probability it was Pappadimitriou, who swallowed his misgivings and stayed on—was found in the language of the will. Christina's father had directed that the shares of "my shipping companies and other companies with headquarters in Panama, Republic of Panama, or elsewhere," be assigned to Beta, but nowhere did he stipulate just what, precisely, the shares in Beta were supposed to represent. Most of the Panamanian companies—Bridgeport Maritime, Lucerne Navigation, Redbank Shipping, and the more than two score of others, representing fifty-six ships, more than five million deadweight tons of shipping, a weight of metal larger than most of the world's navies—existed for the purpose of owning a single vessel. If Christina could invoke the *nomimos mira*, not against the estate but against Alpha and Beta, she would have her ships. The very device her father had invented to deprive her of control would be the means by which she could grasp it.

It remained only to decide whether the ships would be divided singly, with Christina taking half of each vessel and the foundation taking the other half, or whether there would be an actual parceling out of the physical hulls. The latter course was more complicated, but the concerned parties regarded it as preferable. Everyone would gain from the transaction. The officers of the foundation, who in most cases were identical with the management of the fleet, would likewise gain freedom of action, and their holdings would not necessarily be threatened if Christina did something foolish with hers.

The process of allocation began in Monte Carlo, where the ships were matched by weight, age, and debt, a $2 million vessel with a $1 million mortgage paired with a $3 million vessel with a $2 million mortgage and so on down the line. On June 9, 1976, with Christina waiting in her chalet at St. Moritz, the final meeting was held in Geneva. The vessels were apportioned by lot, and Jackie got her money. For once, there was no dissension. It was a year and three months, almost to the day, after her father's death. Christina, playing her hand with consummate skill, had won a mighty victory. The world paid no attention whatever. For the last time in her life, Christina Onassis was upstaged by her stepmother.

"Inexplicably, I feel sad—disillusioned if you will—about Jacqueline Kennedy Onassis," wrote Harriet Van Horn in her newspaper column. "With $26 million, Christina Onassis bought off her mother's threatened lawsuit. And Jackie bought herself another black eye in the public prints. It ought not to disturb us that we suddenly see little green snakes of greed in Jackie's free-flowing hair. No doubt about it, we have idolized her overmuch. A betrayed wife and a gallant widow, she was transfigured in the light of President Kennedy's funeral tapers. . . . I do not see the virtue—or even the sport—in wresting $26 million from the corpse of the husband who was never the darling of your heart. Like Richard Nixon, Jackie will be grist for the mills of novelists and dramatists down the ages. With distance lending enchantment, maybe they'll be kinder than her contemporaries in 1977. One contemporary, recalling Browning's dark thoughts on a fellow poet, scribbled a little elegy beginning, 'For a coffer of silver she left us/For a diamond stuck in her nose. . . .' "

Alexander Andriadis, too, was gone, dispensed with in March and divorced later, a good fellow to the last but totally out of his depth. Unemployed—the government had taken the shipyard as well as the banks—but still trying to make his perplexing marriage work, he smashed up his leg in a motorcycle accident on Skorpios. "Bon voyage, Alexandros, better luck next time," Christina wrote on his cast before flying away to Monte Carlo. At the divorce proceedings, she characterized him as despotic, foul-mouthed, blindly jealous, self-centered, and a motorbike fanatic. She also said that he didn't like her to talk about her fleet. On his part, the object of all this invective seemed bewildered. His wife had a peculiar and dictatorial temperament, he told the court. "She didn't really care about me," he testified. "She also called me a peasant. Due to the short time between our engagement and marriage, I never got the chance to understand her nature." Still, she continued to see him long after the divorce. There were few enough trustworthy men in her life, and Alexander Andriadis was nothing if not a decent chap.

And on one point, she was absolutely firm. "I made the biggest faux pas," recalls one of her friends, "What did I say? I was talking to her, oh God, at a dinner party in November, and she asked me something about, oh God I can't remember, but I said, 'Oh, you know, these Kennedy kids always screw up.' And of course I stopped right in the middle and I said, 'Oh God, I'm sorry.'"

Christina Onassis had given orders that the Kennedy name was never to be pronounced in her presence again.

CHAPTER TWELVE

Mission to Moscow

In March, 1978, one of Christina's friends—who, as was so often the case, preferred to remain anonymous—informed Nicholas Gage of *The New York Times* that she had finally settled down. Christina Onassis had at last outgrown the impulsiveness and willfulness that had so outraged her family. Gage noticed that his informant neglected to accompany the statement with the spitting gesture that, in Greece, is meant to protect the subject of the conversation from an attack of the evil eye.

And yet there was reason to believe that the friend was right, had anyone bothered to look in the right place, although almost no one ever did. She had been as good as her word when she announced that she proposed to devote herself to her ships, and her promising beginning in the business had not been a false dawn. She had continued to do well in extremely trying circumstances. There was no longer anyone to upstage her. The accomplishments were at once genuine and considerable, and while they were not tidily packaged for popular consumption (as her father would have done), neither were they concealed. At the same time, she received no credit whatever for them. In part, this was due to a problem previously noted: Almost no one who writes about wealth for the popular journals has more than the dimmest notion of where the money comes from or how it is managed. In part, too, the problem was due to the obsessive secrecy with which Christina, like her grandfather, cloaked her actions, although the results of her policies were easily discoverable and the policies themselves deduced with equal ease. But the principal source of the difficulty was Christina herself. Simply put, she had never learned how to behave with dignity in public (although she occasionally did so, apparently from instinct) nor had she ever developed a sense of proportion, and she made no attempt to instruct herself in these arts now that she was widely believed to be the richest woman in the world. Her attention span, never long, seemed to grow shorter. As her father had done, she seemed to enjoy the company of frivolous people, but unlike her father she did not form an inner social circle composed of people of substance, like the professor, George Moore, and Gratsos. For reasons of her own, she had retained the executives she had inherited, which made some observers, reasoning backward from her gauche public persona, assume not unreasonably (but incorrectly) that she was a figurehead or a puppet. Her marriage to Alexander Andriadis had seemed a perfect match by Greek standards, but the world was not Greece, and even in Athens it was felt that the arrangements had been made too hastily, with too little preparation and too soon after her father's death to be in quite the best of taste. Moreover, Artemis's involvement made it appear that Christina was being manipulated, and Stratis Andriadis's growing difficulties made her look foolish. That there might be another side of the coin was not an insight that came easily.

Within five months of her father's death, she bought a petroleum refinery near San Francisco in partnership with the UCO Oil Company of Whittier, California. Her father had deeply coveted just such an installation but had consistently gone about obtaining one in precisely the wrong way, either through collusion with dictators, as in Greece, or underhandedly, as in New Hampshire. Christina simply made a purchase. At Olympic Maritime, a company her father had never allowed to mature, a fourteen-man board of directors was established with Christina at its head. Gratsos was out, who had served her father so long and so well (and who had seen his yearly gambling debts paid as a result). Fed up with the infighting, he retired to his comfortable office in Olympic Tower, where he took his calls and reminisced about the astonishing career of his departed friend. Meanwhile, at company headquarters in Monte Carlo, something resembling a modern corporate structure began to emerge. Real power was vested in an inner cabinet of six that included Cokkinis, Vlassopoulis, Pappadimitriou, and Lewis Anderson, the Greek-American managing director whom Christina had

hired away from Exxon, where he had made his considerable reputation as head of the largest chartering subsidiary in the world. The
intrigues so beloved by Christina's father were a luxury that could
no longer be afforded. The times were troubled, and they demanded rational decisions and a flexible response.

Confronted by the exorbitant new price of petroleum, the industrial nations had turned to new sources of supply—in Alaska, in the
North Sea, in the Gulf of Mexico—that were outside the OPEC
network and where supertankers, so recently the kings of the sea,
were not only superfluous but in many cases could not be used.
Smaller ships with shallower drafts were called for, and so were
product carriers, vessels especially constructed to carry the refined
hydrocarbons that would soon emerge from the immense facilities
the Saudi Arabians were building on the Persian Gulf, a circumstance that would profoundly change the nature of the business. It
was time to break up the old ships and buy new ones, but Christina
was stuck with the three VLCCs that her father had ordered in
France, and that had become hopelessly obsolete before their tanks
had been moistened by a single drop of oil. A charter was found for
the first, the 270,000-ton *Olympic Breeze;* it barely covered operating expenses, but it was better than nothing. As the second vessel,
Olympic Bravery, was making her way along the coast of France
to join 400 other idle ships in a tanker graveyard in Norway, her
engines went dead off Ushant, her anchor dragged in a ninety mph
gale, and she went onto the rocks.

Olympic Bravery had cost $35 million; the insurance settlement
yielded $50 million. In a swift and ingenious series of moves, Chris-
tina and her men purchased yet another VLCC from Daniel Ludwig, the American tanker magnate, for $26.5 million, $10 million
less than it was worth, and renamed it the *Aristotle S. Onassis.* They
then bought two older VLCCs from Texaco, sold them for scrap,
and obtained Texaco charters for both the *Aristotle S. Onassis* and
the *Alexander S. Onassis,* the third and last of the new behemoths.
Throughout the complex maneuvering, Christina presided at board
meetings, listened, asked questions, and gave few orders; it was
clear that her men, free of her father's meddling, knew their jobs
well enough, provided they were allowed to do them. Her father's
compulsive interference had stalled many a deal, and stalled deals
were another luxury that was no longer possible now.

It was necessary to downsize the fleet and convert the existing powerplants to diesel from the powerful but inefficient turbines that had been installed in the 1960s, but Christina's father had been bedazzled by the unprecedented profits of 1973, and he had left a flotilla of tankers that were only lightly encumbered with charters and heavily committed in the spot market, where fortunes could be made in good times and shirts lost in bad ones—such as the present. Some of the ships were instructed to save fuel by steaming slowly. Others were scrapped outright. Still others were tied up in drydock or consigned to the so-called graveyards in Greece and Norway. In the late 1970s and early 1980s, a traveler flying over the inlets of Greece and the fjords of Norway could look down on scores of empty ships moored side by side and bow to stern, like boxcars in a marshaling yard. At any given time, as much as 5 percent of Olympic's tonnage was idle, a situation that could not continue.

The remaining charters were good until the mid-1980s, when something would have to be done. In the meantime, perhaps the others could make a virtue of necessity and become trampers, searching out cargoes wherever they could find them, but it was not a secure business. The company was cash-rich—Christina's father had seen to that—and it made at least $22 million in profits during the three years following his death, but it was no longer the bountiful and automatic generator of money it had been in his prime. The future looked bleak. Other shipping crises had lasted a year, two years, five years at the most, but the present emergency looked as if it was becoming permanent. It could not go on forever, of course —the old Greek adage that the sea grew sick but never died remained true—but no end could be foreseen. It was time for a bold new initiative, one of those deft, imaginative strokes with which Christina's father was often credited, but which he rarely executed after the ARAMCO boycott. Perhaps it was time for his daughter to approach the Russians.

Her father had tried it at least once, when Alexander was still alive, dragging his uncomprehending son to Moscow. Apparently nothing had come of the initiative, but it made sense. Through its ship-chartering agency, Sovfracht, headed by Nikolai I. Zuyev, the Soviet Union deployed 7.5 million tons of shipping, but although the heavily subsidized Russians were masters of the cheap charter and the gouged price, they were not well equipped with tankers.

This was interesting. With its world-beating fifty-seven years of bad weather and resulting poor harvest (or so the government claimed), the Soviet Union was a chronic importer of foodstuffs, especially grains, but to purchase these foodstuffs, hard currency was required. The ruble was not convertible outside the Soviet bloc. And because the quality of Russian machinery, machine tools, and consumer goods had also apparently suffered from the bad weather, the country's possible hard-currency exports were limited to minerals (especially gold), furs, natural gas—and oil, of which the Soviet Union was the world's largest producer. Clearly, the architecture of a possible deal existed.

In November, 1975, Christina met with one of Sovfracht's Paris representatives, Sergei Danielovitch Kauzov, at her Monte Carlo offices, but the encounter was not auspicious. "Serge says I wasn't very polite," she recalled later. (She asked him what he, a Russian, was doing in Monte Carlo and on whose money.) They met again in October of the following year when she stopped off in Moscow to explore the possibility of letting Sovfracht have five of her dry-cargo freighters on charter. Most of her executives opposed the deal. The bulk market was as depressed as the oil market, they pointed out; at prevailing rates, the Russians would be getting a bargain. But Christina thought she knew otherwise. Using the good offices of Drewry-Maritime, a Paris firm that was one of the conduits the Russians used when they did business with the West, she lunched with Kauzov and his colleague, Alex Primiloff, at a restaurant on the rue de la Fontaine, closed the deal, and sounded the Russians out on a possible summit meeting with Zuyev. Afterward, Christina drove Kauzov back to his office on the rue des Hussiers in Neuilly. They talked about food; Kauzov, something of a gourmet, recommended a Russian restaurant he knew.

The summit meeting with Zuyev never took place, but the freighter deal became a personal triumph. The market fell even further; the Russians' bargain became Christina's coup. And unaccountably, she found herself falling in love.

Little was known, either then or later, about Sergei Kauzov. He was thirty-five in 1976, with a wife, Natasha, who played the cello, and a daughter named Katya. At 5'4", he was two inches shorter than his newly acquired girlfriend. He had a mouthful of gold teeth, thinning blond hair, and a glass eye that he sometimes removed in public. It was never entirely clear how he had lost the eye; a child-hood accident involving a bow and arrow was spoken of, but he also told one of Christina's disbelieving friends that he had lost it playing tennis. He had never known his father, killed in the siege of Lenin-grad; his mother, Mariya, was a minor functionary at Mosfilm. The London *Daily Express,* one of the world's more excitable newspa-pers, would later award him the rank of colonel and the status of spy, but although nothing was ever proven, other, calmer Western journalists and official intelligence agencies also believed that he was either a member of the KGB (rank unknown) or very close to it. Certainly the indications were suggestive if not conclusive. In most merchant navies, the captain of a ship is the closest thing to an absolute monarch still surviving on earth. In the Soviet merchant marine, the captain makes four daily reports of his position to the ship's political officer. That Kauzov and Primiloff were on their own amid the decadent temptations of Paris was proof enough that they were trusted implicitly. No man could occupy such a position with-out having undergone a thorough vetting by the KGB.

A graduate of the Foreign Languages institute in Moscow, Kau-zov was fluent in English and French. He wore denims (as did his mother) and the then fashionable leisure suits rather than the regu-lation pinstripes. He was fond of good food and fine wine. With Primiloff, he led gastronomic outings to Normandy and elsewhere that were written up in the *Moscow Star* and other publications of the French capitol's very considerable expatriate Russian commu-nity, and yet nothing had happened to him. (Such publicity is usu-ally anathema to the Soviet authorities, and the wise bureaucrat avoids it as though it were the kiss of death or a one-way ticket home, which it very often is.) Although his salary was only $235 a week, he was always well provided with money and was known as a generous and sometimes lavish tipper. He was, in short, a bon vivant, a man who made up in charm and flash what he lacked in looks, and he swam easily in the capitalist sea while giving every indication of enjoying himself.

There was little about his new relationship that was secret. Chris-tina, who was given to developing wild if temporary enthusiasms for certain individuals, was clearly in the grip of another one. She lost weight and cut her hair. They met in the bistros of the seven-teenth arrondissement and, following an old Paris tradition, in apartments lent by friends. She called him Serge and he called her Chrissie, an intimate nickname used by no one outside her family. They walked arm in arm in Monte Carlo and vacationed together in Brazil, a trip Kauzov could not possibly have made without the permission of his superiors. In Washington, nervous Olympic executives met together and coordinated their vacations with the vacations of officials from the navy and the maritime administration in order to ensure that the responsible parties would always be on hand. One thing seemed fairly certain: Christina was playing no deeper game, and there would be no fresh coup. Quite simply but very totally, Christina Onassis had been hooked by a Russian. She was deeply impressed, she said, by his apparent indifference to her wealth, and it was probably true. Bolker, too, had been unimpressed by her money. If Kauzov was charming he was also cool, the aloof, mature man she had always sought and seldom found. When others begged her to consider the implications of what she was doing, she refused. "This is a personal matter," she said. "I do not wish to discuss it." If pressed, she would glare, give one of her father's shrugs, and walk away.

There was genuine reason for concern. With Kauzov installed as Christina's lover, possibly as her adviser, and (if the unthinkable occurred) as her husband, it was at least possible that he would have access to information regarding her fleet from which, by simple extrapolation, his superiors could draw a fairly accurate picture of Western petroleum movements. This was valuable information, with obvious commercial and strategic applications. True, much of the same information was available, for a comparatively modest fee, from the London firm of H.P. Drewry, a fact that was sometimes overlooked, but with Kauzov privy to the thoughts of the infatuated Christina—and, as a shipping expert, able to understand what she was saying—he might also be able to learn her business secrets and gain access to the details of her long-range planning, priceless knowledge that no shipowner divulged to outsiders. Worse yet, he might be able to arrange for Sovfracht to swallow up her ships. Christina was only twenty-five, without guidance, and pliable—or so her marriage to Alexander Andriadis seemed to prove. It was forgotten that she had handled her business affairs faultlessly. It was remembered only that she was inexperienced and impulsive—and that she had cut only one deal with the Russians. (In yet another twist of selective memory, it was likewise forgotten that in it, she had outfoxed everybody, including her own vastly more experienced advisers.) As the panic mounted, there seemed to be no telling what she might be persuaded to do or what the consequences might be. The ships owned by the foundation—52 percent of the fleet—were probably safe despite her status as the foundation's life president. She could be outvoted by the board and probably would be. But where her own ships were concerned, her freedom of action was complete. Nor could pressure be applied. Her American-flag vessels were legally owned by the hospital's trust, and little could be done to effect the destiny of the others, owned in Panama and registered in Liberia. Christina could do with them exactly as she pleased—or anything that Kauzov could persuade her to do. It could only be hoped that her enthusiasm for the man would run its usual course and end with the customary bitter disappointment, as most of her passionate attachments did. The sooner it happened, the better.

If there was a certain amount of pardonable overreaction in the executive suites and chanceries of the West, it was later held as undeniable that the Russians read their quarry with shrewdness and exactitude and played their cards with skill, possibly because Christina was so quintessentially a Russian's idea of a capitalist's spoiled daughter. On December 15, 1976 Kauzov left Paris to attend a conference in Helsinki. While there, he vanished. An uneasy Christina met with a director of Drewry-Maritime, who was in possession of disturbing news. Kauzov had called, the director said. He had been taken back to Russia under military guard. Christina must under no circumstances attempt to join him; it would put him in danger. The director was unable to say more, but a few days later, Kauzov's wife and daughter left Paris on the regularly scheduled Aeroflot flight to Moscow and they, too, did not return. Christina's emotions, always her worst enemies, swung instantly in a new direction. It seemed clear, on the basis of no evidence, that Kauzov preferred the company of his lawful wife, a woman whose photograph Christina had once seen, whereas Christina, who would have done anything for him, had been ordered to stay put, an intolerable situation. At the navy, at the federal maritime administration, at Olympic, powerful men breathed more easily.

At just that moment, mysterious emissaries made their appearance. Just who these emissaries were was a matter that was never made clear, but they claimed to be able to get a message to Moscow. Christina's emotions promptly adjusted themselves to a new heading.

After a certain amount of difficulty at the Russian consulate on the place Malesherbes—obviously staged, some thought—the messengers hastened to Moscow, where they claimed that they cooled their heels for days at the Intourist Hotel until Kauzov finally made contact. Moving about the Russian capital with ease, they met him on a street corner and a plan was hatched. Christina could contact Kauzov at Sovfracht headquarters by using the Drewry telex, but her messages must be in cypher. (The code, a French reporter noted with sarcasm, was so simple that a child could have broken it). Evidently the implications of a Soviet citizen receiving private encoded messages from abroad on the telex machine in his office did not occur to Christina or was never explained to her. (Either that, or the whole episode was the product of a journalistic imagination that was not exactly working overtime, but the truth is hard to discover.) In any event, it was reported in Paris that the Drewry telex had begun to bombard the Sovfracht telex with messages of love. If so, Kauzov never replied.

Christina was reported by the French press to be in contact with aviators and soldiers of fortune; it was said that a commando sortie was discussed, but evidently the practical difficulties of a raid and rescue were finally borne home, and the idea was abandoned. Next, Christina was said to have offered one of her captains $250,000 to put into Murmansk and spirit Kauzov away. Whatever the captain's feelings on the matter, Kauzov was said to have refused, causing Christina to summon a prominent doctor to avenue Foch in the middle of the night and to increase her intake of sleeping pills. Next, the French press reported, she offered an even trade: an oil tanker for Sergei Kauzov. The offer was not taken up.

In January, 1978, Kauzov finally provided her with a Moscow telephone number where he could be reached. There was no direct dialing between Paris and Moscow. So every other day, Christina flew to London and placed her calls from there rather than going through the overseas operator.

However Kauzov explained his actions, it was clear that he made a persuasive case for himself, and Christina—by her own later admission—was not in the best of shape. She wanted to be loved for herself and not her money—the old dilemma, almost in the nature of a cliché, that had been planted in her psyche by her father and his obsessions. Simply put, there were remarkably few men she believed she could trust, while at the same time, like Alexander before her, she clearly regarded herself as the catch of the century, which led her to act in ways that repelled the very partners she wished to attract. She had more or less forced Joseph Bolker to marry her, in part by playing upon his fascination with power and social position and, not least, upon his kindness, but while the marriage might actually have worked, given half a chance, it had been destroyed by her father. The second marriage, to Alexander Andriadis, had been many things, among them (or so she had believed at first) a mutually advantageous business transaction in the traditional Greek manner. The match had foundered on mutual incompatability and, in some unmeasured degree, on the $20 million dollar unpleasantness. Now, in a seemingly irrational turn of events, she had become involved with a man of extremely dubious associations who seemed to represent the very antithesis of everything she had been taught to respect, but under the simple logic that governed all her romantic adventures, the attraction of Sergei Kauzov was actually of a piece with the rest. Infatuation and rebellion no doubt played their roles in the affair, but Kauzov was also a minor member of the Soviet elite, a man with an evident ideological predisposition to despise all wealth and who, therefore, probably did despise it, or was at the very least indifferent to it, although he was fond of the good life. With the Andriadis union, she had discharged her obligations to her father and attempted an obvious solution to her dilemma, but it had been found wanting. Now, for the same simple reason (for how else could she be sure she was loved for herself and not her checkbook?), she was drawn to its precise opposite. And Kauzov, for reasons that were apparently beyond his control, was the one genuine suitor she had ever met that she could not have.

On June 20, 1978 in the London Hilton, she received the call that she clearly believed would change her life. (It was also a call that was apparently overheard by the entire foreign press corps in Moscow.) Sergei Kauzov had left Sovfracht, and he had divorced his wife. Although divorce is a relatively simple affair in the Soviet

Union, he later told friends that he had tricked Natasha into giving her consent by telling her that he had courted Christina under orders from the KGB but had imprudently accepted illegal gifts from her. His arrest was imminent, but if his wife would give him a divorce he would sign over the car and the apartment—precious commodities in the Soviet Union—and thus save them from confiscation. They would remarry when he got out of prison.

Whatever the truth of the matter, while Sergei's mother comforted his ex-wife and Sergei himself moved into his mother's two-and-a-half room apartment, Christina returned to Paris and packed her bags. On June 24, as the story began to break in the world's newspapers, she boarded the train to Moscow, arrived at the Byelorussian Station the next day (which happened to be Sergei's thirty-seventh birthday), and took a chauffeured car to the Intourist Hotel on Gorky Street, where she took suite 1201, overlooking Red Square, for $200 a night. To all requests for an interview, she answered that she never talked to the press. Asked if she was planning to marry, she replied that it was preposterous and absurd. Kauzov was said to visit every day, disguised as a tourist, but her bodyguard made certain that no pictures could be taken. The Russians provided her with an office. Zuyev helped matters along by flatly denying that any person named Sergei Kauzov worked for Sovfracht, and while aides later clarified the situation by explaining that Kauzov had resigned, the news came as cold comfort to the family members, company executives, and government officials who once again found their thoughts focused uneasily on Moscow. "How can she marry a godless man?" asked her aunt Artemis, but in truth relations with Artemis had been rather strained since the Andriadis breakup. And outside the family, the subject of Kauzov's religion was the least of anybody's worries.

If there had been any doubt about his status before, experts on the Soviet system decided, there was none now. Kauzov was almost certainly wired to the espionage apparatus, and while the affair with Christina might very well have begun spontaneously enough, the decision to lure her into a deeper involvement had almost certainly been made at the Politburo level. At the very least, the presence in Moscow of the infatuated daughter of the world's most prominent, if deceased, capitalist was a considerable propaganda coup. It would become a triumph if she married a Soviet citizen and renounced the West. It was normally very difficult for a foreigner to marry a Russian, but no obstacles had been placed in her path —another indication that the regime was directly involved, and another source of worry. In Athens, naval intelligence turned its attention to Skorpios and assessed its uses as a possible Soviet base in the eastern Mediterranean. In Washington, a question was raised concerning the feelings of the militantly anti-Communist Saudi Arabians when they found that a considerable quantity of their oil would be transported in tankers owned by the wife of a Soviet ex-official. A unilateral Arabian abrogation of Christina's contracts might drive the fleet straight into the Soviet embrace, simplifying the situation in an unpleasant new way. In the family circle, there was talk of having her declared incompetent, and a high Greek official was sounded on the possibility of revoking her passport, but there was no hope of that. "There's no way I would do anything that would abandon the only child of Onassis in Russia without a passport," the official said. At Olympic headquarters, spokesmen began to insist that Christina was only a figurehead. Like the Queen of England, they said.

Gratsos—feeling that, at seventy-seven, he was getting a little old for this sort of thing—flew from New York to Moscow to view the situation with his own eyes. As he had expected (Christina called him every day), she could not be moved, but at the same time, she had not lost her head completely. The fleet was in no danger, she said. "There will be no headquarters in Moscow or any of that," she assured him. In fact, Russia did not figure in her plans at all, except temporarily, despite her public declarations of fondness for the country's austerity and its lack of materialism and the refreshing anonymity she claimed to enjoy as she walked the sidewalks. As a foreign businesswoman protected by international treaties, she possessed a multiple exit visa that enabled her to leave at any time she chose, but Kauzov, a Soviet citizen, did not. The authorities had hinted that they might reconsider his status and issue a visa after a period of time, perhaps six months, and although Christina missed her comforts and was apprehensive about the coming winter, she was determined to stick it out until then—but only until then.

Pursuing his enquiries elsewhere, Gratsos learned a number of other things, most of them reassuring and none of them posing an insurmountable obstacle as long as the Russians obeyed their own laws. Christina would not be required to become a Russian citizen. Her husband would be entitled to half her income, but only from the date of the wedding, and it should be possible to devise safeguards that would keep her funds beyond his grasp. (Christina would likewise be entitled to half of Kauzov's income, which at the moment was zero.) No one expected the marriage to last, and in Russia divorce was quick and easy. Should there be a child—and Christina was said to be eager for one—it would qualify for Greek citizenship if it was taken to the embassy. If there was no child, Christina's portion of the estate would revert to the foundation in the event of her death. Under the worst imaginable circumstances, this would be her insurance policy.

On the personal level, Gratsos saw, life in Moscow would be comparatively austere. The authorities seemed cooperative, even benevolent, and with their help it should be possible to find an adequate apartment, a thing ordinary Soviet citizens waited years to obtain. In the meantime, the suite at the Intourist was not intolerable, nor was Mariya Kauzov's small flat, with its paintings and antique mahogany furniture. As a foreigner with plenty of money, Christina could buy prime meat, fresh produce, imported delicacies, and the necessities of life at the UPKD and the beriozka stores reserved for diplomats and other outsiders, using D coupons—ruble certificates purchased with hard currency. The lower bureaucracy might make trouble—it usually did—but the regime was unlikely to do anything that would cause it to lose the propaganda advantage it had gained. (Christina would be watched and her apartment would be bugged, of course, but these were facts of life. Most foreigners in Moscow learned early that important conversations were best conducted in the open air.) If Christina continued to keep her wits about her, the situation could be endured until its inevitable collapse. Gratsos knew from experience that if the Russians tried to put pressure on her—even benign pressure—they would be in for a surprise. And there was this to be said for a police state: The country was an extremely safe place to live.

As his last act in the city, Gratsos took Christina to the Greek embassy and placed her under the personal protection of the ambassador, Pierre Calogeras, and the first secretary, John Fotopoulos. If necessary, he told them, they should protect her from her own relatives.

Christina had once wanted to lead the simple life. Now, it seemed, she was about to do precisely that, although Sergei and his mother could hardly be described as simple folk, and the tasteful little flat in the Lenin Hills was not exactly a typical Moscow accommodation. She and Sergei spoke in English and French, although she planned to take Russian lessons. Meanwhile, she helped Mariya redecorate the apartment. Although friends abroad ridiculed the idea, she also claimed that she had begun to cook, mostly hamburger and chicken, the only good meats available and the only ones whose preparation was within her limited domestic capabilities. She wanted only, she said, to have a baby and to live in peace and quiet. She also wanted badly to get out of Russia, but she was careful not to say so. For one thing, the food was terrible.

Still denying that she planned a major step, she consulted a Russian law firm that numbered among its members the nephew of Leonid I. Brezhnev, the Soviet leader, and she told David K. Shipler of *The New York Times* that she would hold a press conference—something she never did—on Tuesday, August 1, 1978.

"Are you getting married?" asked Shipler.

"Come to the press conference."

"A disaster has befallen us," said a member of the family.

The ceremony took place at the Central Palace of Marriages on Griboyedov Street—the "Street of the Mushroom Eaters"—at 9:45 in the morning of August 1. Christina, wearing an ordinary cotton dress, violet with a pattern of brown and yellow flowers, arrived in a slightly battered Chevvy Nova borrowed from the Greek consul. There were eleven guests, including John Fotopoulos, who stood up for the bride, and the ambassador's wife, Ursula Calogeras. No member of the Onassis family was in attendance. A pair of Russian photographers was admitted while fifty Western reporters, on their best behavior, were kept outside. A string quartet—a common feature at Soviet weddings—played Mendelssohn's "Wedding March." In a civil ceremony lasting fifteen minutes (and costing $2.10), the registrar, Klara G. Lemeshkova, urged the nuptial couple to be loyal to each other. "Wherever you live, do not forget your Soviet motherland," she told Kauzov. "Is your decision to marry sincere and free," she continued, "and can you ensure the full happiness of yourselves and your Russian family? According to the law of the Russian Republic, you are now man and wife."

Leaving the wedding palace to the sound of prerecorded bells, Christina stumbled in front of the reporters. "I feel fine, very good," she said.

"Has she gone crazy?" asked a Russian passerby when he learned the identity of the bride, a sentiment that was echoed in Athens by Alexander Andriadis. Told that his ex-wife had just married a Russian Communist in Moscow, he replied, "You must be joking."

Nothing seemed to go right. Kauzov had trouble starting his battleship gray Volga. When he finally got the vehicle underway, it was pursued by a second car containing two Russian photographers who had, perhaps, read more about the paparazzi of the West than was good for them. Kauzov yelled back at them and ordered them to stop, but they kept on coming, right up to the door of the flat in the Lenin Hills, where they were driven away by Christina's new mother-in-law. (Their effort was in vain. The Soviet press published not a line about the wedding.)

Later that day, as she had promised, Christina gave her press conference. She and Kauzov had returned to the Intourist suite, which she had retained; she had decided not to live in Mariya's $11 a month apartment after all. As usual, she revealed little about herself or her thinking, but in Russia that was always the wisest course. Without mentioning the supposed commando raid, the Murmansk rescue, or the odd lines of communication she had allegedly tried to open to Moscow, she gave a brief and accurate chronology of the relationship. The Russian authorities, she said, had been "very cooperative. I've been accustomed to having everything all my life, but I don't think there will be any great difficulties. All I miss is newspapers. But I don't understand what all the fuss is about." On Thursday, she and her new husband announced, they would board the Trans-Siberian Railway for a wedding journey to Ikurtsk and Lake Baikal, concluding the trip at Magadan on the Pacific coast, 7,000 miles away. It was a curious destination. Magadan, not a resort as far as anyone knew (it was believed to be off limits to foreigners), was deep in the notorious gulag of labor camps and detention centers, and in the past the well-known dissident Andrei Amalrik had been jailed there. What, the reporters wondered, could Kauzov be thinking? And how in the world had he gotten the necessary authorizations?

Christina, a devoted follower of the *International Herald Tribune,* was desperate to learn how her marriage was being taken in Europe and America, something that it was not easy to discover from Moscow, although she must have known that some of her own people had turned against her. A director of the Onassis foundation was said to have resigned in disgust. In London, Nigel Neilson, her own press agent, remarked that "Ari would be terribly disappointed, absolutely astonished that Christina would take up with a Russian." Gratsos, though resigned to the escapade, was hardly more diplomatic. "Kauzov," he said, "is a small cog in an incredibly huge bureaucracy, who has never had to test his ability. Ari wanted Christina to marry an unqualified success [who would] continue his work." No one could be found who believed that she understood the implications of what she had done. "The Russians will woo her and court her, but they'll never trust her," an American businessman recently returned from Moscow told Joan Gage, the writer and wife of Nicholas Gage, *The New York Times* correspondent in Athens. "They'll worry that she might leave the Soviet Union and complain about them. She'll be constantly watched." Only one person, Stavros Niarchos, had a good word for her. "Heaven knows, she deserves some luck," he said.

On Tuesday, First Secretary Fotopoulos was contacted by a Greek businessman who had three of the Athens dailies. The businessman and Fotopoulos met Kauzov in a restaurant around the corner from the hotel and gave the papers to him. (Fotopoulos hid one, *Acropolis,* that carried headlines referring to Christina's marriage to "a one-eyed man.") Kauzov, natty in a dark blue corduroy suit, examined the news photos with pleasure, although he was unable to read Greek. Christina, he said, would be delighted.

Christina was not delighted. She was, in fact, having some very serious second thoughts. Her relatives and friends had sent no gifts. When her new mother-in-law attempted to present her with a garnet bracelet, she said she hated presents and refused to accept it. The wedding ceremony could hardly have done more to satisfy her romantic yearnings for austerity, but the more observant members of the press had noticed the dark circles under her eyes. She later said that she had wanted to call it off, but the momentum of the thing had carried her forward. She had allowed herself to miss Phillipe Junot's wedding to Princess Caroline of Monaco, her neighbor on avenue Foch, and she had passed up the annual dinner of the year at Maxim's—important events in her circle. And now she was facing the prospect of a Moscow winter and more of the same.

Before the ceremony, she and Kauzov had spent their days exploring the city and the surrounding countryside, hardly an encouraging experience. Now she stuck closely to her suite at the Intourist. Thursday, the day scheduled as the beginning of the honeymoon, came and went. On Friday she called John Fotopoulos at the embassy. She knew that the first secretary and his wife were returning to Athens on home leave. Could he, she asked nervously, get her a ticket on the same flight? She said she wanted to see her family.

Fotopoulos did what he could. There was a waiting list of almost a hundred people for the Saturday Aeroflot plane to Athens, but he was able to obtain an additional place. There was no first class; Fotopoulos managed to arrange for the next best thing, a front-row seat near the window. Although the plane was fairly abuzz with talk of her marriage, he and a Greek businessman were the only people aboard who actually knew her, and somehow they managed to keep her presence a secret. Again and again she asked her companions about return flights to the Soviet Union and the necessary paperwork. They did their best to reassure her. Someone produced an iced bottle of Russian champagne, and they drank her health. Christina took a sip and smiled weakly.

She was met at the Athens airport and driven to Artemis's villa in Glyfada. She had returned, her aunt informed the press, because of "an urgent business matter. She is like our own child," Artemis added. "If she has found someone who makes her happy, it makes us even happier." Here was normal life again. The neighborhood swarmed with reporters and photographers. Christina was photographed diving into the villa's pool; newsmen who crept too close to the house were sprayed with a hose by an angry gardener. There was familiarity, too, in the usual spate of unverifiable rumors from reliable sources close to the family, whose impeccable information, again as usual, was partly wrong. There had been a "cooling" between the newlyweds, these faceless sources said. "Friction" had developed.

Meanwhile, as Olympic executives carefully kept their distance, the family marshaled its arguments against the marriage. The experience can hardly have been a pleasant one, but Christina had known few pleasant moments. That, too, was normal. Alexander Andriadis came to call. He was suddenly Christina's "closest friend in the whole world," or so she said. In any event, he was someone she knew and trusted, and there was no harm in him. He reportedly accompanied her on a sudden twelve-hour trip to London, but what she did there (if she went) was not revealed. The customary veil of secrecy was back in place.

In Russia, it seemed that either Kauzov's command of English or his good sense had deserted him. It was only natural for him to be concerned. He had no idea what was happening in Athens, and he made a round of calls to Western journalists in an attempt to find out. He seemed surprised at the thought that Christina might not wish to resume the marriage. "There have been lots of crazy reports, funny stories," he said. "We want to be left in peace. Our plans are our plans. What will happen tomorrow, I do not want to tell you." He explained that he was unable to join his wife in Athens because it might take him as much as two months to obtain the necessary visa. He was, he said, looking for a position as an English teacher. "At the moment I don't have any job at all," he explained. As a teacher, he might make as much as $250 a month. And he confirmed what Gratsos had already discovered. "Whenever a Russian is married," Kauzov said, "he is entitled to half of what he and his wife are earning during their married life. What was mine before we were married is still mine, and whatever was hers will remain hers. Whatever we earn in our mutual life, that's what belongs to us, fifty-fifty." At the very minimum, Christina was entitled to a $250,000 annuity as life president of the foundation. The more Kauzov talked about money, the worse he looked. "She will be back one of these fine days," he predicted.

In Athens, Christina's aunts announced a "wedding party" on Skorpios over the Assumption holidays for twenty of their late brother Aristotle's closest friends in the shipping business. They clearly felt that it was time to roll out the big guns. Christina, they said, would shuttle over to the island by helicopter. But Christina herself had experienced another change of heart. Perhaps the family pressure, after all, had been too much, or possibly it had been poorly applied. Yes, she told her friends, she might have acted impulsively. Nevertheless, she was determined to give the marriage a chance. She told *Acropolis,* the Athens daily, that she was furious over the published reports that Kauzov might be a spy. "I tell you that everything that has been written is false," she said. "I am not divorcing and I am returning to Moscow." At ten in the morning of August 14, nine days after her arrival and one day before the scheduled party on Skorpios, she appeared at the Russian embassy and asked for a visa. The Aeroflot jet leaving for Moscow that afternoon at 2:30 was the last flight for five days, and she proposed to be on it. The diplomats, though often the most obstructionist of men, moved with commendable swiftness. The visa was provided, seating in the front row by the window was again arranged, and she was on her way.

Kauzov was not at the airport to greet her. Catching sight of a friendly English reporter, she asked him to rescue her from the crowd and take her home. But when they pulled up at the apartment building in the Lenin Hills, there was no one home. Neither Kauzov nor his mother had known she was returning.

Four days later, her aunt Artemis's husband, Professor Theodore Garofalidis, died in Athens from the complications of cerebral thrombosis. Christina did not attend the funeral; her three aunts— "their emotions," wrote Joan Gage, "under control"—walked behind the coffin alone. But it was noted with interest that Christina's gynecologist, Dr. Evtychia Arampatzi, was also among the mourners. Christina, it was said on the basis of no firmer evidence, must be pregnant.

She and Kauzov, trying to be inconspicuous, were occasionally sighted in the one place in Moscow where all foreigners eventually gravitated: the hard-currency food market. There would be no honeymoon, Christina explained, although there was a weekend trip to the Black Sea resort of Odessa; she and her husband would stay in Moscow and look for an apartment. The suite at the Intourist was comfortable as such things went, but it was not a permanent home, and Mariya's tiny apartment was impossible. It was only marginally short of an exaggeration to say that the average Russian could expect to have two children and a divorce while he waited for living quarters, but for foreign residents with quantities of money, there was no great difficulty. In record time, Christina and her husband located a seven-room apartment in Tyopoly Stan on the edge of the city near the botanical gardens that, by Soviet standards, was a palace. (Some said that it was actually two apartments with the party wall removed.) The rent was $150 a month, and furnishing the place led to at least one small adventure. Christina, unaccustomed to the Soviet marketing system and far less accustomed to postponed gratification, sought to buy a refrigerator. The clerk at the foreigners' store explained that the model she had selected was for demonstration purposes only. Under the Soviet system of allocating consumer goods—not a high priority in a society ideologically committed to heavy industry—it would be weeks, perhaps months, before another such refrigerator could be manufactured and delivered. Christina insisted. Here was a perfectly good refrigerator, she needed one, and she saw no reason why she couldn't have it now. The clerk's thoughts at this point can only be imagined, but in the end the refrigerator was hoisted atop the Kauzov car and Christina and her husband drove off with their prize. It may have been a Moscow first.

A maid and two chauffeurs were engaged; Christina had never lived without servants. Then, pursuing her strategy of waiting the government out and giving it no provocation, she and Kauzov did their best to drop from sight, and from the headlines. "The less people hear about us," she told a reporter who encountered her in the food market in November, with the Russian winter well advanced, "the better it will be for both of us." David Willis of the *Christian Science Monitor,* who saw her at a dinner given by Juan Antonio Samaran, the Spanish ambassador, thought that she looked overweight, dowdy, and awful. "They were a wonderful pair," says Willis. "Kauzov had his glass eye and Christina drank so much Coke that she probably had her teeth capped. You can imagine them sitting there, Christina polishing her teeth, Kauzov polishing his eye. She was hopelessly naïve to have put the secrets of her shipping operations at risk like that." But her plan worked. Kauzov's multiple exit visa finally came. In the middle of a record −45°F cold snap that disabled her new Mercedes, Christina and her husband finally left Russia.

It was high time that she got out. The Saudis, as predicted, had been made restive by her long sojourn behind enemy lines, and the word in London was that they were threatening to cancel her contracts. With upwards of 12 percent of the fleet now idle, a Saudi cancellation would have been ruinous, and something had to be done about the growing number of laid-up ships. Christina believed she had the answer. Cheap charters were the only ones available. The Russians were expert at extracting a maximum return from just such charters, and Kauzov was obviously a Russian. He would therefore be placed in charge of reactivating the laid-up vessels. This would give Kauzov something to do; her husband still had no job and no prospects. And if he succeeded, he would save the company the $3 million in annual maintenance charges that it was forced to spend with no hope of a profitable return. It was, Christina thought, an elegant solution.

It was at times like these that the wall of secrecy around Olympic became a trifle porous, as executives either boasted of their prowess in dealing with their employer's whims or attempted to influence her through selective leaks to the press. Christina's father, they reminded her, had established stern rules about husbands meddling with the business. (That had been true enough in the case of Joseph Bolker, who—declining to accommodate the Onassis paranoia— had exhibited absolutely no interest in becoming a monarch of the sea.) Kauzov must be kept at arm's length, her executives explained, doubtless with some tact. Christina eventually agreed, possibly because they had invoked her father and not the KGB. They would attack the lay-ups in a more conventional manner, and she would find Sergei other employment.

While she pondered the form that this employment would take, she took Switzerland as her new official residence. As the very center of Western capitalism, the country was the complete antithesis of the Soviet Union, sending a clear message to the nervous Saudis and presumably calming their fears. To protect the couple's privacy when they were in Greece, a sixty-foot wall was erected around the pool at the Glyfada villa, and in a doomed attempt to appease the press, photographers were invited within its confines and encouraged to take pictures. Repeatedly, word circulated that she was pregnant. It was noticed that she had visited Hubert de Watteville, the Swiss doctor who had advised Sophia Loren during the film star's own pregnancy. But Christina was not expecting a child.

On the first anniversary of the wedding, Christina gave her husband a second-hand, 18,000-ton Panamanian freighter, the *Daniela*. Originally it was thought that the vessel would find employment (and keep its new owner busy) by carrying Mediterranean cargoes to the Middle East, but Kauzov was soon able to find an even more profitable task for it, carrying American grain to his native Russia. The compromise seemed to suit everyone. Kauzov, a man accustomed to working for a living, was back in the shipping business and making money, with an agent of his own—Costa Vlassopoulis's nephew—and there was no further talk about letting him examine the books at Olympic. And at the same time, it began to appear that Christina had discovered yet another use, one that had perhaps not been anticipated by the Russians, to which her third husband could be put.

During the first year of the marriage, Olympic purchased two used Russian tankers, the 230,000-ton *Geroy Sevastopolyana* (rechristened *Olympic Splendor*) and the 120,000-ton *Geroy Novorossiyska* (rechristened *Artemis Garofalidis*). A third tanker, the 118,000-ton *Olympic Star*, was acquired from the G. Dimitrov shipyard in Varna, Bulgaria. The two Geroys, built by Britain's Swan Hunter, were splendid vessels, and they were almost new; the Bulgarian tanker *was* new. The Russians and their most faithful satellite, both short of tanker capacity, had sold off three of their finest ships. Olympic, ruthlessly scrapping its older vessels, had replaced at least some of the lost tonnage with tankers employing the latest advances in naval architecture and had stolen a march on the competition by obtaining two of the popular downsized models well in advance of the time it would have taken to construct them from scratch. The terms of the deal were not disclosed, but it appeared that, as long as Christina remained married to Kauzov, the Russians were willing to accommodate her with more than an occasional window seat on Aeroflot.

On August 29, 1979, following the anniversary celebration on Skorpios (which had not become a Soviet naval base), the Kauzovs arrived unexpectedly in southern California with Albert Dodero— repeatedly described in the papers as "the Argentine tugboat king" —along with Dodero's wife, Maria, and their two-year-old baby. Christina, it was explained, had missed the surf. There were no available rooms at the La Jolla Beach and Tennis Club, but the manager was able to locate a suitable three-bedroom house a few blocks away, together with motel accommodations for the servants, who were now routinely referred to in the press rooms of the nation as "a bunch of spies," although no one seems to have gone to the trouble of determining if they *were* spies, or even if they were Russian. In any event, the party settled in for an eleven-day stay and the usual run in the headlines, even though—also as usual—there was nothing to report. Christina was observed romping in the surf on an orange Boogie Board. She played with the Dodero baby. She read documents that were breathlessly surmised to be business reports. And on September 1, she called Joseph Bolker.

Bolker had remarried, not once but twice. His newest wife, Victoria, worked in the exclusive Juschi boutique on Rodeo Drive. She would shortly present him with a son, his first, whom he would name Alexander. He still kept up a steady drumfire of letters to his elected representatives, his mayor, and the local press—Senator Alan Cranston of California, in particular, maintained quite a bulging file of them. Bolker was still honorary consul-general of the Republic of Senegal. (Later, in the early days of the Reagan administration, he would lobby for, and fail to receive, a diplomatic post.) He had also attempted to sell used slot machines to Indian maharajas.

The Bolkers posed with the Kauzovs on the beach and a picture was taken. (Later, Joseph Bolker would press a copy of the print on anyone who expressed a mild interest in it.) Because an anniversary had just passed, Bolker also proposed to host a party of his own at the Costa Mesa branch of 40 Carrots, his health-food chain. Christina accepted, but on the appointed day she called to say that she and her husband would be unable to attend. Her husband, she said, had hurt his eye, whether in an automobile accident or a surfing mishap was never made clear, since both versions were current. Perhaps it was only that she had gotten a glimpse of the menu. The party went on without her, with marachi musicians, balloons, "healthburgers," turkey tacos, and a dessert course of chocolate zucchini cake. (At her annual dinner the following year at Maxim's, Christina served consommé en gelée au caviar, feuilletée de fruits de mer oceane, poularde de Bress aux concombre, and mousse glacée à la vanille, washed down with magnums of Dom Perignon 1973 and bottles of Château Haut Brion 1964.) Christina may have known very little about organizing her personal life, but she knew how to eat. She also knew how to cut her losses, and a few months after the trip to California, she did.

On November 7, amid rumors that she and Kauzov had parted, she was observed dining happily in New York with Princess Yasmin Aga Khan and Mick Jagger. She had checked into a hotel but was actually said to be staying at the Gratsos apartment on Park Avenue, a bad sign for her husband if true. On December 10, with the Russian and Bulgarian ships safely transferred to her flag, she told her lawyer, Stelios Pappadimitriou, to begin divorce proceedings. The grounds—"irreconcilable differences"—were comparatively mild. Although Pappadimitriou tried to bank the inevitable fires of speculation by pointing out that no business complications were likely to be inspired by the divorce, talk went around (and found its way into print) that Kauzov was holding out for either $100 million or $1.1 billion. His net worth, improbably fabulous for a Communist, especially one who had been held separate from his wife's business activities, was estimated at $8 million. It was perfectly true, however, that he was now known as "Captain Kauzov."

As such things went, it was an amiable if curiously incomplete parting. Kauzov kept the *Daniela;* Christina kept the family dog. She continued to see Kauzov regularly right up to the final proclamation of the divorce decree at the end of 1980, and she continued to see him afterward. (An attempt was made to link her name to that of Hubert Michard Pellessier, the lawyer son of her father's deceased French attorney, who had been a friend since childhood and whose mother still lived downstairs in the building on avenue Foch. "Hubert has always been a good friend," Christina said. "We like the same things. Sometimes one seeks happiness elsewhere when it really is waiting right next to us." Nothing ever came of it.) Kauzov became a regular visitor. He was granted unusual permission to live in the West. Despite much speculation, he did not remarry his first wife. He lived in London, visited Paris, and journeyed to the healing shrine at Lourdes. "It's an open divorce," Christina snapped when she was asked for an explanation, and she had one other thing to say on the subject.

"I still can't believe Sergei was a spy," she insisted. "Anyway, what could he get out of me? Do you suppose we talked about oil in bed together?"

That was exactly what everybody thought. On the other hand, she had three fine new ships.

CHAPTER THIRTEEN

❊

"I Think of Only One Thing"

By the spring of 1983, she was—finally—slimmer again, although she was by no means slender and it would not last. With ill-suppressed glee and no compassion whatsoever, the gossip press had exhaustively chronicled her latest and most spectacular battle with her waistline, reporting on the reducing spa from which she emerged fatter than when she entered, alleging that she had asked to have her jaws wired shut, printing merciless photographs of her bloated and almost unrecognizable figure. Joan Rivers made crude jokes about her on late-night American television. Not for the first time, Christina was listed as one of the ten worst-dressed women in the world. But for the first time in years, she actually came to Athens to preside over the annual awards presented by the Alexander Onassis Public Benefit Foundation—an event at which she was usually conspicuous by her absence—and she addressed the assembled dignitaries in passable Greek, even if she said nothing memorable. Still, she was able to draw on reserves of simple dignity that few had suspected and fewer seen, and that befitted her as a person unique in the world, the president of a great charitable institution and the only woman ever admitted to the Union of Greek Shipowners. Unremarked by almost everyone, she had saved her fleet while others were scrapping theirs—and, moreover, had managed to make money while doing so.

If she was lonely—so lonely that she leaned heavily on the friendship of Kauzov and Alexander Andriadis—there was nothing new in that. Her father had chosen his life (even if he lived to bitterly regret the nature of that choice), but Christina had inherited hers. Like her father, she was rootless, but it was not a rootlessness of policy and psychological need. Instead, a life of wandering was her father's gift, like the houses on three continents and the fortune she could not live without. The only real citizenship she had ever known was the nationality of received wealth. Barring the brief experiments in Los Angeles and Moscow, she had always lived in surroundings that had been chosen by others, and she kept them as she found them—all but one. In 1978, shortly before she married Kauzov, she invoked a clause in her father's will and gave the yacht that bore her name to the Greek state for the use of its president. "Christina," explained a friend, "doesn't like boats." As it happened, the vessel also needed an expensive refit.

Her aunt Artemis was now dead. Of all the intimate, corrosive family circle, only Stavros Niarchos still lived, the old "Governor" who chose to exhibit either a new mellowness or his old noblesse oblige by making a handsome gift to New York Hospital. One by one, her father's associates, men she had known all her life, were passing away. Gratsos was gone, dead of kidney failure, and so was Johnny Meyer, run over in Florida by his own car when he stopped at the roadside after a party to relieve himself. Others, like the professor, were elderly or near-elderly, and the professor was deeply engrossed in his new duties as his country's roving ambassador to the Arab world.

"Now I think of only one thing: business," Christina told *Paris Match* in a rare interview in 1982. "I no longer have a fixed idea of having a home. There is nothing ahead for me in that. Ahead isn't the 'poor little rich girl' the magazines write about, but a woman who is suddenly sure of herself." She had never occupied the apartment she had taken on the ground floor at avenue Foch to be near the comforting presence of Mme. Pellessier, the widow of her father's lawyer, during the blackest of her depressions; it was taken as a sign of her recovery that although she kept the rooms, she used them as an annex for her guests. She consulted a psychiatrist and made clumsy attempts to befriend the paparazzi who waited in the street below, riding with them on their motorbikes, pretending that they were really after her neighbor, Caroline of Monaco, and shyly allowing herself to be photographed in a suburban park. She had switched couturiers, abandoning Yves St. Laurent for Christian Dior, who made the ample garments that helped to conceal her thickening figure.

"She always gets fat when she's happy," explained one of her intimates, although others took it as a sign of trouble. "Now she's doing something very good. She's taking care of a lot of cancer problems. It's true that after the divorce from Kauzov she was unhappy and went into a depression, and last year there was another big depression again, but now she's put on a lot of weight and she's much better. She's in a very good mood, too fat but her mind is good, and she spends all day at different places where they have operations for cancer. She sits next to the doctors in her big flowing blouse and they tell her all about disease."

Her fleet continued to shrink, but the ongoing business crisis was hardly apparent in her daily life. On impulse, she might fly to South America for the day. As though following a template laid down by her father and mother, she migrated annually among her parents' homes and offices and favorite cities—three months in St. Moritz, where her mother had crowed in spiteful triumph on Alexander's last Christmas; two months in Monte Carlo, where Olympic still had its offices in the old Winter Sporting Club and there was new trouble with Prince Rainier; two months in Greece, either on Skorpios where she had redecorated the main house but left Jackie's farm untouched, or in the Glyfada villa, where her father had listened to the music of his airplanes all day and half the night; and two months in New York. The balance of her time she spent in the old flat overlooking the Bois de Bologne, with the royal blue curtains, the Louis XVI table and desk, and the general air of opulent shabbiness it had exhibited in her father's time. No trace remained of Jackie. There was the good cook her friends admired; the old butler, Georges; Helene, the maid and companion; and downstairs, the chauffeur-driven Mercedes, a vehicle much favored by the European rich because of its "nonimperialistic" associations. Her nails were cut short; the walls of her bedroom, like those of a teenager, were decorated with posters from the popular newspaper cartoon, "Love Is. . . ."

Like her father, she patronized no art, knew next to nothing about politics, betrayed no interest in literature, and assembled no salon. Her philanthropies, such as they were, were administered by the foundation, from whose ample coffers the money also came. Although Bolker remembers her as an eager consumer of books, she seldom read anything more demanding than her favorite newspaper, the *International Herald Tribune.* A friend in the States regularly supplied her with videotapes of "Dallas." Her favorite movie was *Rocky.*

Like her brother Alexander, she did not drink liquor, nor did she smoke. She still consumed cola drinks in enormous quantities—Tab, now that her weight was a problem again—and despite the clear warning sounded by her mother's fate, she still took pills.

She had neither conquered nor outgrown her early shyness, and she surrounded herself with men whose business it was to preserve her secrets and her privacy. She was not a public figure, her lawyers would patiently explain to the press; her thoughts and doings were not in the public domain, there was nothing of interest to be learned. When a *Fortune* reporter named Lewis Bemans wrote (correctly) that her fortune was not as large as commonly believed, she personally called him and threatened him with the loss of his livelihood. At the same time, she made no great effort to wall herself off entirely. She no longer employed bodyguards, she attended parties and functions, she went shopping, and when she was in New York it was possible to encounter her, if not approach her, amid the flashing lights and colored smoke of Studio 54, lost in the repetitive movements of the dance and surrounded by a blare of music that made conversation impossible. In the morning, if she had spoken and been overheard, perhaps in some quieter area off the dance floor near the bar tended by muscular, bare-chested young men, there might be a quote in the gossip columns, as small but indispensable reminder—such as her father had craved—that men are superior to beasts and the rich are superior to men.

Her father, a hedonist to his core, had expended his fortune on what used to be called vulgar display and had emerged from the experience with the reputation of being a splendid fellow. Christina was a more mercurial but also a simpler person, as untrained in the art of hospitality as she was in domestic science, and for her, Skorpios served a slightly different function than it had in her father's time. Like a pony in the possession of the richest little girl in town, it provided her with an extended circle of friends.

They were a mixed lot, those friends, and almost totally lacking in distinction, although they did not lack for money. At the core of her acquaintance was the small band of mostly younger men, for the most part gainfully employed, who had known her for years and who strove to protect her reputation, but there were others— mainly but not exclusively young women—whose feelings could be charitably described as ambivalent. They declared that she had a good heart while hastening to add that she foamed at the mouth when she talked. They praised her intelligence while failing utterly to recall a single intelligent thing she had ever said or done. They catalogued her eccentricities, repeated her private conversations, and talked about her behind her back. And when the annual invitation to Skorpios came, they went.

"On Skorpios, everyone has to do exactly what Christina wants," says a visitor who seems less than enthralled with the experience. "She doesn't get up until about two in the afternoon, so everyone has to wait around. When she does get up, it's time to call the boats. The servants and the food and the wine are piled into the first launch, and the guests climb into the other, and off everyone motors to a beach of Christina's choosing, where everyone sits around in the sun and eats and drinks until Christina decides it's time to go home, whereupon the process is reversed. In the evening, at the main house, there's dancing to music Christina chooses. Dull music, disco music, except that Christina can seldom find a record she likes, so the music is constantly changing. She chatters endlessly, you know. She can't keep her mind on anything. She asks questions and never waits for an answer, which is probably just as well, since the answers would doubtless be as dull as the questions: clothes, mutual acquaintances of no particular interest, the color of someone's new lipstick, that sort of appalling thing. Trying to talk to Christina is like trying to hold a conversation with a butterfly." Christina was neither willful nor cruel, but simply and totally in charge, and like many people with too much money and too few powers of reflection, she seemed to have difficulty in discerning the point at which Christina Onassis left off and the rest of the world began.

In public, as she had been taught, Christina effaced herself; on her island, she played the role of a benevolent but childish tyrant. Between these poles, in the middle ground of daily existence where the majority of humanity fiddles with the furnace and worries about the income tax, she was—as she had always been—almost completely without resources. It was as though her wealth and the tragedies it brought had afflicted her with a species of cabin fever that had made some of her traits pass beyond eccentricity, to the point where they had begun to resemble symptoms. And her friends, some of them, were the first to carry the news to the waiting world.

Her father had been a notorious insomniac; Christina was unable to sleep without a servant in the room. Day or night, by preference, she was never alone. She bathed compulsively and changed her underwear several times a day, but she never brushed her teeth. She not only talked incessantly but she was almost embarrassingly indiscreet. "She has an enormous chip on her shoulder," says one of her friends, "mostly having to do with men who couldn't or wouldn't marry her or make it with her, which she very openly talks about. Especially Mick Flick. She was really furious that they couldn't consolidate their fortunes. It was the big disappointment of her life, probably because she's impossible to get along with, or maybe because nobody can sleep with her. She talks a lot about people who couldn't sleep with her. But she talks about everything that happens to her. Everything."

"I wish she'd find someone to settle down with and be happy," says Helen Vlachos in Athens. "But for the moment she doesn't seem to have a great talent for choosing partners. I wouldn't be a bit surprised if I read one day that she was found dead, from suicide."

Perhaps, in such an event, Christina herself would have been the only person surprised, and then only briefly. By her thirty-second birthday, according to Joseph Bolker and Stavros Niarchos, she had weathered three overdoses, a number that suggested an almost surreal ineptitude in the uncomplicated craft of self-destruction— provided, that is, that self-destruction was her real purpose, and the evidence was hardly conclusive. Christina had used pills as an instrument of policy and a means of self-expression, a convenient shortcut through certain thickets of life that other people negotiated with guile, diplomacy, willpower, or rage. An overdose, properly undertaken, was an almost infallible way of insuring that attention would be paid, and Christina, having tried silence, tantrums, boorishness, and fantasy, had deployed it with a heedless profligacy that under other circumstances might have been described as misplaced enthusiasm.

All that was behind her now. Her quirks of character may have multiplied elsewhere, but after her father's death there were no more reports of overdoses in the bedroom or bandages on the wrists. And she had run her father's company exactly as he might have wished.

"I know the routes of my fifty tankers by heart," she told *Paris Match.* "Every day I telephone to my directors in Monte Carlo. We speak of our plans, of business. To this I devote two hours daily." She paused to sip her Coke. "I must go back to Monte Carlo. The devil! I detest that city but I have work to do, at least six hours a day at my office."

But in 1982, she no longer had anywhere near fifty tankers.

At the time of her father's death in 1975, his associates had estimated the value of the fleet at around $400 million, and perhaps double that if conditions improved. In 1981, Apostolos Zambelas, the group's treasurer, had hazarded a guess that its worth had grown by "at least 25 percent in real terms" since the founder's departure. The value of the ships, real estate, and cash on hand was pegged in the vicinity of $1.1 billion. This was a heartening figure, but it was wrong. By mid-1982, the fleet was down to forty-one vessels and its net worth had shrunk to an estimated $160 million. The Onassis group's 26 percent share in the troubled Harland & Wolff shipyard in Northern Ireland had been abandoned, sold to the provincial government for a token $250,000. The small Swiss bank Christina's father had bought in 1968 had likewise been disposed of. Olympic Tower, the New York skyscraper that was his most visible monument, had been purchased from Christina's American trust and Arlen Realty in 1979, but by then much of it had been sold off as luxury condominiums, including a fabulous duplex, complete with waterfall, that was owned by Adnan Kashoggi, the Saudi Arabian dealmaker. Thanks to the renewed Manhattan real estate boom, the group's share of the remainder of the building was worth perhaps $40 million.

Christina's father, a cautious man in a volatile business, had always maintained large reserves of unencumbered cash—by some estimates, there was as much as $50 million on hand at the time of his death—but there had been urgent calls on his legacy's resources.

The fleet carried mortgages of at least $130 million, most of them in the form of demand notes bearing interest rates of around 14 percent. In January, 1983, *Fortune*'s David Fairbank White estimated the annual combined debt service at close to $20 million. Fourteen vessels—34 percent of the fleet—were laid up at an estimated cost of $2 million a year. Much of the "A" series—*Olympic Adventure, Olympic Archer, Olympic Ambition, Olympic Anthem, Olympic Accord,* and *Olympic Alliance*—had been sent to the breaker's yard. With the price of a second-hand ship, even a good second-hand ship, running only slightly ahead of its scrap value, the resale market had dried up almost completely. *Olympic Splendor,* bought during Christina's Russian adventure, was trading in the glutted spot market, chasing cargoes at a time when cargoes were rare and the business was dominated by the Japanese and the Scandanavians. So were the *Artemis Garofalidis* and at least ten other tankers.

It was still impossible, as it had been in her father's time, to obtain provable inside information about the group's affairs, but there was no rule against informed speculation. The six VLCCs on long-term charter were probably earning an operating profit of around $25 million a year, a substantial sum but one that was offset by debt service and depreciation; they would not reach black ink until 1985. The older, smaller tankers put out on charter in 1973 contributed between $4 million and $12 million, but the charters were due to expire, and the eleven dry cargo ships may have contributed another $3 million. At best, the Onassis group earned around $15 million a year, at worst around $7 million—respectable enough sums but nothing like the old days. The money machine devised by Aristotle Onassis was a money machine no longer.

But it had survived, and that was something. Between 1976, Christina's first year on the job, and 1981, Middle Eastern oil production dropped by 30 percent—in 1980–81 alone it fell by 16.5 percent —and in 1982 it dropped even lower. In 1981, BP Shipping scrapped three VLCCs with the latest in safety and antipollution devices. "It broke my heart to sell such ships for scrap," said Ronald Ilian, the head of the subsidiary, and he was not alone. In all, no fewer than forty-one VLCCs went to the breakers' yards that year, 5 percent of the world fleet. Taiwan took thirty-two, South Korea took eight, and Gadani Beach in Pakistan, where ships were dismantled by hand, took its first, the 230,000-ton *Brumaire*, built in 1971 and in superb condition. 1982 was even worse. Daniel Ludwig was almost out of the business; from fifty-four ships in 1975, his fleet had dwindled to fifteen. Stavros Niarchos, his fleet reduced to thirty-three vessels, was no longer a member of the industry's top ten. "Why should they care," asked Gratsos shortly before his death, "when they can put their money in a simple bank account and earn a certain 15 percent?" In a business once dominated by Greeks, only Christina and her uncle, George Livanos, remained as major players. And still, no one paid the slightest attention to her achievement.

In large and obvious part, the problem was due to her public persona, the conspicuous half of her character that one might call Christina. Madam Onassis, from whom little was heard, ran the fleet. In part, too, it was a combination of sexism and mythology, the traditional masculine bias not only of the tanker business but of the European upper classes, and the spell her father had woven around himself—it was difficult to believe that anyone, much less his daughter, could replace him. Sensing weakness, two of his old adversaries closed in. Prince Rainier, stoking the fires of his real estate boom, announced plans to replace Olympic headquarters with an apartment tower; Madam Onassis, a far more formidable adversary than he perhaps anticipated, preferred to keep her headquarters where they were. In Greece, the Socialists came to power pledged to combat a national habit of tax evasion that, they claimed, was the worst in Europe, costing the nation $3 billion a year, and they believed they did not have to look far to find an example. On February 5, 1982, the new finance minister accused Christina of dodging $50 million in inheritance taxes and announced that he was dispatching investigators to Panama. (It was left to his conservative predecessor to point out that the minister had just provided Madam Onassis with all the information she needed to hide her funds, short of the investigators' flight number and the date of their arrival. Moreover, there was no tax treaty between Panama and Greece.) Soon thereafter, the foundation let it slip that the Alexander S. Onassis Cardiac Surgery Center, a $30 million project dear to Christina's heart and one that was badly needed in Greece, might not be built after all. The Socialists paused and then retreated to the law courts. There would be no example after all, or at least not that one. (In 1985, Christina settled with the government for $6 million.)

Heedless of these events, the press continued to process gossip. The Onassis money machine may have been a thing of the past, but the publicity mechanism he had set in motion ground on and on, as remorseless and mindless as a clock. Christina was observed with Count Egon von Furstenburg, a man she barely knew, and with Baron Arnaud de Rosnay, another childhood friend. A romantic involvement was suggested with Claude Roland, yet another old friend, and her occasional dates with Yves Coty of the French perfume family were reported as though something of importance were occurring. (She found him frivolous.) In 1979, as Madame Onassis prepared to divest herself of Kauzov while retaining her Russian tankers, Christina was compelled to sue *OGGI*, the Italian magazine, for publishing her mother's alleged memoirs in which it was stated, among other things, that Tina had terminated a pregnancy following an orgy, that her children frequently saw her drunk, and that Christina had caught her making love.

Starved for information and persistently looking in the wrong place, the press processed trivia, glimpses, hints, falsehoods, half-truths, and innuendos until every report came to resemble every other report and her life was reduced to a formless blur. Christina donated $100,000 to the Myasthenia Gravis Foundation and visited her gynecologist. . . . She proposed to recover ancient ships in the Aegean and was seen in the company of Phillipe Junot, who had since left Princess Caroline. . . . She owed Jackie money that she was unable to pay, lost an English boyfriend, and redecorated her house. She had become what she had once instinctively feared she might become, a woman who was famous for being famous, a cypher made interesting because of her money—a process that Christina, with her irrepressible prattle, did her best to help along. Madame Onassis, unless she was in Monaco, was set free only two hours a day, maneuvering her ships in unobserved privacy.

At the age of thirty-one, Christina took up with Nicholas Mavroleon, a man eleven years younger than herself and the scion of the London-based shipping family. The young man had been sent to her New York offices to broaden his experience. Presently, broadening it in ways his family had not foreseen, he was installed in the flat on avenue Foch. "At first, Nicky liked the life," a friend reports. "The helicopters, the wristwatches." But after a while, the friend went on, the helicopters and the wristwatches were not enough. Nicholas was no longer in residence, he did not return telephone calls, and Christina wanted him back. "She threatened that she was pregnant, but she wasn't," says a friend. "He didn't know if she was or not, and she did all sorts of things to convince him, letters from doctors and this and that. I'm glad his father stood up for him. It was a very mean thing to do to a young boy—Nicholas was only twenty. He probably gave her a lot of pleasure for about a year. If he got anything out of her, he probably deserved every cent."

Meanwhile, Madame Onassis, accurately anticipating another fall in the price of bunker fuel and petroleum distillates, diversified away from the oil business by buying four dry-cargo freighters.

And yet, Christina could still surprise. On March 17, 1984, with very little warning, she married Thierry Roussel, a thirty-one-year-old French pharmaceutical heir and venture capitalist whose companies included a modeling agency, a publishing house, and an advertising firm. At the wedding in Paris, she wore a half-million-dollar engagement ring and a quarter-million-dollar bracelet, a gift of the groom, and she was dressed in a silk and linen suit selected by her new husband. Her weight was down to 150 pounds. (A few months before, she had tipped the scales at more than 200 pounds; one report said 280.) "I have told her that she must stick to the diet and she is being very brave about it," said Roussel, "and I'm proud of her." He also chose the wedding date. "I'm a changed woman," said Christina, who had made a similiar declaration before. "I've had ten terrible years since my father's death." Actually, it was nine years. "And the last two years have been the worst of all. Nothing seemed to be going right in my personal life, and I was getting fatter and fatter. I was so unhappy. But now, at last, everything is coming right."

Although for once—and mercifully—a veil was drawn over the details of the courtship, it seemed that they had met on Skorpios a dozen years before, had been briefly drawn to each other, and had drifted apart—Christina into chaos, Roussel into his diverse investments. Christina, huge, ungainly, and miserable, had run into his father at a party, and the rest was history.

Christina's friends, including the greatly matured and remarried

Alexander Andriadis, were both skeptical and hopeful. There had been too many false starts, and it remained to be seen whether Christina had reformed. Roussel, a shy young man, was prepared (or so he said) to make a virtue of necessity. "She's Greek," he said. "That means she can be volcanic, expansive, and sometimes angry. That's what seduced me." She also appeared to be serious. Following the civil ceremony and before the wedding feast at Maxim's, there was a Greek Orthodox service.

The long-sought heir, Athina Onassis Roussel, was born in Paris on January 28, 1985, nine months and two weeks after the wedding, a month early, and jaundiced. It had not been an easy pregnancy, nor had it been an inconspicuous one. Michel Lanvin, the eminent French obstetrician who had been secured for the occasion, issued a vigorous denial of published reports that he had been paid a million dollars for his services. Roussel, who had been in Zurich on business, returned to Paris as yet other stories circulated that Christina had spent $2.5 million to sanitize her new eighteen-room villa in Gingins on Lake Leman near Geneva, and at least a hundred thousand dollars on nurseries in each of her other nine homes. In fact, following European custom, the redecoration of the flat on avenue Foch was postponed until the baby was safely delivered in the cardiac unit at American Hospital (all the maternity rooms being occupied) and transferred to Necker Children's Hospital, with its special facilities for premature infants. Still, although the reports, like the infant girl, were premature, they were not far wrong. Before Athina was six months old, she was presented with a private zoo of her very own.

Christina, who spent the last three months of her pregnancy in a hotel suite in Switzerland, where she believed the air was healthier (there had been alarming symptoms on Skorpios in August, and she had rushed to Paris for treatment) had gained weight again during a confinement that she whiled away by planning the baby's wardrobe with representatives from Dior, not a good sign. When the baby was able to travel, the couple took her to the Roussel chateau 180 miles from Paris, but it was soon observed that the couple were spending more and more time apart from each other. Christina was said to be a possessive mother and, as always, a dictatorial personality. Roussel was said to be seeing another woman. Christina complained that the Roussel chateau was "too old, too

cold, and too miserable looking," and she turned the Gingins villa
—which also featured a swimming pool in the living room—into a
fortification, with patrolled grounds, twenty-four-hour cameras in
every room, and a bodyguard for Athina. Thierry Roussel, who
possessed a very considerable ego of his own, complained that he
was sick of living in his wife's homes.

In June, apparently in an attempt to stifle rumors that were
becoming all too familiar—Roussel had recently been compelled to
tell *France Soir* that he was "scandalized" by published reports that
he proposed to divorce his wife in exchange for a substantial sum
of money—the Roussels summoned a team from *Paris Match* to
Gingins and posed together for the cameras. (Christina, visibly uncomfortable, was also visibly fat. An April visit to her favorite
weight-reduction spa in Marbella, Spain, had failed to work its
magic.) A second session was planned for the following day. Roussel
canceled it. He was planning, he said, to divorce his wife.

The account of the episode, when it finally appeared in the magazine, was very different from the one that had originally been
planned. Indeed, it was said that the article had been drafted with
his cooperation, as an open letter to his wife, a last attempt to save
the marriage. He was unhappy, the article said, with forever being
placed on view in the gossip press, and he detested his wife's
friends. It was also known that he was not pleased when people
called him "Mr. Onassis," and unhappy that his wife did nothing to
correct them, an oversight that she compounded by taking credit
for his business successes. And he wanted her to go on a diet.

When she and Roussel appeared together in Paris at the funeral
of a Roussel cousin, it was said that his strategy had worked, and her
friends confirmed that the two of them were living together again.
At the same time, very little hope was held out for the future.
Christina, it was said, had grown bored with being married. The
thoughts of Madame Onassis were not known.

Index